The Best Kept Secrets of Personal Magnetism

How to acquire charisma and
enlightened leadership according
to the wisdom of ages

(#1 of *"Hints of Wisdom"* series)

Wisdom J.O.Y. Makano

The Best Kept Secrets of Personal Magnetism
How to acquire charisma and enlightened leadership according to the wisdom of ages

Copyright © 2012 by Wisdom J.O.Y. Makano.

All rights reserved. No part of this book may be used or reproduced by any means, graphic, electronic, or mechanical, including photocopying, recording, taping or by any information storage retrieval system without the written permission of the publisher except in the case of brief quotations embodied in critical articles and reviews.

iUniverse books may be ordered through booksellers or by contacting:

iUniverse
1663 Liberty Drive
Bloomington, IN 47403
www.iuniverse.com
1-800-Authors (1-800-288-4677)

Because of the dynamic nature of the Internet, any web addresses or links contained in this book may have changed since publication and may no longer be valid. The views expressed in this work are solely those of the author and do not necessarily reflect the views of the publisher, and the publisher hereby disclaims any responsibility for them.

Any people depicted in stock imagery provided by Thinkstock are models, and such images are being used for illustrative purposes only.
Certain stock imagery © Thinkstock.

ISBN: 978-1-4697-7584-5 (sc)
ISBN: 978-1-4697-7585-2 (e)

Print information available on the last page.

iUniverse rev. date: 06/09/2015

The poems "Only You" and "Only Me" by Dan Coppersmith, first published at www.spiritwire.com (May 2008), are used by written permission of the author.

Quotes from Oregon Masonic News are used by written permission of the author and The Masonic Grand Lodge AF&AM of Oregon

Thank you very much for encouragement. Please Read my Book

The poems "Only You" and "Only Me" by Dan Coppersmith, first published at www.spiritwire.com (May 2008), are used by written permission of the author.

Quotes from *Oregon Masonic News* are used by written permission of the author and *The Masonic Grand Lodge AF&AM of Oregon*

and enjoy

Anberya Makk

wisdom J.O.Y. Makano

This work is primarily dedicated to the following:

To light, truth, wisdom, beauty, strength, love and all who seek them.

To my Guardian Angel, the Great Master within, the True Image of God in me, and the subject of my adoration.

To my worldly source of support and inspiration, especially my lovely life mate, Mwajuma, my daughter, Laliya; my sons, Alimasi, Joseph Jr., Wisdom Jr., and Malaika whose unconditional love and limitless patience sustain my faith, courage, and determination to act upon my daily duty to the best of my ability, maybe not perfectly but at least joyfully.

To my beloved parents, Makano Sr. and Laliya, whom I promised to lead a life they would never be ashamed of and whom I hope and trust are flipping the pages of this work from higher and better dimensions of life.

POINTS TO PONDER

There is contagiousness in every example of energetic conduct. The brave man is an inspiration to the weak, and compels them, as it were, to follow him.
—Samuel Smiles (in Haddock, *Power of Will*)

Keep cool and you command everybody.
—Louis de Saint-Just

When a soul succeeds in convincing others that it is genuinely possessed by an eternal truth or principle, the Infinite steps in and accords him a public coronation as leader.
—Frank Channing Haddock, *Power of Will*

In the fullest sense, a strong Will for control of others is a right Will. Yet it seems true that not all such control is explicable on the theory of plain means and methods. What is the secret of the power which cowes the wild beast, compelling its eyes to wander from the steady gaze of man? What bows the stubborn purpose of the would-be criminal when confronted by the resolute fearless gaze of his victim—"in that deadly Indian hug in which men wrestle with eyes"? What maintains the mastery of family, school, prison, when some quiet sprit walks among their inmates? It is not always fear, for his punishment may not be unduly severe. It is not always love, for he sometimes fails to inspire affection. It is personality centered in unyielding Will-power.

—Frank Channing Haddock, *Power of Will*)

If you would work on any man, you must either know his nature and fashions, and so lead him; or his ends, and so persuade him; or weaknesses and disadvantages, and so awe him; or those that have interest in him, and so govern him.

—Francis Bacon

CONTENTS

Preface		xiii
Acknowledgements		xvii
Chapter One	Introducing Personal Magnetism	1
Chapter Two	The Origin of Personal Magnetism	14
Chapter Three	The Anatomy of Personal Magnetism	25
Chapter Four	The Power of Persuasion	52
Chapter Five	Ingredients of a Magnetic Leadership	78
Chapter Six	A Page from a Master's Playbook	140
Chapter Seven	The Art of Living	186
Chapter Eight	Thoughts, Feelings, and Mental Sight	220
Chapter Nine	Love and Self Confidence	277
Chapter Ten	Loyalty	299
Chapter Eleven	Associates and Noble Characters	318
Chapter Twelve	Golden Keys and The Crown	340
Postscript		363
Bibliography		365
About the Author		371

There are all kinds of people out there, the affluent, the tall, the elegant, the beauty queens, etc... yet, many times the outer appearance or material possession does not make a significant impact at all on the image we project to the world. While physical appearance or material possession may sometimes be helpful, as many people judge the book by the cover until they read the content, the secret of lasting personal magnetism is totally a different animal. Sadly, "money does not buy love" is a lesson many learn the hard way.

Then, what makes it possible for some people to easily conquer the hearts of their fellow men without necessarily physical or financial advantage? Why do the rich and the famous sometimes lose their life mates or friends to the financially less fortunate people than themselves? Where does the power of charismatic people come from? How do they master the art of keeping people happy and craving more? These and many other questions are answered by the author in this book with insightful experience based on lifelong research of ancient secrets of personal magnetism.

We were not all born wealthy, well connected or as attractive as we would like to be; that is a fact. Hence, understanding the secrets of personal magnetism puts the key of opening any social door in your hands, regardless of your social station in life. That is 50% of the battle won in your favor. The other 50% depends on the diligence of your application of the laws herein detailed.

PREFACE

Early on in my life, I started thinking about those mind-boggling questions that have eluded mankind for ages, such as the following: *Why are we here? How did life begin? Who created the universe? Who is God? Does* He *have parents?* And so on. These questions have challenged children of Earth since the dawn of time. While I cannot say that humanity has wasted time pondering questions to which he will never find definite answers, it is my conviction that science, philosophy, religion, and art are direct outgrowths of these inquiries, and that is a good thing.

Whilst those questions have preoccupied my thoughts, I have tried not to torment my mind with something that is better off left to prophets and mythologists. Instead, I sought answers to equally vital yet more practical questions that preoccupied my mind for as long: What does it take to win the hearts of our fellows? Why are some people more popular than others with just little noticeable effort, while others are not, despite great visible effort? These questions are so practical that anyone who invests sufficient time of serious study will see obvious results from his own experience.

Although initially I sought the understanding of these issues for the pleasure of my own curiosity, as I found myself in the course of discovering one precious secret after another behind the mysteries of personal magnetism, the obvious thing to do was to record what I was amazed to be learning. Thus, my curiosity expanded one step further. As I was given freely by sages of old who forwarded these treasures through generations down to our time and beyond, I thought it would be a great privilege to become a tool of those sages—not only to help spread this knowledge among my contemporaries but also to assist in forwarding it to generations to come by putting their wisdom in written form. Thus, the purpose of this work. I have no doubt this work will make great impact on the lives of those who want to extract the most from life by practicing principles herein detailed.

The finding of these principles, of course, required a very good understanding of the mysteries of love. In case you have not investigated, let me tell you, my reader, it is relatively easier for a person to love when his aim is to love others, but it is much harder when he craves to be loved, to find someone who will genuinely love him. To be modest here, it requires more than average effort to love, but it requires extraordinary efforts—sometimes deadly efforts—to genuinely win the hearts of our fellow men. History is full of people who lost their lives prematurely by asking their fellow men for nothing more than love and compassion.

For some reason, when you truly love something and humanity, you can achieve a lot; but when you love and *are loved* by the people of your time, you can not only achieve the extraordinary, but can also literally become a demigod in their minds, entirely adored and empowered.

In this book, I have labored painstakingly to take the scary out of personal magnetism or charisma. Here, you will find fear-free yet powerful, practical, secret wisdom—knowledge of the ages—presented in the simplest terms possible. It will show you how to love and, most importantly, how to win the hearts of your fellow men, gain their total trust and loyalty, set yourself apart as you build an unshakable foundation of your personal magnetism, and rise and shine above the crowds. Thus, out of the many, you will become your true self, a guiding light of the masses.

In your hands, my reader, I place, to the examination of both your inner and outer eyes, these secrets of the ages that took to the mountaintop of greatness those great men and women of old who applied them diligently. They are laws of nature, and laws *do not* apply themselves—their power lies dormant unless applied by man. Recall the laws of electricity: these, too, are as old as the universe, yet mankind never started to scratch the surface of electricity's potential until little more than three hundred years ago. Before then, only their results were felt—through sudden fire, crashing thunder, and the shocks of lightning and certain catfish. Similarly, the laws of winning the hearts and minds of others—which I call the *laws of personal magnetism*—are ancient and universal, but lie dormant.

I have not learned of these laws the easy way; I know them as a result of very intensive investigation that took countless of hours of digging into ancient books, visits to various schools of life, and numerous instructive conversations with some of the most knowledgeable sages I had the good fortune to meet.

The sky is the limit as far as the growth of personal magnetism is concerned for those who will invest considerable time and effort studying this book. I promise you two possible returns: For casual readers, you will have an understanding of how these laws have affected people over time and continue to today, just as centuries ago, casual observers knew about electricity and other wonders of modern science and technology through various spectacles of nature. For dedicated students of self-knowledge, you will have the opportunity to understand and manipulate these laws to your constructive advantage as the growth of your personal magnetism takes off.

What is in the following pages will instill into diligent readers priceless and illuminating wisdom—the know-how to win the hearts of your fellow men beyond your wildest imagination. Dare to enjoy the journey!

Wisdom J.O.Y. Makano

Acknowledgements

Especially heartfelt thanks go to Parkrose Masonic Lodge #179 A.F. & A.M., Portland, Oregon, not only for being such a great lamp of inspiration but also for providing me with an ideal and serene setting where many of the thoughts in this book and my next one, **Exalted Secrets of Brilliant Minds**, currently in review process, were put in written form.

I wish to thank, from the bottom of my heart, all my teachers, as listed in the bibliography section of this work and elsewhere in the great book of my life, whose instructive pens, chalks, thoughts and, words were great sources of illumination, inspiration, and strength.

Deepest appreciations to my elder brother Mboko Ya Makano Ntendetchi for designing such a magnificent book cover that epitomizes exactly the ideals this work endeavors to convey to the world.

Chapter One

Introducing Personal Magnetism

The golden rule—*Treat others as you would like to be treated*—is arguably the finest rule of conduct for all people; it can be found as the highest principle even in the remotest societies on Earth. This ancient tenet was famously offered by the Christian master, Jesus Christ, and it was also taught by ancient wise men and prophets from a variety of persuasions, including Hebrew, Greek, Chinese, and Indian. For millennia, this *rule of rules* has been used as the key tenet for influencing people.

Throughout history, this successful strategy for influencing people has placed those who have been known as teachers and wise men at the center of actions and reactions of human events in every corner of existence. This work will not imply otherwise; it will simply show how this rule, wholeheartedly taught by the wisest of the human race, is a truly dynamite, awe-inspiring bomb of social change when used strategically. We will show that whoever uses it as prescribed will be gladly carried on the shoulders of his or her fellow man to the top of the social pyramid.

Philosophical man is truly a sophisticated creature. The common belief is that man is the smartest living being on Earth. Religious people proclaim that man was created in the likeness of God, and philosophers teach that man is a mortal God, while God is immortal man. In my view, the general characteristics of man make him a unique being among all others.

But does the majority of the human race actually realize the power at their disposal that makes possible such religious proclamations as "we are made in the likeness of God" and philosophical teachings such as "we are mortal gods free of controversy"? What would man be like if he was aware and capable of utilizing all the natural powers at his disposal? All these questions and more are debated and answered to the best of our ability in this work. We analyze what we believe to be the greatest power—greater than intelligence and wisdom, because it is the basis of both—at the disposal of man and how it can be used to make life happier and more fulfilling.

Personal magnetism is that power. We all have it, or at least, we all have equal access to it. But very few people are aware of its existence, and an even fewer know how to utilize it consciously to improve their lives and the lives of those around them. Those who consciously know how to use this power become highly self-confident; thus, they are the ones who rule over the rest of us in business, politics, art, science, and religion.

They make laws we live by in society; they design what we learn in school; they create rules by which businesses are to be conducted;

and they propose the rules by which we conduct ourselves in our family lives. In short, they define pleasure and trouble, heaven and hell for the rest of us, and we happily, sheepishly, or otherwise comply out of fear of becoming social outcasts. Personal magnetism is the power that enables those who have it to run the greatest show on Earth: influencing the free will and minds of fellow human beings for positive ends.

On the other hand, those who are least aware of personal magnetism are left to admire, covet, and even serve those who do. Those who have this incredible power work exceptionally hard in their own private world, but they do not appear to do any work at all in the outward world they share with everyone else. Those who are ignorant of this power do little work in their own inward world, but work very hard in the outward world, usually under the control of their more magnetic comrades, thereby drawing unto themselves all kinds of unwanted experiences.

Why is personal magnetism such a power—the greatest law that man should strive to master, more important than any other power or any quality or anything else, for that matter? It is so powerful because it enables its possessor to attract any quality, circumstance, person, or group of people favorable to his or her desires. Once a person develops his personal magnetism, all that person needs to do is *desire constructively*, and everything else will be added accordingly. Personal magnetism is basically what the Christian master implied when he said, "Seek ye first the Kingdom of Heaven, and everything else shall be given to thee."

But personal magnetism is not just a privilege for the few; it fills the universe. Hence, we all have access to it anytime, anywhere. It is simply possessed by or at least consciously and efficiently used by the self-confident few who, beyond all doubt, keep the rest of mankind happily captive when their desires are constructive. They manage this even after they have passed to the next dimension of life, guiding and inspiring societies decades and even centuries after their passing.

In contrast, the influence of those who use this incredible power unwisely or destructively dies with them, and they are cursed by all but the dark-hearted in time and space. Hitler, Stalin, and Mobutu are prototypes of cruel abusers of personal magnetism; thus, when their names are brought up, many hearts are broken.

Those who use their personal magnetism wisely use their power to better the lives of others. They do this not by handing bread to the weak but by creating opportunities that enable others to realize their potential. Thus, we have philanthropists and big businesses that grew out of the garages of some magnetic people to become engines that are solving problems of the mankind. If we could attempt to develop this power, there would be no need for people to envy each other; envy would disappear from the face of the Earth, and in its place, we would have motivation.

The development of personal magnetism is something that we should all strive to accomplish. It is really the cornerstone of success in any human endeavor. All the greatest people in history were magnetic people—Moses, Jesus, George Washington, Shakespeare, Napoleon, John F. Kennedy, and others. Some people who are still alive today also ooze magnetism—Bill Gates, Barak Obama, and the "greatest," Muhammad Ali. Personal magnetism creates the times or changes them in each generation.

There is no better cause under the sun for which anyone should sacrifice his or her life than personal magnetism. In today's world, this may sound radical or at the very least controversial. But the reality of life is that a fascinating person is always the darling of everyone. We like to associate ourselves with popular or likable people. Those who have a wonderfully charged magnetic personality find almost every door open to them. Even rich people who don't have enough magnetism can hire a magnetic person to lobby on their behalf! How many times have we seen popular personalities sign contracts worth millions of dollars in exchange for appearing in commercial advertisements to endorse products they do not use, much less understand.

While it is usually said that life is not fair, it just might be fair after all, according to some thinkers. One of these, William Walker Atkinson, an American pioneer of the New Thought movement who wrote under different pen names, including Theron Q. Dumont, writes:

There is a law in back of all creation [that] evens up accounts. No one is given all the advantages. There are many young men who have started with almost nothing in a financial way, but who possess a strong, clear magnetic power [that] enabled them to secure credit. Jobbing houses, wholesale dealers, and business enterprises of all kinds are willing to take a chance with a pleasing young man of promise. We meet persons who are well-groomed, persons who possess a great deal of magnetism, but we seldom meet one who possesses all these. (*Advanced Course of Personal Magnetism*, p. 12)

Dumont goes on to say that "when you have acquired all these qualities, you will possess a talisman [that] will open all doors to you."

Why does not nature or the divine allow one to have all the elements of personal magnetism? The answer is easy, simple, and rational. It is so that we can need each other, form families and societies; so that we can learn from one another, and so we can, even briefly, form a more perfect union, so to speak.

Even some of the most magnetic minds that ever lived could not have shined so brightly without the help of others. For instance, there is no proof that Socrates and Jesus knew how to write their names, much less conduct the work that informs us about them. But we know them through their disciples. Alexander the Great, Napoleon, and George Washington could not have had such widespread success as great generals without the skillfulness of their soldiers. We all have deficiencies, and we all need each other. Magnetic people both need more of us and are needed by more of us, because of their abilities to bring people with complementary abilities together and motivate them to achieve a common goal.

We all have weaknesses and need others to reach greatness. But be warned: be careful in life. The road ahead is slippery. Drive safely. Do not be comforted or distracted by the deficiencies of men; strive to be needed rather than to need. The more you need, the less magnetic you will become. The more needed you are, the more magnetic you become, and the more favorable the circumstances, the more people you will attract or will be attracted to you. A magnetic person is like a life-giving sun—everyone wants exposure to it, including the most beautiful roses, the beasts of the jungle, and the creatures of the deep oceans. As we will see in the following chapters, personal magnetism is built essentially by giving rather than receiving, even though the initial giver ends up receiving more than the initial receiver. Thus, unless one strives to develop qualities that society needs, personal magnetism will remain as elusive as the vain pursuit of the wind.

Make no mistake; life has only one goal in the whole universe: happiness is the ultimate end. Happiness alone is the combination of both bountiful supply and perfect health. Everyone wants to share his or her relatively short journey on this planet with those who will help increase his / her happiness. No wonder it was reported lately that a wealthy lady preferred to leave a big chunk of her fortune to the pet that made her happy, rather than to her grandchildren, who may have made her miserable. Joy—not wealth or knowledge or any other quality standing alone—is the key to both the visible and the invisible worlds. Joy alone is a rainbow or manifestation of love, power, wisdom, peace, harmony, wealth, and health, or any other quality that comes to mind. Radiate more joy and you will become as captivating as a life-giving sun. Radiate more joy and you will be needed as much as the inspiration that gives people hope for a better tomorrow. Radiate sadness and neediness and you attract very few people, except perhaps the good Samaritans who want to help you get back on the joy track.

Those who have learned and mastered the art of spreading joy usually win the hearts of even the most difficult people without major effort. They gently but firmly compel others to please them. Many times, we buy things that we do not need because the salesman is mentally stronger than us. And his strength is nothing but mastery of the art of spreading joy by making his customers feel good about themselves and his products. Lovers have done the unthinkable just to please their more dominant mates. Countries have gone to senseless wars just because their allies have used more compelling diplomacy. Magnetic people are not magnetic because they have power over others; they are magnetic because they make others feel that they are finally within the reach of the ultimate goal of life: joy.

But this is too often a trap. When people fall into the trap, they feel obliged, out of their own free will, to return the favor. Craftiness can be hidden behind an ability to create instant friends. Many people will tell you their friends are more charming than their brothers or sisters. This is the case simply because we are naturally powered to choose our friends, while no one can choose his or her brothers and sisters. We all live to please our heart, not head. This applies to loved ones, neighbors, countries, and even our view of the Supreme Being. Even when we do please our loved ones, our neighbors, our countries, or the Supreme Being, we do so to please our own hearts or, more accurately, our inner selves. Thus, the ability to ignite the flame of joy and happiness in the hearts of others is the untold power for which the wisest of men mortgage their souls; once they have this power, not only do they gain mastery of life but also the hearts of men in time and space. Think about it.

This power is no different from the power of electricity or any other power of nature. In the same way that electricity has the power to light or burn down gigantic cities, personal magnetism has the potential to enlighten or destroy. It is no respecter of man. If not used constructively, it will destroy those with evil intent as well as those around them. We have seen how large companies have been quickly brought down because of the greed of those at the helm. Charismatic leaders like Napoleon Bonaparte, Adolf Hitler, Saddam Hussein, Idi Amin, Mobutu Sese Seko, and Muammar

Gaddafi have been toppled from power just when they thought they were the masters of their own destinies.

This power is used in politics, business, entertainment, religion, education, and all kinds of human undertakings. When wisely used, it performs wonders. But when the power of personal magnetism is used for misguided or destructive purposes, it can cause great pain and suffering to men than all the nuclear bombs put together.

As Dumont states, "It has always been a moot question as to just what is the greatest blessing in life." And I would ask what the greatest curse in life is. Dumont answers his own question and hopefully mine too: "It is my conviction that the greatest achievement we need hope for is to raise ourselves to our highest possibilities, to call out the hidden beauties of our natures, and to become more attractive and helpful to humanity instead of being repellent and unsympathetic."

And in the opinion of this author, the greatest curse is the destructive or misguided use of personal magnetism, because the misuse of it brings great pain and suffering to mankind. No country led by a constructive use of personal magnetism has ever stopped growing in peace, justice, and freedom. On the other hand, countries where personal magnetism is used destructively or for personal gain not only stop growing in peace, justice, and freedom, but they ultimately suffocate, disintegrate, or fail. The former Soviet Union is a prominent example, including many countries in Sub-Saharan Africa and Southeast Asia.

It is not my purpose to frighten anyone here. Far from it. I want readers to be attracted to this work, not repelled by it. Fear is the least magnetic quality there is, so I want you to be enthused by this book, not frightened by it. Therefore, I am simply warning those who might be inspired by this work to study and acquire the power of personal magnetism then employ it with discipline. Personal magnetism is a power that must be learned and handled with extreme care, because it can destroy the abuser's body, mind, and soul, but only the victims' bodies. One doesn't need to be born in royalty to develop this power. Anyone can do it. In fact, we are all born with it to some degree.

Some of us develop it consciously, and others develop it unconsciously, but many in society are either unaware of it or unwilling to invest the effort and energy necessary for its growth. Unfortunately, this greatest gift man can have is also the least mentioned in our schools. I cannot think of any knowledge that can make us more needed by our fellow men but least mentioned in public than this power. I cannot think of a more rewarding investment than the energy and effort spent in learning and acquiring the art of happiness. We all want to be popular, but we do not want to carry the inner load that is required to become powerful.

There is no need for people to find themselves in positions they haven't chosen. All it takes is to seek first and then to learn. I know that learning is the hardest of all human activities: we start to learn in our mother's wombs, we grow old, and pass away not even using

10 percent of our intelligence. According to scientists, we seldom learn and develop to our full potential.

But it is essential that everyone learns this art of magnetism. We either learn it or we keep blaming life for its apparent *unfairness*, because no one will flourish in isolation. The biggest trap that all successful companies fall into, regardless of their size, is not how many geniuses they have or how much money they invest in research and development, but their lack of investment in the quality of their customer service. The most valuable asset we have is not the number of degrees we have but how appealing we are to others. Acquiring a fascinating personality is not a choice but a must if one wants not only to be successful in one's profession, but also in getting the respect and esteem of others and in embarking on the easiest route to happiness. One may have the highest degree, with the highest grade point average, but if one goes to a job interview looking awkward, one's chances of getting the job are close to zero—even if one's family owns the company!

Your knowledge may not always open the door to where you want to go, but your magnetic personality will not only open the door for you, it will guarantee you a long stay if you have the necessary competence. So goes the old saying, "the first impression is not only the best but also the most lasting."

Society judges us first by the way we appear, unfortunately. Thus, the evils of racism, sexism, age discrimination, and all other social nastiness. These evils can be lessened or even eliminated by learning how to impress our fellow human beings, how to excite their hearts, and how to reduce their reasons for not liking us. We can thus learn how to make the second, the third, and all other impressions as strong as first one.

Very few people have been blessed with the ability to be innately aware of their magnetic personality. Dumont, who wrote some of the best books on this subject, says that personal magnetism is acquired by studying magnetic people. Since practice makes perfect, one must imitate what one learns from the experts. According to Dumont, magnetism can only grow when the law of nature returns an interest to whatever we joyfully give out. Thus, association with magnetic people is one of the avenues of acquiring this power. We will explore some of these avenues. While some people are born magnetic, those who learn personal magnetism develop a much stronger magnetism.

Now relax, take a deep breath, and let's explore how to acquire this power and, most importantly, how to use it wisely for your growth and the benefit of the society in which you live, hence making your influence grow and live well beyond the grave.

Chapter Two

The Origin of Personal Magnetism

The impression most people have of personal magnetism is that it is nothing more than a superstitious deception. But personal magnetism has its roots in natural laws that govern life and everything that we know—the same laws that, when harnessed properly, provide light in our homes, on the streets and drive us to work and back home again; in short, these are the natural laws that make our lives easier and better.

No amount of money or property can make us happy. Man is happy when in the company of his fellowmen and is happiest when he is among those who enjoy his presence. Thus, a strong magnetic personality is the greatest blessing one can have, because not only does it put us on our way to accomplishing our life dreams, but it puts us at the center of man's strongest feeling: happiness.

With all the praise about wealth, if it does anything for us at all, it is only when used properly. Its only effective use is when it puts us at the center of people's attention—since we all strive to attract the attention of our fellowmen. A magnetic personality will bring man happiness far beyond that provided by wealth and power. It will make one the darling of his family, friends and, for those who are in the public eye, the general public. Nothing else can do this. Wealth cannot do it, fame cannot do it, and the prestigious job cannot do it. An attractive personality will easily draw wealth, fame, and friends, but the opposite is not always true.

We sometimes think that the powerful and the famous are happier than we are, but in reality, many of them just look happy in public, while in their private lives, they are loners or they have broken hearts. To deal with their unhappiness, they have to use drugs and some of them go as far as committing suicide.

Perhaps one of the most amazing examples is Johnny Carson, a popular late-night television host for more than thirty years. Carson was an extremely famous person. All aspiring comedians of his time dreamed of becoming him. A mere appearance on Carson's *Tonight Show* launched many a career. People liked to be near him, but deep in his heart, Carson did not want friends. When he died, it was revealed that he was a loner. To prove the point, Carson requested a private funeral in his will, inviting no friends or fans.

So what is the origin of the magnetic personality anyway? We touched on this question slightly in the previous chapter. Here, we will dig deeper into the topic to give readers a glance at what is to come. To answer that question, let's see what Dumont said about it:

> The secret of being naturally magnetic is to develop your natural love so that you think *love of the world*; you must possess

self-control; you must at all times be above petty meanness; above irritability, above resentment and malice and gossip, and all the weakness which so many permit to interfere with their highest and best development.
(*Advanced Course of Personal Magnetism, p.* 21)

Dumont goes on to say, "You must develop generosity and sympathy, and be ever ready to give a helping hand to the needy. Knowledge is a self-conscious power." From this, we can take the old adage, "As a man thinks, so he is."

So, the first step to developing a magnetic personality is to think about it strongly, impressing the intention of becoming magnetic upon your subconscious. And as you think about it deeply and honestly, you will discover what will make you magnetic, and you will uncover the formula that will work for you. Remember, you may hear great suggestions about how to be magnetic, but in the final analysis there is no general rule that will make two persons equally magnetic.

Just as the universe is infinite, so are the circumstances that will make a person magnetic. No one else will give you the magic key. As you set your intention, you will most assuredly encounter a road map, and you will see traffic signs, but you will have to interpret them yourself to fit your own situation. You will have to take risks when you may and be cautious where you must. You will have to travel the road alone knowing that the guarantee of your safe arrival is entirely in your own hands.

What this work and the works of current and past masters on this subject will do for you is to make you conscious of the power you have and the potential you have of becoming a thunder of influence in the world around you. Nothing will be handed to you on a silver platter; you have to work for it, and work hard knowing that only tireless work will guarantee the enormity and value of the reward.

There is no limit to what those who make every effort can harvest. In the words of Jesus, "Seek and ye shall find, ask and it shall be given you, knock and the door will be opened for you." To that, Dumont adds, "All things come to him who strives with earnest will and unfaltering will."

The origin of magnetic personality is thus within you. It is in a place where only your *inner* hands can reach, where only your inner eyes can see; it is in a place loudly revealed by a voice that only inner ears can hear. If you want to be magnetic, you have to *decide* to be magnetic. Then start trying all the keys of magnetism hidden within you, through every door to unlock your way into the compound of this incredible power.

You will have to watch your spoken and unspoken language, your expressed and unexpressed actions and their impact on others and on yourself. So, let's see how our spoken and unspoken words and our expressed and unexpressed actions can influence each other.

In no way should anyone develop a magnetic personality with the intent of subjecting others to his or her will. We touched on this point in the previous chapter, and we repeat it here as a reminder. Having a magnetic personality has nothing to do with being more intelligent than or otherwise superior to others. It simply serves to bring together people of ideal quality for a common and worthy cause. The deadliest poison to personal magnetism is to consider those around you as less intelligent and less important than you—not only because it is not true, but also because it is the greatest *repellent*, the exact opposite of a magnetic personality. People coalesce because they want to be inspired, so looking down on others does not make anyone magnetic.

Throughout history, it has been taught that greatness comes from serving others, and no matter the advancement of our education or technology, that formula will never change. It has been like that from the dawn of time, and it will probably be so forever. Serving, of course, does not mean *free lunch for everyone!* It means doing what you do best for the satisfaction of those who are willing to invest the energy to deserve your service. For instance, if you are a teacher, a mechanic, a doctor, a merchant, or a janitor, your service must satisfy or exceed the expectations of your patrons. A doctor or a mechanic who does a sloppy job rarely has repeat clients. Anyone who wants to be the center of attraction must be willing to serve everyone else according to their means and abilities. If you're a preacher, you must be able to inspire or your congregation will disappear.

People come together around an individual not because they are worthless people, but because they each have a hole within them and they believe the person they are coalescing around has the ability to fill that gap. Sometimes all they need is to be shown respect for their inherent worth, and the hole is filled.

The majority of the world's inhabitants will give their lives in defense of their personalities. But disrespect for others is the strongest killer of personal magnetism. This may come as a surprise to some, but people do not go to church, synagogue, mosque, or any other place of worship simply to pray to God. They go there because they feel that the priest or the rabbi or the monk and their fellow worshipers can fill the emptiness within them. For that reason alone, priests and rabbis and monks in many part of the world are the beneficiaries of charity from the public and governments, and they are exempt from paying taxes. Because their activities fill people's inner emptiness, church leaders are seen as serving a public good, even perhaps keeping the masses out of trouble.

Nothing provides us with a better lesson than our own experiences. By thinking how we can become useful to the lives of others, we will become a magnetic tower where people will come to seek shelter in troubling times as well as to enjoy life in happy times. This may seem somewhat simplistic to those who deeply suspect mystery behind personal magnetism. But there is no power, above or below, that makes one magnetic besides respect of and service to others. It is that simple. Yet it is a powerful truth and causes many to almost worship their fellow human beings.

All great leaders in history have used that same power. It all starts by serving those around us; their joy will carry our influence to the most remote corners of the Earth. People become immortal by the service they render to others, not by the power or wealth they amass. Serving others in deed and thought is a magnificent act. It releases tremendous energy from the universe that time and space is incapable of undoing. Why can Bill Gates be characterized as magnetic? It's certainly not because of his wealth, but because he has provided a service for reasonable remuneration that has made the lives of billions of people easier.

Devotion to the improvement of the lives of others is the magic key to personal magnetism. This can be evidenced in the achievements of Henry Ford, Bill Gates, and Thomas Edison, and it can be seen in the actions of Mother Theresa, Mahatma Gandhi, and Rev. Martin Luther King, Jr. Or better yet, it can be seen in the work of millions of unsung heroes whose names are written only in the hearts of those whose souls they touched in some very important way.

It's little wonder that we are so aware of the great, historic individuals who have released their energy by lending their support to those who needed them. Respect and service to others can overcome almost all hurdles of personal magnetism, but no tactic can overcome its deficiency.

It is very important that we clarify this point. We cannot emphasize strongly enough the importance of helping or serving. Helping others does not mean that one should deny oneself happiness. Even Mother Theresa never denied herself life for those of others. In fact, this is against the law of nature. A sick doctor will be denied access to his office to treat others. To preach happiness, one must first be happy. To serve others, one must be well. A well-known prostitute or thief will never preach in a place of worship, because no one will listen unless that prostitute or thief changes her behavior. So, to help others, one must practice what he preaches. He must be well—or rather, well enough—neither well at the expense of others nor so well that he shows he has neglected others.

We hear time and time again about how the CEOs of many big companies become social outcasts (despite their wealth) because they pay themselves huge salaries while the workers at the bottom of the food chain who lift the heaviest loads can barely afford to feed their families. While no man is obligated to lift anyone who neglects his or her own well-being, anybody who is seeking a magnetic personality must proficiently understand how to lift those who are trying their best, those who use all the power at their disposal to be reliable members of society. The best leaders are not those who have fought their way up, but those who were carried up by those they served. To be such a leader, one must serve with the interests of one's constituency in mind first and foremost; one must work as if one is a farmer who intends to reap many stalks out of one grain. Except this time, the farmer is sowing seeds in people's hearts. This does not mean that everyone will sing the same song of joy, just like not every grain sown bears fruit, even in the best fields.

While serving others, one must be guided by the unselfishness of one's intentions. It may be popular to say that life is not fair, but truly, life is the fairest of all judges. We are often misled by the appearances of the outer world while ignoring the inner. Life always pays according to our mostly inner efforts. This does not mean that those who supposedly have access to more material make the most sincere effort, because life does not pay off in terms of money or things, but in terms of happiness. Bhutanese former king Jigme Singye Wangchuk, the architect of Bhutan's modernization, coined the term National Gross Happiness (NGH) saying that he cared "less about his country's Gross Domestic Product and more about his country's Gross Domestic Happiness." Why? Because happiness is the real thing, happiness is the true currency of both invisible and visible worlds, though too often mistakenly expressed in terms of what we know as money.

No one can go wrong by targeting happiness. No prophet, philosopher, or seer has ever promised wealth; rather, they promise happiness as long as our intentions are unselfish and have the sole purpose of putting ourselves in a better position to help others. All religions and gods of all cultures promise only one thing to courteous followers: happiness forever after. Blending service with happiness is magic. It generates wings on the shoulders of the servant; it makes one immortal, regardless of what happens to our physical bodies; it lessens our suffering and the most painful events we experience when we meet our so-called death. It plants man's influence in the hearts of his fellowmen for generations.

Matching the joy we serve ourselves with the joy we serve others is truly going beyond the Golden Rule. It is the key to a mystical magnetic personality. A happy servant is to those around him like a sun in a cloudless sky, shining across the universe, and in return, he receives the adoration of those who appreciate his life-giving energy. This does not mean that one should be a blind servant; rather, one should be a fair one. Even the sun cannot shine or warm up those who hide in caves. Effort, on the part of both the giver and receiver, must be presented on the basis of service. The giver should not impose service, and the receiver should not demand it. Effort must be performed by the receiver as well.

It is said that when the student is ready, the master appears. Effort alone must be the currency to buy or sell happiness, as Leonardo da Vinci once said. I have no doubt that until one realizes what da Vinci realized, the magnetic personality will forever be out of reach.

When the hearts of the majority of the people are impregnated by the force of a strong and determined will that is translated into effort, magnetic personality will be accessible to many of us and the world will be a better place. We should thus educate our wills about the mother of effort that buys happiness.

The education of the will, the determination to choose what is right and good, is indeed the beginning of happiness. It is my opinion that the world and the lives of people will be transformed if our education system is more focused on achieving this goal. While emphasizing knowledge as a worthwhile goal, knowledge does no good unless it is in the hands of a willing and determined person. To serve others better, it is not sufficient that we merely hand them out a carrot; we must also inspire self-reliance in their ability to do things, to develop a strong will of their own, and the determination to overcome any obstacle to happiness.

I will close this chapter with a quote from the author Robert Collier:

> The world loves leaders. All over the world, in every walk of life, people are eagerly seeking for someone to follow. They want someone else to do their thinking for them; they need someone to hearten them to action; they like to have someone else on whom to lay the blame when things go wrong; they want someone big enough to share the glory with them when success crowns their efforts. But to instill confidence in them, that leader must have utter confidence in himself. A Caesar or a Napoleon who did not believe in himself would be inconceivable. It is that which makes men invincible—the Consciousness of their own power. They put no limit upon their own capacities, therefore they have no limit. (*The Secrets of Ages,* p. 240)

With Collier's observation in mind, let us get onto the mental plane and get an aerial view of what the field of magnetic personality looks like.

Chapter Three

The Anatomy of Personal Magnetism

In the previous pages, we indicated that personal magnetism has its origins within each one of us. This simply means that everyone who wants to develop this magnificent power has to find it within him or herself. Yes, education does help, and observing magnetic people does help, but these are only reminders. You have to find it inside you and help it to blossom from inside out.

The keys to the inner field, that holds this power, are the use of assertions like *I am*, *I can*, and *I will*. Anyone who can utter these three short phrases and do what they mean will find that the sky is the limit of the strength of his or her magnetic personality.

Whether you are a prince, a movie star, or the heir to a great fortune, no power exists that will make you magnetic if you do not make an effort to become so. History is full of examples of kings, princes, and inheritors of great wealth who lost their power or fortunes because they thought it was their birthright, and therefore, they did not have to perform. As Collier reminds us, people don't just coalesce around an individual because of wealth or power; they only do it because of inspiration.

This may be why Jesus said that "man cannot live on bread alone." Mother Nature knows we have nowhere else to go, but still she changes her outlook consistently, not just so we can pay attention to her, but also so we remain interested in her. In winter, we have cold weather and white snow that please skiers but annoy motorists; in spring, we have nice weather, new flowers, and returning birds that sing for us upon their return from warmer climes in ways we don't understand but that still inspire us. This is how Mother Nature keeps us captivated day in and day out. When we are not impressed by what she offers us, she demands our attention in a catastrophic way. Hence, we see earthquakes, floods, cyclones, and other natural disasters that take lives and destroy property. Then, we take notice!

In no way should this be taken to mean that violence is an acceptable way to seek the Holy Grail of magnetism; it simply illustrates the importance of inspiring people if you want them to come around you. In the case of natural disasters, floods don't always destroy our houses or interrupt our lives, but they inspire us to build better ones, build fortresses along our river banks, and construct better canalization; earthquakes prompt us to build better bridges, roads, and skyscrapers. So, always look at what is positive, not negative, because you can always find the unpleasant side of everything, which ensures you will never accomplish anything.

Now, let us look at the characteristics of man that will make him magnetic and will ensnare others to him like the three wise men who found the star of the new born Jesus.

Desire

I will open this segment with few words from Mr. Buxton, as quoted by the author William Walker Atkinson in *The Secret of Success: Self-Healing by Thought Force*:

> The longer I live, the more certain I am that the great difference between men, between the feeble and the powerful, the great and the insignificant, is Energy—Invincible Determination—a purpose once fixed, and the Victory or Death. That quality will do anything that can be done in this world—and no talents, no circumstances, no opportunity, will make a two-legged creature a man without. (p. 22)

The Earth is round for good reason, to keep unprepared souls lost or wandering endlessly. Unless you know where you are going, you can crisscross this little old planet of ours and look like a fool. So, too, is the power of desire. Without desire, there is no way one can develop a magnetic personality. The power of personal magnetism is a gift from nature that is equally distributed to all of us, but we are left to figure out how to develop it.

The importance of desire cannot be overstated. It is that strong craving to live that makes a disabled man forsake his wheelchair and run for his life in a time of great danger. Unless one has a strong desire to be magnetic, one cannot be magnetic. There is no way a weak person can be attractive or magnetic. People are attracted to others not just because they have some material thing to offer, but also because they make them feel emotionally secure. Unless you can provide emotional security to the people, you will never be magnetic, and nothing will do that for you better than a strong desire that radiates through your person, your words, and your deeds. It is amazing what a man of strong desire can accomplish. Planets, stars, lands, oceans, wealth, power, minerals, atoms, and natural laws have all been discovered by people with strong desire. Thousands of books have been written on this subject.

We are on our way to having an aerial view of a magnetic personality, but before we do, let us take a look at a second element, a twin sister of desire, that makes someone magnetic, and that element is determination.

Determination

In some ancient schools of wisdom, it was taught that desire and determination were the two wings of success. Desire without determination amounts to nothing, and vice versa. Determination is an equal partner of desire in the transformation of magnetic personality. In the same Atkinson book from which Buxton is quoted above, Mr. Forster says of determination:

> It is wonderful how even the casualties of life seem to bow to a spirit that will not bow to them, and yield to sub-serve a design which they may, in their first apparent tendency, threaten to frustrate.

When a firm, decisive spirit is recognized, it is curious to see how the space clears around a man and leaves him room and freedom.

And Mr. Mitchell adds:

Resolve is what makes a man manifest, not puny resolve; not crude determination; not errant purpose—but that strong and indefatigable will which treads down difficulties and danger, as a boy treads down the heaving frost lands of winter, which kindles his eye and brain with a proud pulse-beat toward the unattainable. Will makes giants.

What these thinkers want to tell us is that fate doesn't always come to destroy us; many times it strengthens us. No one can improve his condition unless he is willing to stand up to the sometimes destructive forces of nature we face in our lives.

A man without determination will achieve very little while on this Earth. Unless one has the courage to face the potential danger he will never grow or attract others. When Jacob, alone after sending his family away, met what he thought was a dangerous man, he determinedly wrestled him until daybreak and demanded that the man bless him before he let him go. The King James Version of the Bible, Genesis 32:26 reads: "And he said, let me go, for the day breaketh. And he said: I will not let thee go, except thou bless me." Blessings come in different shapes and forms. Unless you are determined to face all obstacles that stand in your way, you will never develop a magnetic personality.

People are seldom attracted by a novice; they would rather be led by someone who has tried and failed than by someone who has never faced real life experiences. We hear and read it all the time when we are looking for employment. The first criteria employers want is experience, followed by education. Experience is important because that is the proof that the potential employee has had the guts to face danger.

Desire and determination, without which there is no success in anything tangible or intangible, are at the essence of any action. Determination can make anything happen. Those who persisted for a long time against the odds are always among the most admired people who ever lived. People do not win the Nobel Price because they are smarter than the rest of us; they win it because they endured to the bitter end, until they discovered some way to improve people's lives. These tests of endurance are sometimes lifelong quests.

Now let's see how desire and determination become the actions that lead to the development of a magnetic personality.

- **Be principled.**

Having two legs, two eyes, two ears, or any other physical characteristic does not qualify anyone to be a man in a true sense. A person must have a set of principles to consider him or herself a proper human being. This set of principles should not be a set of slogans, but a guiding light of thoughts and actions, a set of values that provide life direction to something constructive and worth living or dying for. While we neither believe nor condone radicalism and fanaticism in any shape or form for any reason whatsoever, we can say that it is worth dying for a rational principle that is not only good for the individual but also for society.

This does not mean that one should stick to one's guns even in the face of incredible odds—adaptability is a virtue when it fits into the needs of society. But flip-flopping does not make anyone magnetic; politicians even use this argument to accuse their opponents of untrustworthiness. If you are unable to pull the crowd onto your side of an argument, you can rest assured that you will at least gain the respect of your opponents if you are principled.

- **Be honest.**

History is full of people who died to defend the *truth* and the leaders who professed it. The pioneers of almost all religions were prosecuted and mistreated; many of them were put to death by stones, hanging, prison, poisoning, or crucifixion. People will not only give everything they have for an honest person, they will give their lives as well. The most irreparable harm that can be inflicted upon a public figure is to sully his reputation with a claim of dishonesty. Very few people will forgive a leader who is lying to them. People follow leaders not because leaders know the way, but because they trust that leaders are honest and sincere.

People need a leader who is able to provide them with assurances about the future by telling the truth about the past and the present, someone they can forgive in case of an honest mistake. Of course, not every truth can be told in public. But make no mistake, truth as well as falsehood fills our auras, and humans have inexplicable ways of reading feelings even if you do not utter a word. Anyone who has a history of lying never has an aura of personal magnetism around him, and when a leader starts being dishonest and people sense an air of deceit around him, it is usually the beginning of the slow death of personal magnetism.

To avoid the danger of being dishonest with people, it is advisable to live a simple, clean and clear life. The price of making life complicated or even sophisticated can be costly. You will have too much to hide, and you will soon run out of confidants to trust with your dirty laundry and places to hide your secrets. In the worst-case scenario, you will become a slave to or captive of those who keep your secrets, for fear of being blackmailed, as the story of founding FBI director J. Edgar Hoover attests.

Thus, instead of developing a magnetic personality, you will develop the opposite, an energy that repels. Honesty has always been cited by psychologists as the most important characteristic of leadership. Dictionary.com defines honesty as "freedom from deceit or fraud." We will leave it up to you to find out how many people out there are likely to be attracted to deceitful leaders.

An honest life is so attractive because it is easy, less expensive, liberating, and worry-free, whereas a dishonest life is always uncertain, uneasy, and full of worries. Most people do not want to live their lives with uncertainties and worries about tomorrow.

A magnetic personality should be an open book rather than a mystery. Make your life a mystery and you will confuse people; make it a reference book and you will guide mankind. Make it a mystery and you will attract fools; make it an open book and you will attract the wise and the rational. Make it a mystery and you will see it on the streets; make it an open book and you will see it in the sacred places. Make it a mystery book and it will light the caves; make it an open book and it will light the universe. Make it a mystery and it will die with you; make it an open book and it will influence generations beyond your grave.

The best illustration of this point is the 2008 Democratic Party presidential primaries in the United States. One of the contenders, Hillary Rodham Clinton, clearly lied when she said she came under sniper fire when she visited Bosnia as the first lady while her husband was the president. She was attacked by the press and the public after footage of her arrival in Bosnia was repeatedly shown on TV with no evidence of the attack. As a backlash, she saw her trustworthiness decline to the lowest level in public-opinion surveys. Even though she apologized publicly, the damage was irreparable and the price was already paid.

On the importance of telling the truth, Dumont writes:

Unless you are convinced that something you have been told is true, do not think of repeating it as the truth. If you do, give the authority where came it from. But even though it be the truth, unless you are ready to say it in the person's face, do not say it at all. The square man will never state facts other than they are. *(The Advanced Course of Personal Magnetism,* p. 35)

Legends of many cultures and religions say that the search for the truth is the cause of the conflict between man and the Spirit. Nothing irritates man's nerves more than the untruth. The truth is the only body through which the visible and the invisible, the living and dead, live forever. It is the only door through which the dead come back to life or die again and again. It is not a toy to play with; it is a truly double-edged sword and we are free to play with it at our own peril. It may be useful to close this point by reiterating Dumont's observation: "Men and women of 'genuine' qualities are everywhere in demand, and will be more and more so in the business world. Genuineness develops magnetic qualities of the very highest kind." (*The Advanced Course of Personal Magnetism,* p. 39)

- **Have faith.**

Both scientists and philosophers teach that with faith we can achieve anything. We can move our inner mountains as well as solve some of society's most excruciating problems. Faith is indispensable for anyone, religious or nonreligious.

We are not talking about faith in an almighty old-man-in-the-sky scenario. We are talking about faith in one's own ability to perform. Not that faith in God is less important, but it is not the scope of our work.

Why do we bring faith into this equation anyway? Atkinson states:

> It is a cold, hard truth that each and every man must work out his own salvation in the matter of success . . . but the individual must accomplish the real work. He must carve out his own destiny, and there is no power above and below that will do it for him if he refuses to perform it himself. (*The Secret of Success,* 65).

As the quote clearly implies, if you cannot do it for yourself, you must forget about succeeding in anything. You either do it yourself, or you become a failure.

As harsh as it may seem, the world may be willing to *lend* you a hand, but it will not *give* you a hand, even if it has a spare one. You must use your own hands for your salvation. We were all equipped with two hands at birth, and we must use them first before we can ask others to lend us one.

How do we do this? We do it by casting off our fears. Fear is said to be the biggest enemy of mankind. A fearful person does not trust anything except what he can see. But if a person does not trust what he does not see, he cannot achieve anything, because the world we see is far smaller than the world we don't see; the world we know is far smaller than the world we don't know; the invisible provides the visible. The invisible is actually the source of the visible. Everything we are or have, was first invisible.

Everything came out of the invisible, including us, our food, and our clothing. We must believe in something, especially the invisible. You must have faith in the invisibility of things if you want to be magnetic. That faith in the invisible must start with faith in your courage to face obstacles, your self-confidence in your ability to do something. If we do not have faith in our ability to do something on which we are focused then there is no way we can accomplish anything meaningful. As Dumont wrote, "A fearful person does accomplish anything neither for himself nor for those around. He does not love himself even if he thinks he does and is hardly loved by others."

The person who thinks he has strength equal to his obstacles and trusts his abilities to overcome them will rarely fail in his undertaking. It is good to believe in God, but it is said that God wants us to believe in ourselves first for He believes in those who believe in themselves.

Many great religious teachers have taught that God does *for* us only what He can do *through* us. So we should not use God as an excuse to hide behind, we must have faith in ourselves if we want to develop a magnetic personality. By having faith in ourselves we invite others to have faith in us, and the more faith people have in us, the more magnetic we become. It is that simple.

For that reason, we should strive to take care of our bodies first and foremost. Women are more magnetic than men, especially in their youth, because women spend a great deal of time and resources looking after their bodies. The amount of time and effort women spend on the management of their bodies encourages others to have faith in their beauty. As faith in their beauty grows, they attract men, sometimes more than they desire. As women head into their twilight years, in general observation, they seem to be less preoccupied, compared to how they did in their youth, with physical appearance. As a result their personal magnetism tends to fade as time goes on. Not to say that older women are unappealing, in fact they are more magnetic than they are given credit for, because older women's confidence in their *inner* beauty, strength, and wisdom grows as they age. However, unfortunately as it is many times the case, when the beauty of youth is all that is recognized in someone, older women's magnetism is affected by the cultural view, as surely as when person's worth is unfairly determined by race, class, creed, or ancestry.

An aspirant of personal magnetism must give his body a great deal of attention. He must shower at least twice daily; smooth his body with lotion, cover it with clean and nice clothing; and supply it with healthy food. He must make sure the body has sufficient air, not just the air we breathe to sustain life but through deep and safe breathing. A body that is treated well will be admired when seen though the mirror. And the more one admires one's body, the more faith one will have in oneself. Thus, a clean body must be wrapped in nice and neat clothes; these should not necessarily be expensive, but unconditionally well-maintained.

After meals, we must brush our teeth in addition to brushing them in the morning and before going to bed. A measured consumption of water all day long is also an essential element of the development of a magnetic personality. Of course, it would not make much sense to eat well-cooked and good-tasting food from dirty dishes; the maintenance of the physical body is the beginning of the growth of faith in oneself.

Our bodies are actually the best tool we have in the success of any enterprise. In the Bible, the body is called the Temple of God. Of the body, professor Dumont says, "The physical body represents the storage house. Your success in life depends upon your ability to handle this power."

Ralph Waldo Emerson adds, "Every man is a doorway through which the infinite passes into the finite, through which God becomes a man, though which the Universe becomes individual."

One who strives to develop a magnetic personality should always look for the best that is performed by other people. By watching how others maintain their bodies and perform their acts, we can correct our own mistakes and avoid even more in the future. No human being is perfect; we all have our shortcomings. By becoming aware of them and improving ourselves, we increase faith in ourselves as our magnetic personality enhances itself. The best examples in life are not necessarily the best we do, since we are seldom infuriated by our own deeds.

- **Develop altruism.**

Let's be clear from the outset. Nothing prompts faith more than selfishness. We advocate the importance of some kind of selfishness in this work: the selfishness that is balanced between a person's joy, health, and the good of others is extremely warranted. No one can be useful to society unless he or she is healthy, resourceful, and happy. However, a fully selfish person does not attract people, even blood relatives. To develop a magnetic personality, one must aim to develop a caring aura around oneself. People will do anything for any person who takes an interest in the well-being of others.

Earlier in the book, we discussed the magic inherent in the Golden Rule as the first rule of personal magnetism. To take that a step further, nothing will get you beyond the Golden Rule faster than treating people not just the way you want them to treat you, but the way they want to be treated. Making people happy according to their values is exactly what the Golden Rule is all about.

No one can earn the love and respect of others if his or her aura radiates selfishness. Few people out there can stand the company of a selfish person. Just as light attracts all eyes of all beings, service to others or sharing your *blessings* attracts people and keeps them orbiting around you like planets around the sun.

Of the magic of giving, Ralph Waldo Trine writes:

> It is not especially commendable in me to give a pair of old, worn out shoes that I shall never use again to another who is in need of shoes. But it is commendable, if indeed doing anything we ought to do can be spoken of as being commendable, it is commendable for me to give a good pair of strong shoes to the man who in the midst of a strong winter is practically shoeless, the man who is exerting every effort to earn an honest living and thereby take care of his family's needs. And if in giving the shoes, I also give myself, he then has a double gift, and I a double blessing. (*In Tune with the Infinite,* p. 153)

Even though this kind of altruism described by Trine is rare, it is the kind of altruism that builds a magnetic personality. Giving to others must not just make the giver happy; it must also free the receiver from future needs. A Chinese proverb simply wraps it up in these few words: "Give a man a fish and you feed him for a day, teach a man how to fish and you feed him for life."

Handing out carrots to the needy may be admirable, but it may not be necessarily rewarding. Inspiring people is always both admirable and rewarding. By inspiring people, we not only free them from immediate need but, most importantly, we also make them entirely independent for the rest of their lives, which makes their lives even more enjoyable. A magnetic personality is basically mastering the art of uplifting people.

Most people guard their pride with their lives; they love those who don't hurt their feelings; they defend those who give them hope; and they immortalize those who inspire them. To be altruistic is also to be tactful—be careful that you do not hurt people's feeling. Some people anger others when they are convinced that they are simply helping. Anger on either the part of the giver or the receiver is a strong repellant of personal magnetism. A man who cannot be inspired will never be satisfied with all the food in the world.

- **Resist fear.**

I have never heard or read a serious work that praises fear in a positive way. I doubt if there is such a work anyway. Fear is the most destructive emotion a man can experience. Throughout the ages, generation after generation, man has always warned his offspring against the emotion of fear. A fearful man is never remembered once he passes away. Nothing constructive gets done with fear. All over the world, millions of traffic accidents are caused by fear every year. Fear is destructive and deadly just as certainly as bullet and cancer. The suffering of man is entirely blamed on fear. Life coaches say that fear destroys man not just physically, but also mentally. Without his self-confidence, man cannot progress.

People are never attracted to fearful people; they are attracted to more confident people, because they feel protected when around them. As soon as they feel insecure while in the presence of a person they thought was confident, their attraction starts to evaporate. Fear really enslaves and kills man, also obstructs all achievements. In social relationships, the person who is more fearful is either more submissive or a hindrance to joy in the relationship. A great number of marriages have disintegrated because fearful spouses obstruct harmony in the household, either by being too cautious or by simply taking advantage of the submissiveness of the partner, therefore making the conjugal life horrendous.

In *Mind Power: The Secret of Mental Magic*, William Walker Atkinson portrays fear as "the most negative emotion in the being of man" and its opposite, fearlessness, as "the most positive quality" (p. 162). To combat fear, he suggests the cultivation of an "I Dare—I Do!" attitude. He writes: "Fear is one of the most negative emotions in the being of man. Fearlessness is one of the most positive qualities, just as fear is one of the most negative. Cultivate the "I Dare—I Do!" attitude. People seek protection because of the uncertainty of tomorrow. All their lives, despite their wealth or power, people are always seeking someone who can give them some type of assurance for a better tomorrow.

In a recent example, we saw a member of the British royal family, Prince Harry, being sent to the front lines of the war in Afghanistan, but he was secretly and harshly evacuated when his whereabouts were published in the media. The British government feared for his safety despite all the gun power, the wealth, and the prestige of Great Britain. When it comes to tomorrow, we never know; that's why people are attracted to a personality that lessens their fear of it. No one can repel people faster than a fearful or an angry man, the former because he cultivates fear, the latter because he instigates it.

To fight fear for the purposes of building a magnetic personality, one must always think of its opposite first, which is fearlessness. It is not enough to think about fearlessness—after all, what a foreign concept that is to someone who is afraid—one must draw oneself up into the image of courage through will, words, and deeds. Feelings are internalized realities, and people don't see them. So by talking and acting fearlessly, despite any fear you might project magnetism that will make your personality more likeable, inspiring, and pleasing to the world around you.

The negative impact of fear can never be overstated. On Wall Street, fear not only drives the market into the tank, but the most fearless investors are also the most prosperous. In democracy too, the most fearful candidate not only has trouble attracting supporters, but his fearless rival inspires a huge following and ends up winning the contest.

- **Deliver yourself.**

A magnetic leadership is not always developed by attracting others; it is sometimes developed by delivering oneself into the hands of others. Resistance to other people's influences can be a very harmful ingredient to personal magnetism. Can you imagine a garden that attracts colorful birds if its soil is too hard for the roots of rose bushes to penetrate? If you want to have a magnetic personality, you must be just like a garden; you must let the roots of roses, as weak as they are, to penetrate the center of your heart. Let those roses feed themselves and flourish even at your expense.

People are attracted to those who pay attention not only to their needs, but also to their pastimes, beliefs, and cultures. How many times have we seen political leaders traveling to foreign lands dress in the local custom and dance to the local drums and traditional songs? A person who wants to develop a magnetic leadership must learn how to accommodate other people's points of view; he must have an open mind to stomach even what he does not necessarily agree with but what is correct in the minds of others; he must be quick to play by local rules, otherwise he will be out of step: he will look strange, or he will seem like an invader and will face forceful resistance.

Sometimes, wisely delivering oneself into a trap led by others may prove to be the best weapon against them. It is a well-known fact that it is much easier to influence people by living among them than by living outside. "When in Rome do as Romans do," is a well known adage. This will always prove to be a tactful move as long as it is done wisely, because by so doing you will be able to touch the weakest side of human beings, the emotional side, from which we all mostly act and react consciously or otherwise since many times our emotions have the power to override rational decisions. When you understand and are able to supply the needs of the people, you are absolutely in a position of strength.

Jesus was almost certainly referring to self-delivery when He counseled his followers "to resist no evil" (Matthew 5:39). It is not always an easy approach, but there are techniques to help you *resist no evil and turn the other cheek*, which we will discuss later.

But to give you a clearer idea on the power of self-delivery, consider the example of two sailors: one chooses to resist the wind and forces his way to his destination, and the other chooses to adjust his sails and lets the wind fight itself. Certainly, the latter has an easier time of it, which might be what wisdom is all about.

- **Develop self-control.**

Self-control is one of the mightiest powers a single man can utilize to shake up the whole human race. This is not an overstatement. It has been said time and time again that no one can control others until he controls himself first.

There is good reason for this. Emotions, language, and body movement are the tools we use to truly communicate effectively with others, and people are attracted to others depending on the message sent out through those channels. An angry man impresses no one. A man whose eyes, legs, hands, and other body parts are relentlessly moving stupefies everyone. Until the body is under strict control, the task of building a magnetic leadership may come at a high cost if it ever comes at all.

A man who often finds himself irritated even with insignificant incidents, a man who has an unbalanced temper, and a man who does not get over minor displeasures will hardly develop a magnetic leadership. Therefore, one must always avoid or at least keep his anger under strict control if magnetic leadership is to be developed. Anger is the emotion that annihilates mental aptitudes the quickest; it is also the closest state to madness. Therefore, it must be avoided at all costs or subdued with all legitimate means. Emotional self-control is paramount to effective communication.

Energy is what life is all about. Nothing can exist or even move without energy. Anyone who has the most energy and uses it wisely will not only be the strongest in society but will attract almost anyone in his path. The more energy one has, the longer life he or she will have; the better one uses it, the healthier, smarter, wiser, and stronger he will be. We spend our energy in so many ways consciously and unconsciously by thinking, looking, talking, breathing, walking, and working. But nothing drains our energy faster than uncontrolled movement of the body.

Uncontrolled actions of the body, mind, feelings, and speech not only use up our energy but also impede concentration, blur vision, sidetrack hearing, and most of all, keep people away from us, since it gives them the impression that we are not interested in listening to them, looking at the them, or even caring about them.

Impulsive actions of all sorts, big or small, suck energy from the body in the same way that a vacuum sucks dirt from the floor.

As hard as it is to totally put the self under the submission of will, every effort must be deployed not to let one's body or thoughts move uncontrollably. Yogis spend a great deal of their lives in the Himalayan Mountains submitting their bodies to their will, controlling even the slightest movement of their fingers or toes, including such semi-voluntary acts as breathing, and thereby gain discipline over their thoughts and feelings as well. As a result, they go on living well beyond a hundred years in a healthy, happy existence.

The significance of controlled eye contact is inestimable in the building of a magnetic leadership; its reward is priceless. Some writers have suggested that the human body is a microcosm of the universe. In other words, everything that is in the universe is also in the human body—fire, water, minerals, air, space—literally and metaphorically speaking. With the naked eye, we can see the beauty of the shimmering sun at noon, the sadness of an eclipsed moon, the joy of the roses celebrating the springtime. But how do we observe the attitudes of the universal elements that hide in man? The answer is simple: through human eyes.

Our eyes are the true windows to the outside world. They reveal our joy, sadness, courage, fear, anger, hypocrisy, honesty, sincerity, and so on. They expose the highs and lows of our fellowmen as well as our own.

Sometimes, we are less interested in what we declare and more interested in what is behind it. Therefore, to keep people from getting confused by our message, it is extremely important to avoid expressions that send ambiguous messages. In order to enforce a magnetic leadership, one must get into the habit of looking people straight in the eyes to enable them to read the sincerity and self-confidence that makes us human beings.

Without looking people straight in the eyes, they will either be suspicious of you or will be confused by your point of view and lose their interest in you. As a consequence, your leadership, if you have any, will never be magnetic. It is important to mention that we are not saying that you should stare at people all the time, which would not only be distasteful but also frightening, we are saying that, in order to ensure a magnetic leadership, it is necessary to maintain eye contact, the only window through which the rest of the world can see the universe in you.

And let us not underestimate the impact of speech and language in the development of a strong magnetic leadership. How many times have we heard that well-intentioned people have been misunderstood and consequently rejected at best and persecuted at worst? People often eat and digest bad food, but they have a hard time digesting the bad words that come out of other people's mouths. Our words cannot only build gigantic social edifices but they can also ignite mighty conflicts.

Many times, it is not what we say that drives people away from us, but how we say it. To form your words in a way that makes people feel respected—not necessarily loved or flattered—will go a long way to increasing the fascination of people toward you. Profanity, belittling people, and outright lies will drive people away from you with the speed of a bullet. An aspirant to magnetic leadership controls his words with all he has, including his life.

I cannot help but repeat myself here, and I really feel the need to do so in order to strongly impress the point I want to make. Looking people in the eyes is very difficult for the vast majority of people, but it does go a long way toward bringing you to the same mental plane with others. It is not an easy exercise to look people in the eyes. It is easy neither for the commoner nor for the king.

There is a reason why kings demand those who approach them to bow and look upon the ground. Straight looks take out the power and myth of the powerful; it diminishes their aura and exposes their mysteries; and it weakens their egos. To shield kings and the powerful from revealing their fragile, human sides, those who dare to look them in the eyes are not well regarded.

So, too, dictators such as Mobutu of Zaire, Saddam Hussein, Joseph Stalin, and Ivan the Terrible sent to death those who challenged them through eye contact. In democratic societies, those who challenge the boss through eye contact are quietly demoted; the lucky few are usually reassigned to unpopular outposts. In any situation, ancient or modern times, democratic or autocratic societies, eye contact rarely goes unpunished. The degree of penalty may be different, but the bottom line is that it is never tolerated.

Many theories, myths and mysteries attempt to explain eye contact. It is said and believed by students of truth that when two human beings come in contact for the first time, there is a duel to evaluate the possibilities of getting along. This contest is a double-headed dragon. It is fought at the inner or subconscious level and outer or conscious level. At both levels, the sparring can be bloody; though, at the inner level, it is relatively short, and common ground or lasting reconciliation is easily attained. At the outer level, this duel is carried on through eye contact; it can be bloodier, long lasting, and end more ambiguously, with both sides powerless if no one comes out victorious.

Of all the senses, only vision helps form an idea of infinity and God. No sense reveals the mysteries of life to man faster and more accurately than vision. It is believed that many people have heard the voice of God but none has seen Him; still we all long to see Him (yet are powerless to open our eyes in front of Him even when the opportunity is given us) rather than to hear him.

Moses is reported to have heard God but bowed down in order to avoid making eye contact. While the hearing and other senses give us a sense of the Presence of God, only vision helps us conceive his Presence in the likeness of fire, blazing light, a gigantic, white-bearded old man, or whatever. No matter how often you hear someone on radio you have never seen, you can never possibly conceive a correct likeness of him or her. Vision alone gives man an idea that takes him on a ride to distant planets, stars, suns, galaxies, or systems of worlds. No other sense has the power to strengthen faith in ourselves or the Supreme Being in the way vision can. "Seeing is believing" is an all-too-common expression to be ignored. (Caution: We are not undermining the value of other senses by any stretch of imagination; they are all equally dear to life. However, we are simply emphasizing the importance of eye contact.)

Vision enables man to trust himself, to be his own best friend who can be trusted with the most sacred secrets in the world without having to worry about self-betrayal. The benefits of eye contact cannot be overstated. Not only does it instill self-confidence, it also helps in the most tremendous way in gaining the trust and respect of others.

Because of this, it is very important to learn or reinforce the habit of looking people, if not directly in the eyes, at the very least directly between their eyes. Make eye contact with anyone who crosses your path of life a habit; then it will become as easy as walking or breathing, and before long, eye contact will bring many to bow to your majestic spirit.

Chapter Four

The Power of Persuasion

Communication as an Instrument of Magnetic Leadership

An Egyptian proverb says, "Make yourself a craftsman of speech, for thereby thou shall gain the upper hand." More than anything else, the power of speech has been responsible for all the transformations of human civilization, including the creation of the universe, if religious teachings are to be believed. In Genesis, it is written that God said, "Let there be . . ." and everything was. In the New Testament, John tells his readers, "In the beginning there was the Word, and the Word was with God, and the Word was God."

We are not professing any religious view in this work, and we will not try to prove this point from a religious viewpoint, but since religion is the fabric that binds the lives of billions of people; it is perfectly rational to use some scripture to demonstrate longstanding viewpoints. Beyond that, we must caution anyone who wishes to develop a magnetic leadership against ignoring the religious viewpoint of this rule of personal magnetism. The spoken word has such a tremendous power that it is beyond description. I hope this is not a revelation to anyone. Many people are able to resist the power of a bullet that may kill them physically but happily bow to a speech that may destroy not only their bodies but their spirits and their souls, as well as their and others' cultures.

It has been preached, written, and sung by the wisest of the human race that persuasion is better than physical or mechanical force. Persuasion does not come in any other way but speech. It does not make enemies, but makes those who would be enemies happily surrender, regardless of their power, wealth, and prestige. It is so powerful that when it is used, no one in search of peace of mind can resist. In religious terms, it is called praising the Lord; in politics, it is diplomacy; in business, it is negotiation; and in social encounters, it is called sweet talk. Persuasion may make potential enemies feel uncomfortable but rarely angry or vengeful toward a shrewd opponent.

In the history of literature, nowhere is the power of speech illustrated better than in the Aesop's fable retold by French poet Jean de la Fontaine, in his extraordinary poem, "The Crow and the Fox," taken from ublwire.com website.

The Fox and the Crow

A Fox once saw a Crow fly off with a piece of cheese in its beak and settle on a branch of a tree. "That's for me," said the Fox, and he walked up to the foot of the tree. "Good day,

Mistress Crow," he cried. "How well you are looking today: how glossy your feathers; how bright your eyes. I feel sure your voice must surpass that of other birds, just as your figure does. Let me hear but one song from you that I may greet you as the Queen of Birds." The Crow lifted up her head and began to caw her best, but the moment she opened her mouth the piece of cheese fell to the ground, only to be snapped up by the Fox. "That will do," said he. "That was all I wanted. In exchange for your cheese I will give you a piece of advice for the future:

Do not trust flatterers.

When asked how one should pray for the prayer to be answered, Jesus taught his followers this famous prayer, known as the Lord's Prayer, Pater Noster or Our Father:

> Our Father which art in heaven,
> Hallowed be thy name.
> Thy kingdom come.
> Thy will be done in earth, as it is in heaven.
> Give us this day our daily bread.
> And forgive us our debts, as we forgive our debtors.
> And lead us not into temptation,
> but deliver us from evil: For thine is the kingdom,
> and the power, and the glory, forever. Amen.
>
> —Matthew 6:9-13 KJV

It is no accident that these two pieces of text are placed side by side. The first one, of course, is a fable emanating from man's wisdom; the other is a prayer from divine wisdom. The former is mocked as a flattery, while the latter is honored as an appeal to God. But deeply observed the missing link between the two is that they are both instruments of persuasion: one to man who, many times, undeservedly insists on glorification, and the other to the divine source whom man owes everything and from whom man gets his life, health, wealth, and happiness. Therefore, when well used, the words persuade both man and Spirit.

Aesop's fable may be called flattery and Jesus' poem a prayer, but their common strategy as instruments of persuasion is that they start talking directly to the hearts of their listeners by praising their splendor in every way they know how. They show their total, absolute surrender, and by so doing, they get sympathy along with the prize—be it from fellow men or from God.

That is the power of excellent speech. When a speech makes people feel good about themselves, shows respect for others, praises people's worth, it becomes, indeed, the most important instrument of magnetic leadership.

A person who is in search of magnetic leadership has to learn all the means of acquiring the mastery of this kind of speech. Very few people are immune to the power of persuasion. We are told by the New Testament that even Jesus fell victim to it on the cross at the very end of his life on Earth. He granted *amnesty* to a criminal who confessed his transgressions but uttered kind and persuasive words to Jesus about His innocence.

On the other hand, profanity destroys a magnetic personality faster than lightning can burn a forest to ashes, and disrespectful language dries up personal magnetism like heat evaporates water in a kettle. The power of the spoken word when used effectively is such a strong power that it multiplies personal magnetism at an incredible speed. The power of persuasion or the feel-good speech is irresistible. We are all, without exception, vulnerable to it. The most powerful among us is the one who knows how to manipulate this power.

Even one of the craftiest politicians who ever lived, the man who is considered by many thinkers to be the father of Western political philosophy, Niccolo Machiavelli, confessed the powerlessness of princes to this force when he writes:

> One important point we do not want to overlook concerns a failing against which princes cannot easily self-protect unless they are especially prudent or have good advisers. We refer to the flatterers with whom the courts of princes are crowded. Because men are so easily pleased by their own qualities and are so readily deceived in them, they have difficulty guarding against these pests, and in attempting to guard against them, they run the risk of being scorned. For there is no way of avoiding flattery (highest form of persuasion) except by letting men know that they will

not offend by telling the truth; yet if every man is free to tell you the truth, you will not receive the respect. (*The Prince*, p. 81)

See, you're damned if you do—"surrender to persuasion"—and you're damned if you don't, according to the "devil/angel" politician. The alternatives to persuasion boil down to begging or the use of force. By begging, one becomes the slave of the giver, because the beggar never earns respect from anyone, including oneself; whereas by force, one creates enemies faster and longer while making one's own life extremely uncomfortable.

Persuasion has the potential to make enemies or friends, but it transforms both your enemies and friends into your admirers. Admirers do not necessarily love or hate you, but they are your best students—and we all know few relationships are more magnetic than the relationship between the teacher and student. It is equal to the bond between parent and child; for we are all the students of our parents, just as teachers are the parents of their students.

To make persuasion always work in our favor, we must study the qualities of those we want to attract and then appropriately reflect those qualities to them. Nothing makes women vulnerable or more easily succumb to men than telling them how beautiful they are, making them feel good about themselves. On the other hand, nothing makes men more submissive to women than being told that they are great husbands or lovers. Persuasion accelerates the vibratory speed of joy, which is (as we have already stated) the highest vibration anywhere in the universe, in all of us.

Study the qualities of those around you if you want to develop your magnetic leadership, and then let them know that you see those qualities. It will neither do you any good nor increase your magnetic leadership if you keep the qualities of those around you a secret. If you tell your lover how sexy he/she is, he/she will literally submit his/her passions to your will; if you tell your subordinates what a great job they are doing, you will inspire them, sharpen their minds, and you will get the credit for all their work; if you tell your friends how supportive they are, you will never know faithless friends; if you tell your so-called enemies how much you respect them, you will disarm them.

No mind is immune to this power. It is the only power that a slave can effectively use to submit to his master, and the only power that drives kings, queens, princes, princesses, presidents, governors, high priests, or the mega-rich to go to bed with their servants. This may seem like an outlandish and thoughtless statement to some, yet it is absolutely true. Hence, we confess this to be such a bold claim and not so easy to back up, probably. The goal here, of course, is not to impress readers with some sensational ideas, not at all, but to honestly bring to your attention the scale of the power of persuasion, so you can use it constructively as often as possible, regardless of the apparent obstacles.

Now, using more recently revealed secrets, let's see if we can support this bold claim. Here is what ABC News and the *Los Angeles Times* reported about the former California governor Arnold Schwarzenegger:

> Mildred Patricia Baena is the woman with whom former California Gov. Arnold Schwarzenegger fathered a son about 14 years ago, ABC News has learned. Birth records show Schwarzenegger's son Christopher and his newly revealed child were born less than a week apart. Known as Patty, Baena reportedly worked in the family home as a housekeeper and assistant for more than 20 years, until January. (http://abcnews.go.com/US/mother-arnold-schwarzeneggers-love-child-revealed/story?id=13626896 [01/01/2012])

> Schwarzenegger fathered a child with longtime member of household staff Schwarzenegger's wife, Maria Shriver, moved out of their Brentwood mansion earlier this year after the former governor acknowledged the child was his. The staff member worked for the family for 20 years, retiring in January. (http://www.latimes.com/la-me-0517-arnold-20110517,0,4552508.story [01/01/2012])

And the New York Times reported this about the Prince of Monaco:

> PARIS, July 6—In what is either a fairy tale come true or a true confession of an expensive indiscretion, Prince Albert II of Monaco on Wednesday officially recognized paternity of a boy born to a French-Togolese woman nearly two years ago, automatically conferring on the boy the eventual rights to a thick slice of his billion-dollar fortune. The prince, who assumed royal powers in April upon the death of his father, Prince Rainier III, issued a statement through his lawyer saying he "has and will continue to face up to his responsibilities" after having fathered the child with Nicole Coste, a former flight attendant whom he met in July 1997 on an Air France flight to Paris from the French Riviera. (http://www.nytimes.com/2005/07/07/international/europe/07monaco.html?pagewanted=all (01/02/2012])

What do you think caused such a powerful man like Schwarzenegger, married to journalist Maria Shriver, niece of President John F. Kennedy, to fall in love with his housekeeper or the Prince of Monaco fathering a child with a flight attendant? We will let you think about it.

Shrewd salesmen and politicians know and utilize the law of persuasion every time an opportunity presents itself; so can you to your own constructive advantage. It is no accident that we hear politicians on the campaign trail praising the American people—not just their constituents—but all Americans. How many times have you heard "the American people are a great people; they are magnificent; they are a smart people"? But what happens after a politician gets elected? He stops listening to his "smart American people," the ones who elected him, and he starts listening to his smart contributors, who will fund his campaign during the next election. What did the fox do after the crow dropped the cheese? Think about it.

The mysterious power that makes the cunning word irresistible is all hidden in the voice. To many people, it is not what you say but how you say it. On the importance of the voice, Dumont writes, "A well-trained voice is a big asset and one that is well worth cultivating . . . . A man with a well-trained voice can use an infinite variety of ways in which to express his thought," (*The Advanced Course in Personal Magnetism*, p. 41). Political leaders and those who make their living influencing people spend a great deal of their energy and money mastering this art. They spend a lot of time practicing not only the content of their public speeches, but also the tone with which they deliver the speeches.

They do this because they know that good words are like a shapely and beautiful young lady going out naked. She won't disgust or repel everyone, but she will cause an uproar. But if that young lady is clothed in beautiful garments, she will be the object of curiosity for many as though she were the masterpiece of a famous artist. That is the power of the tone that builds a magnetic leadership.

While natural tones require less effort, the best tones must reveal your pure intentions. If your voice reveals anything contrary to your true feeling, it will spell disaster for you. The best way to do this is to gently feel what you mean. Why? Because gentle feelings are very attractive. Unless your tone discloses a gentle feeling, it will sound harsh. For this reason, experienced public speakers do not speak when they are angry because anger is a very strong repellant feeling, second only to fear. Because an attractive tone must reveal the feelings of the speaker, as a general rule, it is better for speakers not to speak or at least speak less when they are engulfed by negative feelings such as anger, fear, hopelessness, weakness, discouragement, powerlessness, doubtfulness, uncertainty, shame, and arrogance, or they risk overwhelming the *inner self*. Even if there is something you can gain by speaking while feeling negative, it will harm your own magnetism.

While the power of the spoken word is very powerful, it is sometimes rendered less potent by the physical position we take while speaking to others. No matter what the subject of your message, no matter what the tone of your voice, people will be less attracted to you if you avoid making eye contact. We spoke of this earlier, but sometime repetition serves to reinforce the point. Looking above the heads of the audience, below their chins or simply avoiding eye contact will send a very strong negative feeling to people, and they will most likely reject the message and become less attracted to you. Avoiding eye contact sends a message of self-doubt, dishonesty, and incompetence.

Of course, staring at people directly in the eyes can be frightening too. But looking at people's faces or precisely between their eyes will make your audience comfortable enough to lend you their ears and harmonize their feelings with yours. It makes the audience feel that you are truly concerned about their problems first and foremost and that you are talking to the best of your knowledge. Allowing people to look *you* in the eyes gives them access to your inner self and enables them to hear the sincerity in your heart, not just the words that dress your feelings. Thus, when talking to people, we must sit down properly with both feet steady on the floor or we must stand up straight. These postures allow your body to support your voice, enhancing your ability to project gentleness.

Less is more. The power of the spoken word can get us almost everything and anything we desire but it can sometimes be a double-edged sword. Just like when a strong man who uses his power or threatens to use it very often ends up losing the respect he once had from the community, anyone who speaks too much, especially when it is not necessary, will lose the power of persuasion. It is amazing how speaking less can be more eloquent than speaking too much.

It is natural to want to say too much; people like to talk about their life experiences. We all want to tell others what we have been through, how good or miserable our lives have been, or how fortunate or unhappy we are. Every human being has a deep desire to be the center of attention of his fellowmen—not just so he/she can win the sympathy of others, but because our true divine nature makes everyone of us the center of his/her universe, hence each one of us is the center of universe from where the ray of light goes to the infinity of creation. That is why speaking less and listening thoughtfully while giving others more opportunities to tell you about their lives attracts people to you and strengthens your magnetic leadership.

A great leader must be willing to be led, too. It is said that a great speaker must also be a great listener. By thoughtfully listening to people, we not only discover their weaknesses, strengths, and desires, but we also fortify our own argument as we motivate others to give in to our requests. Master Fox could not have taken the cheese had it not given Master Crow the chance to show off his singing skill and opening his beak.

It also takes less effort to talk than to listen, so it is easier to draw people toward you by listening than by talking. Talkers are like sheep; they are led to the river to drink water or to the grazing land by a shepherd who listens to them, studies their needs, understands their worries, and then decides where to lead them. Listen more and speak less; be a shepherd, and you will, by the law of nature, attract more sheep around you. Cultivate more of what people want and less of what they do not want, and they will gather around you like sheep around the shepherd. Even if you think you have a brilliant idea, foisting it on people by talking too much will not bring people around you. Inseminating people's minds with gentleness and tenderness may take longer, but its fruits will stand the test of time.

- **The Power of Listening**

    One must study to know; know to understand; understand to judge.
    —Apothegm of Narada, as quoted by Phylos the Thibetan

    (p. 25)

Speaking and listening are incredible powers that man can possess if used methodically. They are two faces to the same coin. Despite facing away from each other, they do not oppose one another; instead they complement one another. A talent for speaking is fortune, and it is possessed by few people; listening, however, is mastery, and though it can be learned, it is possessed by even fewer. Those who possess both skills walk in the narrow path of greatness.

No one understood this better than John Jacob Astor. In its "Collector's Edition: The Secret of the Super Rich," *US News and World Report* described Astor in the following terms:

> Before Bill Gates and Donald Trump, before the Rockefellers, before Andrew Carnegie, E.H. Harriman, and Henry Ford, there was John Jacob Astor. America's first multimillionaire. When Thomas Jefferson imposed an embargo on all foreign trade, Astor tricked the president into making an exception for him. When James Madison blundered into the war of 1812, Astor lent the US Treasury money to finance the conflict and thumbed his nose at both sides by floating part of the war loan in London . . .

Astor was not eloquent and had little talent for flattery, but from an early age, his character commanded trust and confidence. He was not a man who lost his temper easily, nor was he given to bragging. He was formal and guarded but knew how to lead people almost without their knowing where they were being led.

Like a shepherd, Astor led his sheep not with speeches but by listening to their concerns. He then led them, knowingly or unknowingly, where he chose. Who in the world thinks that Astor tricked a man as smart as Jefferson? (The point here is not in defense of trickery; it is not to be condoned. We are simply demonstrating the power of silence and listening.) Before persuading someone, as Astor did, one must understand them. Astor had to have understood what Jefferson needed.

The most precious things in the universe are invisible and silent but are revealed to the wisest among men; the most precious things to the wisest of men are kept secret but are revealed to the sincere truth seekers; and those who hold these secret truths are the true light bearers of the world. Heed this age-old lesson and you will develop an invaluable magnetic personality.

By no means are we diminishing the power of the spoken word here, we are simply showing how to strengthen it by combining it with more potent powers, such as listening and silence. By listening thoughtfully to others we gain more than the speaker.

We get more inspiration and develop a strong magnetic personality by the simplest of all mathematic laws. There is no argument that 1 x 1 x 1 x 1 x 1 x 1 x 1 x 1x 1 = 1, but 1 + 1 + 1 + 1 + 1 + 1 + 1 +1 + 1 + 1 = 10. Thus, by listening to yourself over and over again you will just know what you knew before, but by listening to ten people, you will know what ten people know and end up being more knowledgeable than all of them. That is just simple arithmetic. This rule works in personal magnetism exactly as it works in mathematics. Try it, and you will never be disappointed.

So listen to as many people as you can, and you will understand more people than most. People are easy to lead when they are being led by their own values or at least adjusted values. Get yourself educated by people you want to attract, study their needs, and understand their concerns, and you will have an unmatched magnetic personality.

Among the most amazing realities is that one of the deepest desires of all men is justice. We all want to be treated fairly and equally. The truth is that there is no justice without law enforcement. Everyone wants justice, but the vast majority of us are skeptical about law enforcement. Consequently, law enforcement is one of the *least* magnetic professions.

Whenever police officers are seen, be it in traffic or in the neighborhood, people start to feel uneasy and search their souls for evidence of wrongdoing. You would think it was a given, but many police departments have gone the (unnecessary) extra mile to purchase advertising to show people that they can trust the police in their neighborhoods. On the other hand, the entertainment industry, which harbors many bad guys or at least bad role models, but offers the stories about justice that people want, is one of the most magnetic professions.

There is no question that the police play an indispensable role in society. Without justice, we would be back to the law of the strongest, the law of the jungle. We would all have to work without salaries and our employers would get away with it. Yet most of us have a love–hate relationship with law enforcement. Why? They inspire fear even among innocent people, and they lead us in a direction that we would never voluntarily go. It is always *their way or no way*. Not that they like it that way, but that is the nature of their job.

On the other hand, the popularity of entertainers such as movie actors and sports stars cannot be overstated. Why? Entertainers listen to the people; they understand that people crave for happiness, so they design their products solely based on how to make people happy. Whether it is true or false, that is a question for philosophers to mull over. They do their job to feed hungry hearts, and then they move on.

Listening attentively has a tremendous impact on building a strong magnetic leadership. But before going forward, it is important we make clear here what we mean by listening. Simply put, a magnetic leadership is an illumining leadership, and where there is illumination, there is less danger. We all know that darkness naturally inspires fear and uncertainty, while light inspires hope and confidence.

This is because in darkness we see neither dangerous nor safe things, but in light we see both; therefore, we can make an informed choice about what we want. By listening attentively to people, a leader aims to attract followers by giving them an opportunity to light their hearts, thus making admirers feel cared for and cherished.

Unless you find a formula for making people really feel treasured and cared for, magnetic leadership will remain elusive. Once you are aware of this fact, you must always choose what makes people happy or at least what has the potential of doing so. The happiness I am talking about here is not a "plastic surgery" sort of happiness; it is a genuine one.

People are far more easily attracted to someone who emphasizes their values than to someone one who professes unfamiliar values. Thus, if you want to develop a strong magnetic leadership, especially if the objective is to make it a long-lasting magnetic leadership, the surest way is through timeless values such as freedom, justice, brotherhood, and self-reliance. Make them look new, like you just invented them.

Ancient leaders learned that the fearful lack courage, the doubtful lack self-confidence, the nervous lack self-control, the deceivers lack honor, the dishonorable lack honesty and integrity, the faithless lack trust, the uncertain lack decisiveness, the ignorant lack knowledge, and the pessimistic lack optimism.

By listening courteously to people, they provided appropriate medicine and appropriate doses to their constituents. In return, their leadership was charged with personal magnetism. They helped people gain what they lacked; the fearful would gain courage, the doubtful would gain self-control, and so on . . . To this point, Dumont writes in *The Advanced Course of Personal Magnetism:*

> The world needs noble characters. Men and women who will stand for what is right, first, last and all the time. Men and women whom money cannot buy. There is a big opportunity awaiting for those who can qualify . . . Try to win the respect, friendship, and confidence of every person with whom you come in contact . . . Don't be agreeable merely because you want to impress a person, but because you feel kindly toward all. (p. 45)

Dumont implies that nothing will develop a more magnetic personality than inspiring others and reinforcing the good qualities they already have for the good of society and never for personal ambition.

While we are on the subject of power of the spoken word, it is extremely vital to mention the importance of humor (more on humor in chapter 11) in the development of a strong magnetic personality and leadership. As a note of caution, keep in mind that magnetic leadership is a fragile thing, as fragile as an egg. Just as alcohol and driving do not mix; profanity or cheap language and magnetic leadership do not mix. It gets blown away by profanity and cheap language. Using profanity humorously has never been a technique that can build a magnetic leadership. No magnetic leader can use profanity without severe consequences.

Laughter (more on laughter in chapter 11) is said to be the universal language, some even suggest that it is the best medicine; it cures many illnesses. Mignon McLaughlin, author of *The Complete Neurotic's Notebook*, says, "A sense of humor is a major defense against minor troubles." A man with a gift of humor and the ability to use it at the right time, in the right way, and the right place is blessed with one of the most powerful weapons to cause hearts of men to surrender almost unconditionally, without fight or struggle of any kind. When skillfully employed, humor plants seeds of joy, hope, and even life itself in the hearts of men.

In the words of Hugh Sidey, author of *Profiles of Presidents*: "A sense of humor . . . is needed armor. Joy in one's heart and some laughter on one's lips is a sign that the person down deep has a pretty good grasp of life."

Psychology used to be defined as a study of the soul. Not until the beginning of the twentieth century did it come to be known as a behavioral science, supposedly because the soul is better understood through behavioral observation. But let's go back before psychologist John B. Watson and define it again as a science of the soul. What good is revealing the darkness of someone's soul? Many times bad language does just that. It may be what he is, but a criminal never likes to be called criminal; a thief never likes to be called a thief; and a prostitute never likes to be called a prostitute. Reveal to people their dark sides, and they will never be attracted to you.

Bad language is the first-born child of selfishness. To avoid this killer of personal magnetism, it is advisable to consider the world (your constituency) as a team and you as just a team member. No matter what you do in a team, you are not more important than your teammates. Even if you are the most prolific scorer, you do what you do because everyone else is playing his part and plays it well. What is true in sport must be true in real life, and if it is true in real life, it is imperative to stop embarrassing people; instead, uplift people and encourage them to escape their moral lowliness. Only then will you grasp the premise of the Golden Rule and consequently you will build an indescribable magnetic leadership.

Building a magnetic leadership is a serious business. Those who succeed become immortal by building a strong magnetic leadership that goes beyond their graves. Take for example Andrew Carnegie, one of the richest men who ever lived. Despite his wealth, Carnegie never looked other people down, at least not in his heart. "He was also a shrewd judge of character and superb talent scout," *US News and World Report* writes of him (July 2008). When he passed away, he left his vast fortune to all his equals, including you and me. When searching to find what prompted Andrew Carnegie to give away his money, his biographer, David Nasaw, wrote:

> One of the reasons Carnegie gave away all his money is the simplest of all: He never thought he had earned it. He said time and time again that he knew people who were smarter than he was. Westinghouse, James Watt, Edison—were people who really invented. He also knew that he was a middleman—he didn't mine the coal, he didn't ship the ore, he didn't stoke the furnace, he didn't mold the steel into rail. Someone else did that. So, who created wealth? Wealth is created by the nation, by the community, by the collective. And then it ends up in the pockets of a couple of people who have specific talents. But it ends up in the pockets only as trustees to give it back to the community. He writes: "This is all luck." And with all these skills that I have, if I had ended up somewhere other than Pittsburgh, if I had been born twenty years earlier or twenty years later, none of these skills would have counted. I ended up at the right place at the right time.

You may not share Carnegie's view on luck; you might agree with Louis Pasteur who asserted that luck "comes to prepared minds" and see that Carnegie gained his wealth thanks to his incredible energy, his absolute self-confidence, his unbeatable perseverance, and, yes, his superior skills. Yet, this man who achieved wealth in legendary proportion, humbled himself and called himself equal to all of us, many of whom will never have the slightest idea of the kind of wealth he created.

Today, from his grave, Carnegie still has a very strong magnetic leadership that is inspiring the philanthropic industry. He has come to be the person that people such as Bill Gates, Warren Buffet, Michael Bloomberg, and other members of the super-rich class want to emulate. Why do you think more and more wealthy people have dedicated their fortunes to charitable and nonprofit causes? They have come to realize that, like Carnegie, pursuit of money can be a pursuit of the wind unless it is put into the service of a common good.

This kind of magnetic personality is achieved by those who consider whatever fortune they have as simply a privilege rather than an advantage, much less a superior attribute, over others. They are grateful for whatever nature has entrusted them and mindful of the equality we all have at birth and death—we all come and go the same way, regardless of who we are or have acquired between those two landmarks of human life.

- **Body Language**

Beyond the uses of the spoken word and silence, let us focus now on the messages our bodies send through our dressing styles and body movements. Fair or not, society judges people by appearance first. There is a reason why beautiful clothes are expensive. *L'habit ne fait pas le moine*, says a French proverb: "the clothing doesn't make the monk"; or, to put it another way, "you can't judge a book by its cover." In fact, when it comes to personal magnetism, the clothing does make you a monk until proven otherwise. People admire elegantly dressed people. Unless you want to make a unique statement, pertinent to a specific cause, like Mahatma Gandhi did, dress well. Anyone who is trying to build a magnetic leadership and does not understand the impact of dressing is really headed in the wrong direction.

The way we dress in style and color influences how people perceive us. Three simple illustrations can help put aside the doubts anyone may have on this point. First: bullfighting, a very popular sport in Spain and other Spanish-speaking countries.

To arouse anger in the bull's mind, the toreador raises a red flag. As soon as the bull sees the red flag, and the bull is released, the fight begins. At close range, the toreador begins to vex and distract the bull by waving the red flag in front of it without intent to cause injury. But the toreador is often injured or killed when the bull becomes mad due to arousal of an awful anger caused by the red flag.

Second: newborn babies are said to be very sensitive to red and black. And stories have been told of patients who experienced relief from excruciating pain at the view of doctors dressed in white or any other hope-vibrating color. If the color of clothes can stir the mind of an animal or a child, if they can comfort a patient, how do you think it will affect the minds of mature people?

Third: when the head of the Catholic Church meets with cardinals, one person is dressed in white to distinguish him from the rest of the entourage, and that person is the Pope.

The point we are trying to make here is that the way we dress can make or break our personal magnetism. Unfortunately, there is no general rule, but a clean and good outfit defined by the occasion will always be helpful in increasing magnetic leadership. Expensive or luxurious clothes don't always add much to a magnetic leadership, particularly if they seem out of step with the occasion. But well-cared for and clean dress will go a long way toward magnetizing a personality.

Dressing is a powerful magnetic leadership device because it lets us reveal our human side to those who may not know us well. Imagine being an executive at a prestigious accounting firm and going for a jog in a suit and tie or going to work in a running outfit. In these cases, not only will you be physically uncomfortable, but you will look like an alien to those around you.

Dressing is a major instrument in strong magnetic leadership development; one can ignore it at one's own peril. Only three rules are worth remembering when dressing: the clothes must be clean, must fit, and must be appropriate for the occasion. While dressing expensively may attract some individuals around you, it may never attract the kind of dignified people you might be looking for.

Truly, valuating people by the way they dress alone is a very poor method of judging them, yet it is the quickest and most popular way we are judged and judge others. The so-called *love at first sight* is a good illustration, and men are the most frequent victims of it. Men usually see women on the street and fall in love with them without knowing anything about of their values; by the time they discover the truth, it is usually too late.

Chapter Five

Ingredients of a Magnetic Leadership

We have seen how communication plays such an important part in the building of a strong magnetic leadership. Now, we will examine the *secrets*—the nuts and bolts—of magnetic leadership. We will see how by improving these components on a regular basis, one can create a very strong magnetic leadership. We will start with what we believe to be the central point of magnetism; the rest of the features will come in random order and not necessarily in the classification of their importance, since we believe them to be equally critical.

Attitude

No doubt you have heard it is said that *attitude is everything,* and indeed it is. Attitude is the most cherished secret of a strong magnetic leadership; it reflects the wisdom, intelligence, and temperament of an individual. It is really the whole package. It is the sum of everything that constitutes a strong magnetic personality. It does not matter whether a vehicle is new or old: unless it has all its parts in place and functions well, it is a vehicle only by name.

So, attitude is that well-running new or old car with all its parts in place. Attitude is how we show our inner world to the external world.

Courage, optimism, honesty, wisdom, and self-control are all invisible, but the external world determines which of these is at the forefront through observation of an individual's attitude. It is that window through which we allow our inner world to be displayed and admired or detested by our fellowmen. It is a well-known fact that many educated and productive people lose their jobs just because they display a negative attitude in the work place.

Again and again, human-resources managers tell researchers that the most important attribute an employee should display is the ability to get along with others. Employees can only function as parts of a team if they have the ability to fit in. This ability enables workers to overcome all other challenges in the workplace. Serious companies spend millions of dollars investigating the backgrounds of their prospective employees. They don't just investigate criminal records; they also go through employment verifications to find out how an employee performed in his previous team (s).

To protect themselves and to oblige recruits to facilitate background checks, companies force recruits to sign forms allowing the release of all information from former employers. They do this when recruits are applying for a job in order to get them to give up their rights against possible legal actions.

An acquaintance of mine—I will call him Carlos—worked for one of the most prestigious agencies of the federal government, which does most of its dealings with private financial institutions in the United States. One of Carlos's duties was to travel all over the country to meet with top executives of big banks. He visited a different state practically every week. Carlos was a smart man and performed his job with the highest admiration of his superiors. He spent his nights in the best hotels in every city he visited. Because of the nature of his job, Carlos was sometimes allowed to travel with his family and stay in family rooms in the hotels at the expense of the government.

He loved his job, but his supervisor was not totally happy with him. Even though she evaluated Carlos as a competent and good performer, she complained about Carlos's volatile temper and lack of courtesy when speaking with colleagues. After several failed attempts at persuading him to change his attitude toward his coworkers, the supervisor asked Carlos to voluntarily resign to avoid being forcefully fired—and all the consequences that come with it. He refused to resign, and so he was fired. As to the reasons for Carlos's disassociation with the agency, the supervisor wrote, "violent, physical threats . . ." True or not, those two remarks followed Carlos everywhere he went thereafter.

Carlos was turned down for every job he applied for, and he had to watch as less-qualified applicants were being offered positions. When Carlos discovered that he was being turned down because of the negative information on his file with his previous employer, he immediately took legal action against his former agency. The lawsuit asked for reinstatement and financial reparation. To make a long story short, Carlos did not win the case; he never got his job back and was never paid a dime, but the judge demanded that the agency pay his legal bills and remove the negative remarks from his file. Shortly afterward, Carlos got a job with another federal agency and has never been happier.

Wise people protect their reputation with their lives, but that is not always necessary if a good attitude is maintained. Our attitude is the way we display the climate patterns of our lives; it is how we let the weathermen (our fellowmen) tell or predict whether there is or will be sunshine and mild temperatures, gloomy or cold weather, or even a hurricane. The more we let people know that there is sunshine in our inner world, the happier the people we will attract. Simply put, the more we display an attitude that agrees or disagrees with people's needs, the more likeminded the people we will attract or repel. It is that simple. So, here are some of the components of attitude beneficial to magnetic leadership.

Courage

Some people will tell you that life is an adventure, an activity that should make us all happy. Yes indeed, as we said earlier, happiness is the true goal of life both above and below. But here is where life becomes a whole new and different ballgame. The search for happiness can sometimes be perilous. Some intellectual adventurers have made it a purpose of their lives, the search for the Holy Grail. But there is no holier grail than happiness. Anyone who finds true happiness can become totally free, not only from pain but also from want. A legitimate search for happiness can be terrifying, but it is worth everything. The hunt for happiness has dangers along the way, but the will to face those dangers will not only reveal some of the *imaginary* obstacles, it will also reveal an important ingredient of magnetic leadership: courage. The fearful suffer for nothing; on the other hand, the courageous suffer for hope and the suffering is usually short-lived.

Courage is the opposite of fear; it is the antithesis of panic. Courage and fear are like light and darkness, like two faces of the same coin; they don't know each other because they never meet. Nobody can have them at the same time. You either have one or you have the other. As we said before, the search for happiness, the ultimate goal of life is by nature perilous. Because it can be dangerous, very few people dare to go for it. The majority of men would rather enjoy the fruits of labor that they did not perform. At the same time, many people would rather be killed by fear than face it head on.

It is said that fear attracts pain and miseries while courage attracts peace and harmony, the two elements without which happiness is unattainable. The one or two percent of the world's population that spend their lives in the realm of audacity depend upon their self-confidence for survival, and the rest of us depend on them for our survival. It is almost a law of nature: the brave depend on their Higher Self or Inner God, and the weak depend on the brave. It does not have to be, but it is so, and it will be so until people realize the indispensability of self-reliance. We all make a choice to cultivate courage or fear. Those who choose courage over fear don't only find happiness, they also find the magnetic force within themselves; they attract us, and our joys and miseries literally depend on theirs.

Courageous people are always magnetic leaders in their fields, because all those around look up to them for relief from sometimes real, sometimes unfounded fears. Inspiring fear, on the other hand, is a sure way to become repellent. Since a truly courageous person inspires hope, faith, and self-confidence, he becomes a magnetic leader with the help of joy seekers. Therefore, one of the best kept secrets in the whole universe, known only to a few self chosen students of self-knowledge, is to depend completely on the inner self, also known as the higher self, whose voice illumines our hearts, souls, intellects, and feelings by telling and showing us the constructive way of life. These few chosen ones do not rely on the lower self or the human that induces us to obey our senses.

Courage does not necessarily mean embarking upon extraordinary things like Columbus, Napoleon, or Alexander the Great did, or being like the shrewd, young, biblical warrior David, who brought down the legendary Goliath with just one stone.

Being courageous can also mean taking on simple things like looking your fellowmen in the eyes when talking to them rather than avoiding eye contact. It can mean casting out the fright of public speaking that overcomes many of us. It can mean having the audacity to admit one's mistakes and accept the consequences. It can mean just appreciating a job well done by others, even our competitors. It can mean being able to subdue our passions and control our tempers, or just keeping quiet while actively listening to others. It can mean forgiving and loving our enemies. In fact, it takes a tremendous amount of courage to truly and sincerely love one's enemy. It does mean undertaking both small and big things.

In appropriate forms, courage is a very powerful factor of magnetic leadership. Of course, just because one is courageous does not mean one will give people happiness, but one will certainly give them the hope of happiness and that is what makes bravery such a central element of personal magnetism.

It is all right to praise courage and laud the work of its achievement—how it transforms the world and how it alters lives—but we believe you will benefit even more if we suggest some ways of cultivating and acquiring it. We will try to describe the two best ways we know of to cultivate and acquire this indispensable quality, and we hope that you will be satisfied; if not, we hope to at least set the foundations for future investigations.

In his book, *As a Man Thinketh*, James Allen writes:

Man is made or unmade by himself; in the armory of thought he forges the weapons by which he destroys himself; he also fashions the tools with which he builds for himself heavenly mansions of joy and strength and peace. By the right choice and true application of thought, man ascends to the Divine Perfection; by the abuse and wrong application of thought, he descends below the level of the beast. Between these two extremes are all the grades of character, and man is their maker and master. (p. 7)

There is no better way of acquiring courage than building a mental image of courage around oneself and thinking of courage constantly—and even more strongly when one is overwhelmed with fear. All it takes is a thought and a feeling, followed by an *act* of courage. Continuous applications of these simple but powerful steps can build an aura of invincibility around a personality. It does not take muscles or physical power. Neither Napoleon nor Joan of Arc had a threatening physical appearance. As James Allen clearly lays out, unless one continuously thinks the *thoughts* of courage, *sees* plainly with inner eyes the beauty of courage, *visualizes himself acting* courageously, he can never acquire courage no matter what school or teacher teaches him how to fly.

There is no over-the-counter or prescription drug out there that will make you courageous. It simply does not exist. If it did, it would come from inside out, not the other way around. There is no miracle or shortcut to acquiring courage. Only through thinking, feeling, and acting courageously does one acquire courage.

All courageous figures in history that performed extraordinary things did so by getting rid of all thoughts of fear and then thinking and feeling themselves as fearless. On this method of acquiring courage, Genevieve Behrend, the author of *Your Invisible Power*, writes:

> There are a few who have found it worthwhile to study this simple, though absolutely unfailing law, which will deliver them from bondage . . . . But if you will insist upon seeing yourself surrounded by things and conditions as you wish them to be, you will understand that creative energy sends its plastic substance in the direction indicated by the tendency of your thoughts. Herein lies the advantage of holding your thoughts in the form of a mental picture. (p. 32)

This method of visualizing courage, taught by the ancients as well as more recent speculative schools of wisdom, is still the best way to acquire it.

Breathing exercises are the second most powerful way of developing courage. Breathing, the most important requirement for life here on Earth, is second only to spiritual needs. Breathing is so important that nature assumes the responsibility of supplying oxygen freely—consciously or unconsciously, depending on your beliefs—and equally to all living beings until the last breath. But more is available from breathing than just survival.

Since the earliest civilizations of man, special breathing techniques have been taught to the chosen few, and many seekers have traveled hundreds of thousands of miles just to find someone who would be willing to teach them. In the Far East and in many schools of life around the world, people spend lifetimes learning how to breathe correctly, and through this alone, they acquire spiritual, philosophical, and even scientific knowledge. They acquire the true knowledge of life; they purify their spirit and extend it at will.

Today, wisdom seekers everywhere spend at least a part of their day performing breathing exercises. They do it in the privacy of their homes, at work, or even outdoors while taking a walk on the street or in a more secluded place like a park, the woods or on mountaintops far away from the noise of the city.

For most people, breathing goes on unenhanced from the first inhalation, when we let out that cry we make at birth to send a sign of earthly life, to the last exhalation we eject to mark its end. And for that reason, for most people, life is controlled by negative emotions. But breathing was not meant to be an entirely unconscious performance. Unconscious breathing is usually irregular and incomplete. It is either too fast or too slow, often held at the wrong times, and is never deep enough to feed our lungs to the point of allowing that organ to grow and function to its fullest capacity.

Thus, on a daily basis, our bodies are fed insufficient amounts of oxygen and energy until Mother Nature intervenes and puts us to sleep. In our sleeping state, we are forced to pull in sufficient energy at regular and deep enough intervals before letting us awaken stronger and more fearless.

Of course, it would not be realistic to spend all day every day engaged in continuous breathing exercises. Thirty or forty minutes of serious breathing is sufficient, supplemented with four—or five-minute mini exercises each waking hour. The benefits of breathing methodically are beyond words.

Of all the four elements of nature that make life possible: liquid, solid, fire, and air, the latter is the one that resembles God the most, if the statement "God is everywhere" is our canon. The correct consumption of air is very important to life. Man can live as long as forty days without food; seven days without water, a few days without heat; but it takes less than five minutes for man to die without air. Air is thus the most critical, for it has the quickest impact on our lives.

One of the most visible, but rarely noticed, benefits of breathing correctly is the suppleness of our bodies. Serious students of wisdom throughout history have maintained the shape of their bodies through continuous breathing exercises. Breathing exercises not only keep the body healthy and in good shape, but they also quicken man's relationship with God; the source of human magnetism. Are we not told Jesus spent forty days praying, meditating, or more accurately, performing deep breathing exercises? John the Baptist spent most of his life doing the same in the desert. Why? As stated above, breathing braces positive visualization and draws man to God the quickest of all methods.

Nothing, besides an aid in the form of a Guardian Angel, makes man see and team up with his inner or higher self faster than the practice of persistent and correct breathing. Thus, the more air we correctly and consciously pump into our lungs and then release correctly, the better shape we get into; the better shape we get into, the more self-confident we become; the more self-confident we become, the more we love ourselves; the more we love ourselves, the more trust we have in our inner power; the more trust we have in our inner power, the more fearless we become, the more courage we develop and the more magnetic we become; the more magnetic we become, the more happiness we give to others; the more happiness we give to our fellowmen, the more magnetic leadership we provide to the world; and the more magnetic leadership we provide, the easier and faster people will build imperishable wonders, peaceful and harmonious civilizations.

This explains why athletes are some of the most attractive people in almost every society. The main reason is merely the breathing techniques their training imposes upon them. Through conscious or unconscious effort, athletes shape their bodies, and the rest is automatic. Unfortunately, this does not happen all of their lives. Athletes eventually get too old for their sport and many abandon their breathing exercises; they get into bad shape physically, and poverty returns as inner journeys are barricaded by the return of less proficient breathing. It is amazing how proper breathing can invigorate human life. Not only does it render someone fearless, it increases intelligence and also makes it easier to penetrate the world within, the legendary kingdom of H . . . (fill in the dots) through the deep silence it generates.

And for the lack of better understanding, the masses accuse governments of unverifiable conspiracies.

I once took a federal agency recruitment test. On the very front page of the test, the agency offered advice to the applicants: "take three deep breaths and then relax for a few seconds before taking the test." Ancient leaders did the same thing; they found their inner power using this technique to develop their magnetic leadership. Then they inspired the masses to find their own inner power so they could build legendary constructions with their bare hands and great civilizations with simple words and directions from the kings.

It is not enough for us to call your attention to this incredible power without suggesting some methods of breathing. I will not claim to be an expert on this subject, but I hope I can provide you with some traffic signs to a better understanding and use of this incredible power. Rich bibliographies exist on the topic of breathing, many of which teach something unique. If you can bring together the important points offered by each writer or master, you might be in a better position to master this amazing power. Unlike other vital body activities, such as digestion and blood circulation, breathing is both an unconscious and a conscious activity. Be it conscious or unconscious, all breathing sustains life. But there is nothing more vitalizing than conscious, slow, comfortable and, most of all, thoughtful breathing.

The key words here are conscious, slow, deep, comfortable, and mindful; that's why exercises make a big difference. By mindful, I mean clearly and purposely seeing yourself becoming the person you would like to be, seeing your improved or improving self.

When we sleep, we breathe slowly, definitely not consciously or thoughtfully and not necessarily deeply enough to take advantage of the potential of our inner strength. Nonetheless, we get some benefits when we wake up: we are more energized, refreshed, and ready to gain our daily bread, but that is just about it.

The most beneficial breathing is conscious, slow, mindful, comfortable, and accomplished by taking a good number of deep breaths, one at a time and holding it until the body expresses the need to exhale, releasing the air through the teeth tightening the jaws slowly as if you want to whistle.

Another way is to hold your right nostril shut and inhale a deep breath through the left nostril as you mentally picture yourself in the most harmonious, peaceful and joyous conditions as you possibly can. Then hold the breath while you picture yourself positively. Exhale through the right nostril, always seeing and feeling peace and harmony in and around you, and then hold without breathing for the same length of time. Repeat the exercise alternating nostrils until you have done several times comfortably. Caution: this exercise should never cause or allowed to cause fatigue or anything like it. It must be stopped immediately whenever a feeling of fatigue or discomfort seems to occur.

Twenty to thirty minutes of conscious breathing, complemented by seven to eight such breathing exercises several times a day will go a long way toward transforming life in all its dimensions. However, never hold the body hostage by forcing it to breathe deeper and longer than necessary; not only is it unwise, it invites disastrous consequences.

The best breathing exercises are done in an isolated location, the farther from noise the better, and the fresher the air the better. Some people like performing these breathing exercises on mountaintops where the air is fresher and purer. I strongly advise those who have time to really go that extra mile; it is really worth it. But the quest for perfection should never be an obstacle to progress. Some of the most charismatic people in history have developed their magnetic energy by psychologically isolating themselves from the masses and practicing their breathing exercises wherever they are: on the streets, at work, even while driving on the road. However, whether you practice breathing on a street or on a mountaintop, some special time just before bedtime and early in the morning in the silence of your bedroom is priceless and can never be encouraged strongly enough.

When performed inside the house, it is necessary to open the windows to let the fresh air in. It is also preferable to take a shower first and be at your freshest. Then lie on the bed face up and relax every muscle and joint in your body. Breathe in deeply, holding positive thoughts of fearlessness, love, peace, and joy. Breathe out. Continue for several minutes in this way. After you feel your breathing to be comfortable and rhythmic, and you have completely relaxed, breathe in deeply once again and hold it, raising your legs slightly as you do so. This will stir up the awakening of the solar plexus, also known as the abdominal brain, the point of exit of low-vibration emotions such as fear, anger, doubt, hate, discouragement, ineffectiveness, and envy; and the point of entry of high-vibration feelings such as hope, courage, belief, trust, love, persistence, and patience. Lower your legs and exhale. Repeat this exercise for several minutes.

Special attention should be called to this deep breathing. By no means do we imply that you should hold your breath more than is necessary or out of your comfort zone. Seven to eight seconds are sufficient but the level of comfort may vary depending on the health and proficiency of the individual. It is highly advised not to go to the extreme with exercises, because breathing beyond the comfort zone can be harmful.

Thirty to forty minutes should be the maximum per session, but fifteen to twenty minutes can produce great benefits. Breathing exercises do not just dispel fear; they also get rid of anger (the twin sister of fear.) Like all things invisible, such as dreams, thoughts, electrons, energy, and electricity, air can make life an enjoyable experience beyond description when used effectively.

- **Optimism (manifestation of hope and expectation)**

With all the thousands of philosophers, prophets, and seers that the human race has produced since the beginning of recorded history, it is amazing that no one has shown us how to predict the future accurately. And despite our so-called scientific progress, almost all the products of our modern industry come with warnings of known and unknown side effects. Still, the teachings of prophets, philosophers, seers, and scientists teach us two things: hope and faith. And there is nothing that embodies hope and faith better than optimism.

Optimism is the undistinguishable flame that burns in our inner world; it stimulates us, moving from action to action regardless of apparent impediments. Developing a magnetic leadership is simply attracting people around you, and there is nothing that attracts sincere people around someone faster than optimism. Optimism is seeing the good side of every situation no matter how bad others think of it.

Tomorrow is unknown and unpredictable to all of us, thus the weak live their lives with constant fear, but the strong among us live with hope and go on to become our leaders. Those who live with fear are always in search of someone who can give them a reason to live; not just anyone, but an optimist. An optimist, on the other hand, is not a magician; all he does is cause you to remove your own mental barriers by injecting some hope and faith in your mind and, in return, you agree to follow him.

I will go to the extreme to illustrate this in order to make the point I am trying to convey here. Suicidal people get the urge to kill themselves because they cannot see the light at the end of tunnel, often after what they believe to be a catastrophic event in their lives. Seeing life always as empty or half empty, suicidal people are never able to see the positive impact that tragedies sometimes have on an individual life and civilization in general; they resort to ending their lives violently.

In the minds of optimistic people, the glass is never half empty but half full all the time, no matter what. While tragedies are not always good for individuals, they have been goldmines for civilizations. They destroy the attitude of laziness that tends to make us ineffective in times of comfort and implant the seed of creativity that transforms and improves our way of life for the better. Tragedies enable us to rediscover and rely on our reason rather than our instincts as animals do.

Let's say this upfront: with all the social uncertainties going on around the world, it is very easy to overlook all the progress mankind in general has made in the last two hundred years, at least, in peace, justice, politics, and other social dimensions of life. Without these, in our opinion, advancements in science and technology would not have been able to achieve what they have achieved so far or promise what they are promising for the future. It is our view that because of the progress (not final solution to end all social problems but *progress*) that has been made so far on the social fronts, we can say today the world is relatively at peace.

Of course, we still have a long way to go, but considering what we have gone through: cannibalism, human sacrifice, conquests, systematic extermination, tyranny, genocide, slavery, colonization, imperialism; now at least we are *talking*—we underline *talking*—about the r-word: *rights*. That is, human rights and equal rights etc . . . . This is truly encouraging and gives hope to future generations.

Our planet is going through an initiation of love, and indeed it shows. Every year, every decade, every century is getting us closer to the oneness of human family—of course, slowly . . . but surely. With that in mind we will say what we are about to say, fully aware that many of our readers will be skeptical or even want to challenge us. We welcome the challenge, go ahead and make your point. Here is ours:

The proof of this can be seen in the fact that we live in a relatively peaceful world today because we have endured so many wars in our history that have killed millions. All of this tragedy has taught man how to better defend himself by developing some very cunning weapons to the point where even the strongest army is reluctant to attack a relatively weaker enemy for fear of the unpredictable, thus forcing most political conflicts to be resolved diplomatically, and commercial disagreements resolved by negotiations. Europe is relatively united, peaceful, and prosperous because of their undeclared common and deep desire of preventing the rise of a Hitler-like leader on the continent. [N.B.: This passage and in fact most of this book was written before the worldwide financial meltdown of 2007 (though this edition was completed in December 2011) but everything in this book is not about life at a particular point in time and space, but a broader overview of the whole of human history.]

Thus this: We live in a world that is relatively financially stable because of the lessons learned from all economic phenomena in the past including trades, slavery, industrial revolution, the Great Depression, the impact of the disastrous policies of communism and the side effects capitalism in the twentieth century etc . . .

We drive safer cars, and we have better traffic laws, better roads and bridges because of traffic accidents that killed millions over the years. We live in relatively, technologically advanced and healthier societies because of the lessons learned from the epidemic diseases that have taken their toll throughout history. Thanks to the numerous setbacks we suffered throughout history and optimists who are always able to see the light at the end of the tunnel, we have better communication systems, better medicines, and better transportation.

Even when faced with some of the events that are considered calamities in human history, such as slavery, tsunamis, cyclones, hurricanes, colonization, and world wars, optimists recognize that those events may have been nightmares for the individuals who experienced them, but they have brought political, technological, medical, and social progress of today, and they will continue to do so in the future. In short, tragedies make us hungry for knowledge, optimistic about the future, and enthusiastic about our endeavors; they make optimistic people more faithful, hopeful, courageous, smarter, and wiser, despite the obstacles they have to overcome.

Even in the middle of the night, optimists see the sunrise; on a cloudy day, they see the sun behind the fog; during a snowstorm on a winter day, they see a sunny summer day; and in every disaster, they see the brighter side.

To this, Thomas A. Buckner adds:

The pessimist is half licked before he starts. The optimist has won half the battle before he begins his approach to a subject with the proper mental attitude. The optimist may not understand, or if he understands he may not agree with prevailing ideas; but believes, yes, knows, that in the long run and in due course there will prevail whatever is right and best. (In Kleinknecht, A vol. XV, p. 197)

Drawing people toward oneself is what magnetic leadership is all about, but people are always unlikely to be voluntarily drawn by someone who plays on their fears. There is no easier way of developing magnetic leadership than giving people what they truly want. People want to be guided by hope and inspiration just the same as their masters; so one embodies the ideal man to most people, not only by giving them hope, but also by showing them how to realize their aspirations, and intentionally or otherwise, being bound to becoming a magnetic leader.

A good number of public speakers know this law very well. We have seen how politicians try to become everything to everybody, even to those with two completely opposing needs, like employer and employee, pro-choice and anti-abortion, etc. By giving hope to each side, the politician keeps both sides gravitating toward him like atoms around a nucleus, peacefully and without hitting each other. We have seen how preachers have made churches, synagogues, mosques, or any places of worship sanctuaries where people can go for rest and comfort by just appealing for hope, faith, and action rather than cynicism and inaction.

Most people may be fearful, but they hate fear by nature. A magnetic leadership can never be developed by clinging onto the weak side of others—this may be successful sometimes, but certainly for a very short time. Where there is fear, instill courage; where there is mistrust, inspire trust; where there is a lack of discipline, restore discipline; where there is laziness, inspire work; where there is weakness, insist on determination, persistence; where there is indecision, show decisiveness; where there are mistakes, acknowledge them; where there are errors, take responsibility; and where there is gridlock, encourage creativity.

This may not be easy, but in the end you will prevail and people will be attracted to you like flies to the light; you will stand in the minds of many as a savior, and even your one-time antagonists will find excuses to side with you. Practice the art of giving people not what they *want*, but what they *need*, even if it is a bitter medicine. They will probably be dissatisfied with you for a short time, but they will be glad that their life paths crossed yours in the end.

Being optimistic does not always translate into being right; optimism is not synonymous with correctness, but it is identical to eagerness to keep learning and acting until the best solution is found. An optimist emphatically sticks to his position even in the face of more compelling evidence, but he concedes only to the truth. Optimistic sailors do not go against the wind, they adjust their sails. Being an optimist truly means being humble, because humility is a major component of magnetic leadership; arrogance, like anger, is poison to a magnetic leadership.

A magnetic person has very little problem borrowing good ideas from others and using them as his own. The mastering of the art of borrowing good ideas from enemies and even stealing them if necessary is what saved former US president Bill Clinton when his own personal indiscretions nearly got him ousted from office.

After losing both chambers of Congress in November of 1994, Newt Gingrich became the Speaker of the House of Representatives and, arguably, one of the most powerful politicians in the country.

Emboldened by a hugely impressive victory, Gingrich appeared with some inspiring ideas. The majority of the country seemed to be on his side, and the president seemed like an alien amongst the people. The only power the president had left against the Republicans was the veto and the consolation power of the filibuster from fellow partisans in the Senate.

Blinded by his newly acquired power, Gingrich and his squad of Republicans started to overstep the mark, forcefully setting the agenda. All Clinton could do was watch and steal ideas one by one. By the time of the budget negotiations, Clinton had espoused virtually all of the Republicans' ideas, enhanced them, and used them against Gingrich. While negotiating the federal government budget, Clinton effectively used Republicans' ideas against them and quickly achieved the upper hand. As a result, Gingrich was upset, and negotiations ended in a stalemate that caused the government shutdowns. Clinton's magnetism grew, and he gained more popularity, despite recent defeats in both houses of Congress, while Gingrich was cast as an extremist and became very unpopular, his image was used to defeat other Republicans in upcoming elections across country. In the end, Clinton was reelected to a second term and Gingrich resigned from office in disgrace.

Here is how Wikipedia summarized the whole story:

> The 1995 shutdown of the United States federal government was a major political crisis in which the federal government,

as a result of a failure to pass a budget bill, stayed nonessential services from November 14 through November 19, 1995 and from December 16, 1995 to January 6, 1996. The major players were Bill Clinton and Newt Gingrich.

EFFECT

During the shutdown, major portions of the federal government were inoperative. The Clinton Administration later released figures detailing the costs of the shutdown, which included losses of up to $800 million in salaries paid to furloughed employees. The first budget shutdown was resolved with the passage of a temporary spending bill, but the underlying disagreement between Gingrich and Clinton was not resolved, resulting in the second shutdown.

RESULT

The shutdown, however, was generally considered to have resulted in a victory for President Clinton. During the shutdown, Gingrich's complaint that he had been ignored by Clinton on a flight back from the funeral of Yitzhak Rabin was widely reported, resulting in the perception that Gingrich was acting in a petty, egotistical manner. Later polling suggested that the event badly damaged Gingrich politically. (http://en.wikipedia.org/wiki/federal_government_shutdown_of_1995)

That is the power of optimism with both heart and head; this is what makes it such a fascinating building block of a powerful and strong magnetic personality.

- **Enthusiasm**

    Just as at the entrance of the ancient temple of Apollo at Delphi where the term *Know Thyself* was inscribed, a banking service center where I once worked had a huge inscription on the entrance wall that read, "Start with enthusiasm and you will end up with success." With more than 150 years in operation, this banking institution is one of the oldest in the United States. It seems like, for all the years that this financial institution has been in business, the secret of its success was largely based on the enthusiasm of its employees.

    One can very well argue that knowledge is more important in the success of enterprises. But what does knowledge bring without enthusiasm? Like any successful venture, this banking institution knows very well that knowledge does not guarantee success unless it is accompanied with enthusiasm.

    The question is, why only enthusiasm and why not any other quality? The answer is simple: enthusiasm is the mother of action and nothing gets done without action; inaction, in fact, has never produced anything since the beginning of time and never will. Enthusiasm is for action what gas is for automobiles; more precisely, enthusiasm is to action what electric current is to the light bulb—it produces the light.

With enthusiasm, everything is possible and everything possible is easier: learning is possible and doing is made easier. Enthusiasm sustains determination, persistence, learning, hope, love, faith, and many more qualities that empower man to achieve the so-called impossible. Given all the tools necessary, an enthusiastic person can move mountains. Life is full of examples of knowledgeable people who either failed or lost their jobs because they lacked enthusiasm.

Man's ability to perform a task is seen through the enthusiasm with which he carries out assignments, and the outcome of his job is usually predicted through the enthusiasm with which the job is being done. A man's capacity to attract other people to join his venture is made possible by the enthusiasm with which he or she executes it. No other quality inspires humans like enthusiasm. People see the glint of the treasure hidden in a person's heart through the exhibition of enthusiasm. On enthusiasm, C. F. Kleinknecht, author of *Gems of Thought Encyclopedia,* quotes Emerson: "Nothing great was ever achieved without enthusiasm . . . Every great and commanding movement in the annuals of the world is the triumph of enthusiasm," (p. 243-244).

In the same work, the *Davenport Spokesman Review* is quoted: "Enthusiasm is one of world's greatest assets. It overwhelms and engulfs obstacles. It is faith in action," (p. 243-244).

It is amazing what a person can accomplish with enthusiasm. Because of its ability to enable man to overcome obstacles and realize something that is viewed by some as impossible, enthusiasm is an inestimable ingredient of a strong magnetic leadership. Ancient leaders, many of whom started their kingdoms with only one spear and a sword, became enthusiastic about their gambles and went on to inspire their fellowmen and ended up conquering huge foreign lands beyond their imagination.

No magnetic leadership can be developed without enthusiasm, for it is the cornerstone of personal magnetism. Learn how to become enthusiastic or forget about magnetic leadership altogether. The celebrated English politician, poet, playwright, and novelist Edward Bulwer-Lytton once said, "Nothing is as contagious as enthusiasm . . . It moves charms. Enthusiasm is the genius of sincerity, and truth accomplishes no victories without it," (Kleinknecht, p. 243).

Magnetic leadership is about attracting people to your cause and, as we all know and as cold as it seems, a loser is the least attractive of all men. Enthusiasm achieves victories, and victorious people rarely do it alone. The secret of their success is usually the ability to attract likeminded—but usually more knowledgeable—individuals than themselves. To do so, potentially victorious folks learn and practice the art of enthusiasm and in the process charge themselves with an incredible amount of personal magnetism. Thus, it is really in the best interest of anyone who seeks to develop a strong magnetic leadership to learn how to do everything enthusiastically, for nothing can be accomplished without it.

Enthusiasm is not always natural; rather, it is an achievement. It has to be cultivated and maintained by self-confidence, self-reliance, and faith of inner power. Unless these prerequisites are in place, there can never be enthusiasm. Enthusiasm is not competitive; but if it were, you would be competing against yourself and your ever-growing faith and self-confidence. It can be taken away from you by no one else but you. It is measured by the joy felt when performing a task, regardless of its difficulties. But just as speed is useless if the destination is unknown, enthusiasm without thorough understanding of the activity at hand is like driving blindfolded.

Magnetic leadership is about offering people what they need or what you know or have. As a result, in order to develop a magnetic leadership, it is imperative that you learn and acquire knowledge before taking action. That way, not only you know the goal but also when, where, why and how it is to be obtained. Otherwise, not only will you be deceiving yourself, but you will also be demagnetizing your personality, and no one, including your blood relatives, will be attracted to you.

History is full of physically disabled people who led countries and organizations to greatness. Former US President Franklin D. Roosevelt is one of them, to illustrate the point. But there is a reason blind people are rarely placed in leadership positions.

Knowledge must be blended with enthusiasm, which must precede magnetic leadership and not the other way around. Enthusiasm must never be a blindfold. It must never be used as an excuse to reject the views of others off-hand without serious consideration. If it is used as a shadow to obstruct vision rather than a light to see better and more widely, it will be a mortal blow to magnetic leadership.

The best way to close this segment is with a quote from H. W. Arnold, about whom little seems to be known but is certainly one of the wisest seeds of the human race: "The worst bankruptcy in the world is the man who has lost his enthusiasm." Measure yourself against the truth as well as you can; know it and the demands of life and you will carry on where ancient leaders left off by completing the unfinished pyramids and temples in the hearts of men that have eluded even some of the sharpest minds.

- **Integrity**

Imagine how hard life would be if we did not trust the spring season to be damp enough to allow us to cultivate the land and plant the seeds that will produce the food that will sustain us during the winter. Imagine if we did not trust the rainy season to bring the water that nourishes our farms and allows our seedlings to grow. Imagine if we did not trust nature to deliver its promises. Imagine if we did not trust banks to keep our money safely, or if we did not trust our employers to pay us for services rendered. Imagine how long it would take us to drive from one end of a major American city to the other if we did not trust the traffic lights. Just imagine if we did not trust the government to enforce the law. In all those examples, the answer is the same or almost the same: life would be very difficult or nearly impossible. Without trust, chaos would reign. It is said that order is the first law in Heaven and here on Earth; order, the mother of peace and harmony and progress, is the foremost preoccupation of any decent government.

True order does not depend on the stick-and-carrot approach, but on trust first. Trust binds not only people together, but people with spirit. Despite the invisibility of God, man prays because of his trust in him, he trusts that he listens and will respond in due time. Without trust, everything else would fall apart.

Nothing in man inspires trust like integrity. Trust is, in fact, the fruit of the tree in the middle of the garden called integrity. Corrupt the garden with harmful substances and your garden will bear no fruit, and you will suffer hunger at the very least.

The importance of integrity in the development of a magnetic leadership cannot be overstated. The lack of integrity or proof of its shortage will easily and permanently destroy the binds that exist among men. Even our own blood relatives are very often reluctant to associate with us when they are convinced of our deficient integrity. In their book, *The Leadership Challenge*, Kouzes and Posner assert that honesty is the most essential value, and we all look for this personal trait or characteristic in our leaders. They write:

> It's clear that if we're to willingly follow someone—whether it be into battle or into the boardroom, into classrooms or into the back of the room, into the front office or to the front lines—we first want to assure ourselves that the person is worthy of our

trust. We want to know that the person is being truthful, ethical, and principled. We want to be fully confident of the integrity of our leaders, whatever the context. That nearly 90 percent of constituents want their leaders to be honest above all else is a message that all leaders must take to heart. (p. 22)

They go on to say that integrity is not just saying what pleases people's ears but the evidence that is noticeable through actions. If the road that leads a leader from "Word City" to "Action City" is deemed smooth and therefore safe, there is no question that his integrity will be the biggest attraction of his kingdom. However, if the road is bumpy and uncertain, not only will his kingdom almost certainly not be visited, but it will be deserted, and it will experience a slow, agonizing, and certain death.

A person, a company, or even a country that does not hold integrity as its most treasured characteristic is doomed to fail in every activity it undertakes. Integrity is the soul of every successful activity. Without it, success is only temporary, if it ever comes at all. Integrity inspires trustworthiness, dependability, and faith. Governments around the world invest their most precious dollars in the enforcement of integrity—simply put, into enforcement of the law.

No company, regardless of its portfolios, can live a long life if integrity is not at the heart of its practice or if it operates in an environment where integrity is not highly valued. With lack of integrity comes corruption, and with corruption comes painful but assured death of every human undertaking. George Washington, the first US president and widely called the father of the country, said, "I hope I shall always possess firmness and virtue enough to maintain what I consider the most enviable of all titles, the character of an honest man." The Phoenicians, who were among the craftiest business people in history, prospered not just because of the quality of their goods but because of the honest practices of their craft.

It is deeply important to note that integrity and truth are not identical twins, though they are certainly related to each other and not to falsehood. The definition of each of these terms may be helpful in order to shed some light on what we mean:

Integrity is the truth to the best of our knowledge, which may not be the truth at all, but our sincere awareness of matters related to the facts. Should our sincere knowledge happen to be false, it will always be forgivable. As long as we conduct ourselves to the best of our knowledge, magnetic leadership will suffer little harm if any at all.

The definition of the truth engenders an endless discussion. Countries and religions have gone to war throughout history in defense or imposition of what they believed to be the truth. I will not pretend to give a *universal* definition of truth here, but I will make an effort to offer a *local* one for the purposes of this work.

Truth is perfect knowledge, not merely what exists according to the laws of nature and not confined to the conventions of men.

It may not be possible to know the truth entirely, but it is possible to believe you know the whole truth and still not know its entirety. Falsehood is absolutely the opposite of the truth, pure and simple.

Naturally, people do not look for a perfect man to follow but a man of integrity, a man who is sincere about what comes out of his mouth. A man of integrity must always aim for perfect knowledge. Man being man and imperfect, this will not always be possible, and when this is not possible, he may utter the truth *as it seems*, to the *best* of his knowledge, which may not result in an intentional falsehood but possibly an honest mistake. For this reason, constant and unending education is what a man of integrity arms himself with, first and foremost. As much as falsehood is poisonous to magnetic leadership, ignorance can be equally lethal, especially when it appears as a falsehood and behaves as a falsehood.

Integrity means doing everything with high moral purpose in mind—acting according to a deep belief or a set of principles that you obey regardless of consequences. This set of principles must include an objective of service to the community, helping to improve the lives of your fellow man or giving back to the community all that it has given you: inspiration, justice, education, love.

- **Humility**

As it is said, "charity starts at home," it is totally irrational to love others without loving oneself; you must first love yourself before you can love others. Your individuality is your higher self, but unless you serve yourself for the purpose of better serving others, magnetic leadership cannot be developed.

Without truly and honestly loving and serving yourself, you will never be able to love and serve others. Even the Golden Rule models love of others from the love of self. It is worth noting that love of self is not to be confused with selfishness. Of course, a sick doctor can treat no one and an ignorant teacher can never be trusted, much less allowed to teach. But a doctor who seeks treatment for himself in order to be able to treat others and a teacher who spends hours seeking more knowledge to pass on to his students are the backbone of society.

To better serve yourself in order to serve others, one must practice humility, and there is no greater enhancer of magnetic leadership. The absence of humility breeds arrogance, which is a sure killer of magnetic leadership.

But a humble man is like a peaceful ocean or lake. Calm water attracts a multitude of fishermen who try to catch as many fish as they can, as safely and as inexpensively as possible. A humble man is a goldmine that wise and smart men are willing to explore and dig into at the expense of their own lives.

Humility is one of the best tools that a person seeking to develop a magnetic leadership can and should foster. It enables a person to perform wonders in the eyes of his fellow man and yet assure them that nothing extraordinary has happened that they could not perform as well. Humility is the art of downplaying achievements at least; at best, a genuine understanding of greater forces at work. Jesus, for instance, who according to the Gospels resuscitated the dead and compelled obedience to the forces of nature such as the wind and water, shrugged these miracles off, assuring common men that they, too, could do all things he did. He assured them they could even move mountains if the level of their confidence reached that manifestation.

One of the biggest overachievers of our time, Bill Gates, looks like anything but a super human. When we see him on television or in person, his presence assures us that he is just one of us who happens to understand the laws of nature. Achieving great things with humility is like unveiling a bright star that shines across the world and makes one truly attractive; covering success with a cloak of humility is the true power of magnetic leadership.

A boastful person, however, is in most cases the subject of hatred and diminished love. An arrogant attitude is a sure destroyer of magnetic leadership, no matter how wealthy, smart, or powerful one may be. There are so many reasons why arrogance is not only detrimental to our own inner growth, but also to our personal magnetism. Writing about leadership in the *Oregon Masonic News*, the Grand Master of the Masonic Grand Lodge of Oregon, AM & AF, Dennis D. Johnson writes:

> To be a good leader, you must be a good follower. Most of the time, when leadership is mentioned, people automatically start

thinking that leadership is unidirectional—that is only from the top down... To the contrary, leadership can take many different pathways.* (May 2008 edition)

It is clear what brother Johnson is saying that a good leader must sometimes allow himself to be shown the way by his followers, just like a good shepherd must understand when his sheep are thirsty, hungry, or frightened; and let himself be led to the river, to the pasture, or to safety. Unless this multidimensional aspect of leadership is understood and effectively practiced, the relationship between the sheep and the shepherd will greatly suffer.

In the case of magnetic leadership, unless one is willing to be attracted by the beauty of life that manifests through other people, one will attract very few people.

Here is what some consider being the greatest law of the universe, the law of attraction: "like attracts like," the law says. One who wants love should not seek the company of hateful people; instead, one should seek a loving person, otherwise one will attract hate. Those who want peace should let themselves be attracted by peaceful people; otherwise, they will attract upheaval.

Those who seek joy should let themselves be attracted by joyful people; otherwise, they will be attracted by sadness. No one seeking sunrays can benefit from them by staying inside a cave. The only

---

* Quote used with permission from the author and the Masonic Grand Lodge of AF&AM of Oregon.

way they can enjoy the sunrays is to expose themselves to the sun. Unless we let ourselves be vulnerable to sincere love, joy, and peace that come from the hearts of others, we will find it incredibly hard to develop a magnetic personality.

Brother Johnson proceeds in his essay by saying:

> No leader has all skills. Effective leaders have two or three leadership skills that they do rather well. Effective leaders also realize that in some areas their skills are weak . . . . Now, I've often heard some teachers tell that for us to succeed we must work to improve our weaknesses. This may come as a shock, but effective leaders don't do that. The reason is because no matter how hard they work, they might take a particular skill from 2 out of 10 to maybe a 4 or 5 out of 10. That's just barely average at best. And it took a great deal of their time and effort to maybe get the average. Because they are just not good at that particular skill. So effective leaders acknowledge weaknesses but let them go. Effective leaders will work on their strengths to make themselves even better in those areas and improve their effectiveness as leaders.[*]

The statement leads to some obvious questions: How can Johnson suggest that we should not work on our weaknesses? Why

---

[*] Quote used with permission from the author and the Masonic Grand Lodge of AF&AM. of Oregon.

and how do we let them go? And most importantly, how do we improve them? The evident answer here is just as Johnson answered the question in the minds of his readers: time. Humans are such imperfect beings that we find it practically impossible to perfect ourselves while here on Earth. Our imperfections are countless, and it is hard if not impossible to make ourselves faultless.

The average living person spends only eighty years of his life in a relatively meaningful, conscious and healthy state. At least the first eighteen of those years go by while we are in a state of youth and hardly conscious of the responsibility we must uphold. Fifteen or so of those eighty years are spent more or less in retirement, a period of decline in many aspects. So, we are left with less than fifty years of life when we are relatively capable of working on our weaknesses. Of those, only thirty years are truly dedicated to real work, and of those, only twenty years are very useful. In the United States military, service members are granted retirement after twenty years of active duty, with immediate pension payment regardless of age until they die.

If we take Johnson's reasoning as the basis of our logic we have to ask, should we spend our most precious twenty years of life working on our shortcomings or should we spend them helping to change the world through our strengths? There is no question that it is the latter, not the former. Otherwise, we would either spend all our life working on our weaknesses or doing less than we would have done had we focused on our strengths.

The question now becomes how do we let our weaknesses go? Answer: *humility*. Acknowledge our shortcomings and then assign those among us who are blessed with the relevant strengths to take charge. Avoid the can-do-all attitude. In every successful enterprise, this is called *teamwork*. Humility is at the basis of teamwork.

Teamwork is the secret of success of every social organization, from the smallest families to the biggest governments. Even the best and brightest scientists at NASA seldom act alone when performing the wonders they have been tasked to do. In fact, one could say the whole nation—from the babysitter to the highest politician in government—works together to achieve NASA's goals, directly or indirectly, not only through taxes but also through moral support, interest, community service, and of course all the work that holds together the network of NASA employees.

Let's take another example: we all know that a great bridge is not built by genius engineers alone, but by politicians, teachers, workers, drivers, administrators, miners, and so on. Even the weather forecaster on television may not be aware that he contributes by predicting the weather that determines the safety of the workers.

By being mindful of our weaknesses, then, and letting ourselves be attracted to those who have the strengths we lack, we complete ourselves while building an immense magnetic leadership that will stand the test of time; we will not only attract our contemporaries but also future generations.

A lot is involved in building a magnetic leadership, but this is the truest—discover the pearls hidden in your fellowmen, trust them until they prove you wrong, and work with them by enabling them to unearth the treasures buried in them and yourself, thus bringing only their best and yours to the world while minimizing the deficiencies of all team members. Through this process will you become as magnetic as the physical sun; only by seeking the merry sides of others will people orbit your leadership like planets joyfully and tirelessly orbit the sun.

- **Gratitude**

Before painting the mind with the images of gratitude, let's see what the wise people of history thought about it:

> A thankful heart is not only the greatest virtue, but parent of all other virtues. (Marcus Cicero)

> He that urges gratitude pleads the course of both God and men, for without it we can neither be sociable or religious. (Lucius Seneca)

> Blow, blow thou winter wind/Thou art not so unkind/As man's ingratitude. (William Shakespeare)

On His way to Jerusalem, He was passing along between Samaria and Galilee. And as He entered a village, He was met by ten lepers, who stood at a distance and lifted up their voices, and said, "Jesus, master, have mercy on us!" When He saw them, He said to them "Go and show yourselves to the priests." And as they went, they were cleansed. Then, one of them, when he saw that he was healed, turned back, praising God with a loud voice. And fell on his face at Jesus's feet, giving Him thanks. Now, he was a Samaritan. Then Jesus said, "Were not ten cleansed? Where are the nine? Was no one bound to give praise to God except this foreigner?" And He said to him, "Rise and go your way; your faith has made you well." (Luke 17:15-19)

This work is by no means a religious lecture. Our intention here is simply to show how ingratitude is such a negative force that strongly stirs the winds of both the visible and the invisible worlds that surround us, how it explodes both worlds like the strongest earthquake, and it undercuts the development of a magnetic leadership. It may sound extreme to the ears of many to hear that human language cannot do justice to the wonders of gratitude.

There is no investment or capital worth one tenth of true gratitude. Of course, some kinds of gratitude are forced like salaries to employees. These are not the forms of gratitude that are the subject of this investigation, because they come from outside in, and the world is transformed from the inside rather than from the outside. Thus, we will focus on the gratitude that comes from inside out, joyfully and without any pressure. We will discuss the kinds of gratitude that come from the heart.

I will, of course, illustrate gratitude with real-life examples, but before going on, let's see how one more source explains the power of gratitude to illustrate how magnetic leadership blossoms when the feeling of gratitude is judiciously used. In the *Voice of I AM,* a magazine published by the Saint Germaine Press, Inc., there is a discourse on gratitude that reads:

> There is perhaps no other quality of feeling, which is really a phase of Divine Love, that releases to mankind such blessings as does that of Gratitude; because when you are grateful for something, every bit of energy in your emotional bodies is not only harmonious, but now notice—every time you feel grateful for something, there is a release, an expansion and a giving forth of the light of your own Life Stream. That is why gratitude brings such gigantic blessing to those who will make themselves a "CUP" of its Mighty Flame and Out-pouring of Dazzling light, to all they contact everywhere without reservation. (January 1945)

When we buy merchandise, we hand over coin or paper money to the merchant, but sometimes this money is resisted, depending on the location. Many foreign currencies are not accepted by merchants and some banks as well. But gratitude, the truest currency, is never resisted by either men or Spirit. One of the reasons why the world is engulfed with wars, crimes, and unhappiness is because most of us just want to receive, but hardly any want to give.

So, we could all be enthusiastic about giving gratitude back for the life we have received, not just for the material possessions we possess but for more meaningful gifts like our health and that of our loved ones, peace, the knowledge that enables us to carry on our daily tasks, the roads we drive on, the light provided by the sun and moon, and the good sleep we enjoy at night. We could be grateful for all things visible and invisible that surround us and make our lives livable and without which we would easily fall into despair and misery. By being grateful for small and big things that cost absolutely nothing—a greeting from a stranger on the street, the air we breathe, our health, the praise we get from supporters, and the warnings we get from opponents—we strengthen our magnetic leadership, because we are engaging with the weakest side of both men and spirit, the love of appreciation and glory. Do you know a single normal person who would be offended by appreciation? I don't. Gratitude is universally irresistible. Many people owe their careers to creatively expressing gratitude to their coworkers, superiors, interviewers, and of course, God too!

Anyone who is seriously working on their magnetic leadership must study how to imaginatively express their gratitude along the way. Gratitude may be expressed through a postcard or in any other material form; but by itself, it has no substance. It must come from within; it is a feeling from inside; it must be truly heartfelt, sincere, and it must never be faked. If it is not sincere, it may irreparably destroy personal magnetism. The flip side of gratitude is hypocrisy. Few things demagnetize leadership like hypocrisy.

Very few people will stand for the cause of a person who employs double standards. It is far better to express your gratitude on a small postcard than to offer a big promotion to a supporter with the hidden intention of causing harm or creating a scapegoat for your own misdeeds.

Gratitude, of course, does not have to come in the same currency in which we received the service. In other words, do not always render services in return for something, but don't fail to honestly provide the same joy you received from the services provided by others. The truth of the matter is that we are all happy or offended when someone we assisted sometime in life has done good or ill in appreciation or lack of it for something positive we have rendered them. Two illustrations will try to shed light on these two situations.

The first example is the case of a medical doctor in the northwestern part of the United States. I will call this medical doctor Peter and his wife Jane. Peter and Jane were happily married for more than fourteen years. During their happy marriage, they had three children and bought three houses.

Like many unfortunate unions, Peter and Jane's union grew loveless. Then, one morning, Jane decided it was time to leave. She had once worked as an insurance agent but had quit work to raise their children. Eventually, Jane filed for divorce. In the divorce decree, the judge ordered the couple to sell one of their houses and to share the two remaining. Jane was given custody of the kids, and Peter was ordered to pay child support and spousal alimony.

Peter protested the ruling by walking out of the court. The judge ordered him to return or be charged with contempt of court. His legal counsel pleaded with him to return. When he did, he had to endure the further wrath of the judge.

After a couple of years, Peter found himself paying most of his income in child support and spousal alimony to an ungrateful ex-spouse, who was by now enjoying her new life with her new friends. Enraged by anger rather than jealousy, Peter quit his job. He soon defaulted on his mortgage, lost his house, and stopped meeting his financial obligations. His ex-wife went back to court.

The judge ordered child support and spousal alimony to be paid from Peter's savings. Since Peter had voluntarily quit his job and then refused to go back to work, he found himself homeless on the streets and swore to live such a life instead of working to pay his ex-wife. On the streets, Peter could never live an anonymous life. Soon he was noticed by some of the patients he had treated when he'd worked at his former job.

To cut a long story short, Peter's former patients were so grateful to him that they provided him with financial help and shelter. They pleaded with Peter to go back to work. He did. But he didn't do it for himself; he did it to show his gratitude to the dozens of former patients who helped him get off the streets. Peter started meeting his obligations again, but not because he was ordered to do so by the judge. He did it because he felt obligated to his grateful patients.

That is the power of gratitude; that is its miracle. It transforms the world from inside out joyfully, peacefully, and harmoniously. Happiness can be a very elusive thing. Many people have a lot of material possessions that others would die for, but still they are unhappy and even distressed. Gratitude brings happiness not only to the receiver, but also to the giver. Unless one knows how to appreciate what one has—starting with one's health—not only will happiness prove elusive, but solace will also be hard to find, and one will never develop a magnetic leadership. Gratitude is really the magic ingredient of a magnetic leadership.

Anyone who is working to develop a magnetic leadership must ask him/herself these questions: What prompts people to volunteer in nonprofit organizations? Can the biggest companies survive if they do not show their gratitude to their workers, customers, and the community? Do wages alone help recruit and retain the best and the brightest? The answer to all these questions is the understanding that life is more than just material accumulation.

"Man cannot live on bread alone," said Jesus. Hundreds of thousands of medical doctors, teachers, and other professionals volunteer their skills for little or no pay; they do it to experience the joy of serving and the satisfaction engendered by the appreciation they get from those they help. Soldiers gladly put their lives on the line in return for a thank-you from a grateful nation. The understanding of gratitude is one of the most powerful elements of the art of magnetic leadership. It is practically impossible to build a magnetic leadership unless we let those who helped us along the way know how we have been touched by their assistance. It is even more important to let the community at large know your gratitude (depending on the scope of your position) for its support. And this is done by giving something valuable back to them. It is no accident that streets, highways, public places, cities, and states are named after local and national heroes because enlightened governments have known the secret of gratitude for centuries.

It might do you some good to know what keeps many people from being grateful and what blinds others from accepting hearty gratitude expressed by their fellowmen. Human beings are very complex creatures. Sometimes you just don't know the cause of joy or sadness. When you decide to befriend or work with someone, all that protects you is the hope that your new comrade will return the favor.

Man is a very ambiguous being. You must accept living in that reality. Man is like a mouth that the hand feeds, but it still finds reasons to bite the same hand that feeds it. Yes, humans are like that, many times it is not our worst enemies who do us harm, but our closest and most *trusted* friends. History is full of examples of trusted friends who turned out to be double agents. Perhaps, you have seen, known, heard or read about a friend backstabbing another friend for as little as thirty pieces of silver . . .

Ingratitude is part of human nature, unfortunately. Sometime, somewhere, a spouse, a partner, a friend, a doctor, a lawyer, a team member, a security guard, a sister, or a brother will let down those who placed their faith in them. Anyone who is trying to build a strong magnetic leadership should always give people the benefit of the doubt and never see the evil side of man, but rather the positive side.

Physical isolation is exactly the deathbed of magnetic leadership, while spiritual isolation is its charging station. A magnetic leader will always be willing to trust others in order to attract them until he is proven wrong; and when he is, he must also have the same magnitude to graciously move on without hard feelings and recognize the episode as another chapter of his life that must be forgiven. It mustn't be forgotten, but remembered as a rich lesson about man's unpredictable nature. Doing this will not only increase one's magnetic leadership, but it will also keep one mentally healthy and physically fit. It will wear off the hard feelings that influence the thoughts and actions of others, and stop one from worrying about the things one cannot control, which is the source of ill health. This may be easier said than done. Ingratitude is a very difficult feeling to bear. According to Shakespeare, ingratitude is far less kind than the wind of winter. It is not easy to get over it; it is upsetting, and it breaks the bonds of social intercourse.

Many indications can cast light on possible ingratitude and enable us to lessen its shock. One of those indications is the understanding of life itself, by nature, as a classroom. In fact, this is the only classroom where you are both teacher and student. Without that understanding, you will never be able to enjoy life, because you will go from one misery to another.

If you take life as a classroom and be eager to learn positively from the thoughts and actions of others, regardless of their impact on you, you will not only minimize the effect of ingratitude, you will certainly be grateful to teachers you meet at home, at work, at your place of worship and on the street.

Bad or good, the actions of our fellow human beings have one major purpose, and that is to shed light on us so we can avoid doing to others what we do not like done to us. Does that sound like the Golden Rule? It does indeed. That is the power behind magnetic leadership. That is how ancient leaders were able to tell their followers "Follow me," and see them come in multitudes to construct the wonders of the world.

Bad actions in many cases may turn out to be the blessings you have been looking for. Let me express it differently: as much as man hates pain, pain is good for man. Why? Without pain, life would be hazardous, perhaps meaningless; man would be incapable of assessing injury, illness, even risk, and practically incapable of feeling joy. Without the ability to feel pain, life would not only be joyless, and a constant danger since no one would be able to distinguish painful from joyful experiences.

On this specific point, Esther and Jerry Hicks, authors of *Ask and it is Given*, write, "We do not want to imply that feeling of negative emotion is a bad thing, because, very often, in the feeling of negative emotion, you are alerted to the fact that you are in the process of negatively attracting. And so, it is like a warning bell. It is part of your guidance system," (p. 254).

What can guide man better than knowledge? Who is a better teacher than life itself? And if you take ingratitude or rudeness, shown to you or betrayal done to you as opportunities to learn, you will certainly overcome their effects, and despite the shock you might feel, you will build more relationships and repair the ones that have disappointed you.

A magnetic leader is a good student of life; he understands that the ingratitude he suffers is so he can do to others what he would want them to do unto him. By looking at ingratitude as a lesson rather than a curse, one will always be grateful to and less ungrateful to others; therefore, one will keep building a magnetic leadership by holding captive the minds of many and becoming the darling of their hearts.

Another way of lessening the impact of ingratitude, while empowering the seed of gratitude, to enable magnetic leadership to take roots is to see ingratitude as a pest, a nuisance; that is what it really is, a bug that disturbs even the loveliest of flowers. The quote above from St. Luke is a perfect illustration—even Jesus Christ was troubled by ingratitude. No person is immune to it. It is damned by every culture of every society.

What would you do to keep this monstrous iniquity from affecting your magnetic leadership? One way is to act like a wise salesman who refuses to let the margin of profit dictate the longevity of his art. Countless books have been written about the power of expectation, and few explain it better than James Allen. In *As a Man Thinketh*, he writes, "The vision that you glorify in your mind, the ideal that you enthrone in your heart—you will build your life by; this you will become."

Not to disagree with Allen, but in the case of gratitude and ingratitude, it is usually better to expect neither. Not that you are trying to avoid both, but because when the unexpected comes, you will be well-equipped to deal with it, especially when the unexpected is also the worst-case scenario. Of course, it feels good to learn that someone to whom you have rendered a service is ever grateful. It lets us know that our gift has been fully received, which is the most satisfying part of giving.

When I worked for a big bank, I encountered an eighteen-year-old man who wanted to start a business using his first credit card as his source of capital. The young man, let's call him John Doe, barely understood how credit cards work. He did not understand that the bank would expect monthly payments and charge interest. Full of anger, panic, and frustration, he called the bank one day, and I picked up the phone.

After lashing out at the bank using all kinds of colorful language, I asked him to calm down so I could explain the situation in such a way that he could understand me better. The young man agreed. I started explaining how it works: "Do not do this . . . do not do that . . . never this . . . never that . . . do this . . . do that . . . always this . . . always that . . . . If you have any doubt or question, please call us twenty-four hours, seven days a week."

Through the phone, I could feel the young man's demystification. He exclaimed, "Wow . . . I did not know that . . . incredible . . . . Next time, I will do better. Wow! You really saved my life; now I know . . . . This will never happen again . . ."

In my mind, I thought I simply did the job that I was paid to do, but in the mind of the young man, it was a life-saving experience. The next day, still amazed by the service that he received, the man called back to talk to the manager. The manager was off, but he left a message on his voice mail that said something like this:

"My name is John Doe Jr.; I am calling because yesterday I spoke with one of your employees, whose name is [Mr. Makano]. This man really saved my life. He explained to me a lot of things in a professional and easy-to-understand manner . . . . I will never get in trouble again. I will use your service wisely . . . he saved . . . he is a valuable employee! Thank you . . . ."

When the manager returned to work after a few days off, he played the message in front of all our team members. I really felt very good, not just because of the gift certificate I received from the bank, but because of the unexpected gratitude from a person whom I thought I was just rendering a usual service. How would I have felt if that young man, like so many others, cared less about my service? Indifferent, of course. Why did I feel humbled by his gratitude? Because it was unexpected and sincere.

That is the power of unexpected gratitude; it stirs joy strongly from inside out. Ingratitude stirs strong anger if gratitude was expected. The anger stirred by unexpected ingratitude is usually more manageable if no gratitude was expected. We all know how it feels when you happily buy a gift for someone you care about, and be met with ungraciousness. Imagine the feeling of an experienced worker who, after training a new employee from college, is laid off by his long-time employer as soon as the novice is barely able to manage the task. Unexpected ingratitude is shocking when you are expecting gratitude, while unexpected gratitude is always uplifting.

Indeed, nothing is more disappointing and discouraging than ingratitude. Life is sweet when you sow less but reap more, and it is bitter when you reap less than you sowed. Farmers always expect the amount of grains they planted. In the same way as farmers are disheartened when they harvest less than they planted, those who expect gratitude or praise from beneficiaries of their good deeds put themselves in a position where disillusionment may be unavoidable.

Instead of viewing life in terms of farming where giving less and expecting more is the common law, why not view it in terms of a mirror used by an attractive young lady to build her self-confidence before going out and charming onlookers. Life should be a mirror where our imperfections are reflected and corrected with effort, but it should not be like a farm where more is gained for less given. We are told that what one man of average intelligence can do, all men can. We are all guilty of either breaking or bending the law at some time in our lives, even lawmakers and law enforcement agents.

In fact, the major difference between those who live behind bars and those who live in freedom is that the convicted felons were caught in the wrong place at the wrong time. If none of us is guiltless, why expect more for less, and why not reflect the shortcomings of others as potentially our own and then work assiduously to keep from repeating them. If we aim to learn from the mistakes of others rather than condemning them, we will expect less for more instead of more for less and we will rarely be shocked or discouraged when our expectations are not met. Thus, we will always work our hearts off to reach our ideal goals and sharpen our magnetic leadership, keeping it ever shining throughout space and time.

All these suggestions of escaping the savagery of ingratitude and erecting our own gratitude attitude regardless of what is thrown at us is to instill the idea that magnetic leadership is a conscious choice of serving just one master: society.

Seeing society in general every time you serve a person or a community is an effective bulletproof coat against ingratitude. A magnetic leader sees every person as a representative of society, so every time the opportunity comes up to serve someone or a community, he takes advantage of it to the fullest because he knows he is serving his master—the society—not just the physical individual before him. Individuals may always be thankless, but ingratitude from society is rare, for it never forgets its heroes.

Serving society through individuals and then expecting all your compensation from society will always allow you to keep brightening the star of your leadership. The name of the game is to aim for the nobler goals, that way whatever you hit will always be worthwhile.

A few instances in history illustrate situations when societies have been ungrateful to their benefactors and many of those instances have been corrected:

Charles de Gaul liberated Nazi-occupied France, but he was thrown out of office after he restored the pride of the French people. After his death, the French people immortalized him in many different ways. That's how society corrects is wrongs.

On the other hand, countless instances have occurred when individuals have been ungrateful to their friends. With all its ugliness, when viewed as a lesson, ingratitude sometimes changes the course of history, for the better. We are all familiar with the so-called kiss of Judas, which ended up becoming an example of the power of forgiveness despite the agony one may suffered due to the ingratitude of a once-trusted ally.

No one knows what Europe would be today had Napoleon not been betrayed by one of his most trusted confidants: Charles

Maurice de Talleyrand. What is certain is that lives were saved, and Europe was spared further destruction.

Far from defending ingratitude, these examples are meant to call to view life as a mirror where you can see and improve your own shortcomings so that you might do good for the sake of society rather than individuals; hence, you will always be grateful despite the ingratitude of others and your magnetic leadership will forever grow.

- **Self-Pity**

The most vicious harm that most people do to themselves is succumbing to self-pity, which is the highest form of self-betrayal. The reality is that, many people betray themselves every day. Their self-betrayal keeps them suffering atrociously for a long time. Self-pity is the ugliest form of betrayal that most of us do to ourselves. Self-pity alone is responsible for countless crimes committed to society every day; it is responsible for the deadliest enemies of mankind: fear and poverty. People who feel pity for themselves in the hope that the world will be more sympathetic toward them end up disappointed and discouraged, and consequently, they contribute very little to the progress of society. Self-pity causes people to die poor while blaming everybody else for their miseries, by feeling the world owes them everything, as they consider themselves victims of injustice. Seeing only what is wrong with life, many self-pitying people spend their lives imprisoned in their own imaginations, discouraged and cursing life and helplessly waiting for the final blow to come, to which they surrender without resistance.

The damage caused to life by self-pity is by all means indescribable. Its disappearance from the face of the planet would be the single most important event since the appearance of light. It could change our lovely little home in the universe, the planet Earth, into a crystal globe that could illumine distant stars and a totally self-sufficient home where pain and suffering would disappear like the prehistoric dinosaurs. Self-pity keeps the vast majority of mankind in the service of the tiny minority; the most self-confident segment of the world population decides the fate of the majority. Words cannot adequately describe the crime of self-pity.

Self-pity will never win the sympathy of man; much less attract favor from the gods. It is a dangerous enemy of man and must be dealt with head on with all your being and power. As a shadow instantly vanishes at the appearance of light, so does self-pity at the appearance of happiness and passion. A fight between self-pity and happiness would not be a fair fight. Self-pity is defenseless in the presence of happiness; it melts without a struggle like heated ice. Self-pity kills the body, the soul, the mind, and the spirit just as happiness shines the body, brightens the soul, inspires the mind, and frees the spirit. The so-called diagnosis of depression is a prime example of self-pity. It leads to suicide, underperformance at work, and total chaos at home and in the environment. It must be fought, not necessarily with prescription drugs, but with the seeds of happiness that no one can sow in your heart but yourself.

These seeds can be found when you compare yourself to other people who are much less fortunate than you in terms of health, friends, and opportunities. Rather than seeing negativity in everything, try to see the positive. For instance, rather than feeling pity for yourself when your car breaks down on the freeway, why not be happy it was not a deadly accident? Rather than feel bad for being dumped by an abusive partner, why not be happy for the second chance life has given you to meet or start over with a more appreciative and compassionate partner? With this attitude, self-pity or sadness will disappear defenselessly like a shadow. Happiness, the vibration of the highest feeling in the universe, is not only the key to the hearts of men; it is the key to the door of the universe. A happy heart pleases man and God.

Students of life have learned and developed many effective ways of ridding themselves of self-pity. One of the most philosophical lessons taught in schools of wisdom is this:

The world pays every one of us in our own currency. If you sow corn, you will harvest more corn, no beans or rice; if you look sad, you will reflect sadness, not happiness or courage; if you smile or laugh, you will reveal joy. In other words, as teachers of life might say: *reaping what one sows is an exact, mathematic formula. You cannot multiply two by two and have a number other than four.*

Nothing is more disastrous than self-pity or sadness, yet people are sad when all it takes to defeat a feeling of sadness is to substitute it with a feeling of happiness, and in a second it is gone. It is important to know that those who suffer from self-pity, depression, or sadness have the power to stop it: all they need is to engage their will. Self-pity can be a conscious or an unconscious emotion, but it is fought and subdued by a conscious effort. This battle cannot be fought in terms of "fire with fire" but rather "fire with water or water with fire." It must be annihilated at once without escalation before total surrender. The more overwhelming the water the firefighters have, the better chances they have to put out the fire; the heavier the rain, the sooner the flames of the forest fire are extinguished. On the other hand, the higher the heat, the sooner the water will evaporate. Water and fire or heat never cohabit, it is one or the other, never both together. The Amazon jungle will always be wet as long as its water reservoir is plentiful; and the Sahara desert will suffer drought as long as there is no rain.

There is not a more effective way of fighting depression, sadness, or self-pity than enjoying the brighter side of life. No matter where you stand in life, whether you are a king, a movie star, a laborer, a refugee, or a poor person, there is something good and bad in your life. If you do good, you will always be happy; if you look to the bad, you will always be sad; if you look to both, you will have a mixed bag. Make up your mind where you want your true north to be.

Self-pity is also the product of an inferiority complex; therefore, it cannot be fought either with more of itself or by its direct opposite, the superiority complex. Fighting an inferiority complex with a superiority complex is like undressing Paul to dress Peter or vice versa. It involves serious problems that we do not have time and space to solve here. This is just a warning. An inferiority complex is fought by the feeling of being equal among all men.

If you feel that all men are equal before the law of nature, you will never let your spirit bow to another person's spirit nor lord it over him; you will treat people with respect and demand that they treat you with the same respect you show them. The forces of nature distinguish no man. When the snow or rain falls, it falls on Wall Street and Main Street, on the White House and on the remotest Indian village in Alaska; the kings and presidents of the world are subject to life's tragedies in the same way as refugees at a camp in Africa. We are all equal before the law of man when correctly applied; we are all born naked, and after we die, our skeletons will not show our former social or physical differences. This feeling of equality with all men wins more than half the battle against self-pity and makes other steps a matter of formality.

The question here is: what is the true secret of effectively purging self-pity, sadness, and the inferiority complex? Sometimes things are easier said than done, and this is not an exception. But paying attention to what Dumont once said can reveal a masterpiece of the operation. He writes: "There is no royal road to anything worth having. We must work for what we get. The prizes are not for weaklings and triflers, but the persistent, earnest individuals who will 'hang on' until they succeed," (*The Art and Science of Personal Magnetism*, p 9).

However, it is extremely difficult for weaklings and triflers, as the quote says, to beat depression or an inferiority complex. It is even harder for those who are consistently looking for excuses to fail. Persistence is magic. It is a concentration of all the knowledge, wisdom, poise, courage, faith, determination, and desires accumulated until it can powerfully explode in the face of an ignorant and miscalculating enemy called failure and a kingmaker of a beloved prince called success.

Persistence propels orphans to the top of the pyramid of power, it is truly the door through which we enter the hearts of people and rule them. Unless the feeling of happiness and equality is persistently felt, self-pity, depression, and an inferiority complex will slip in and mistreat you, this time more harshly than before.

I will close this segment with few words from an authority on this subject: "...self-pity is an extreme form of egocentrism, and usually a result of a very selfish perspective of the world. People who regularly engage in self-pity are miserable, and they tend to make others quite unhappy, too." So there you have it folks, self pity makes others unhappy. Trust me; no sane person will be attracted to someone who will certainly make him or her unhappy.

Chapter Six

A Page from a Master's Playbook

Henry Ford, a master of the game of life, wrote his name in stone onto the book of life by aiming higher and for a nobler goal; as a result, he built a magnetic personality that will always be honored by every generation to come. Through his labor philosophy, Henry Ford embarked on one of the most revolutionary employment perspectives of his day. He undertook this gigantic task against the established forces of the day, forces far bigger than him.

Early in its infancy, the Ford Motor Company suffered heavy turnover, which caused the loss of qualified manpower and an endless circle of training and retraining. Faced with the possibility of seeing his dream vanish before his eyes, as the world events of 1914 unfolded, Ford decided to go against the greatest forces of the capitalistic system—Wall Street and labor unions. He initiated his own system, known as Welfare Capitalism, in which starting pay more than doubled to bring workers into a Ford Company consumer class.

Henry Ford was able to withstand these powerful forces because he served his own interests by putting the interests of the Ford employees first and, through them, the interests of the community at large.

At the time, when many Americans were wracked with labor practices that forced some workers to toil for up to thirteen hours a day and many others until t*he end of work*—whenever that was, Ford slashed his company's work time from nine hours to eight hours per day, or forty hours per week, and increased the starting pay from $2.34 to $5.00 per day, effectively establishing what we today take for granted: a living wage. He raised his minimum wage to the annoyance of his fellow industrialists and Wall Street investors.

On the other hand, Ford went out of his way to confront unions to the bitter end; he believed the unions did not necessarily have the best interests of the workers at heart and that they were the major force that restricted productivity. Rather than taking instructions on how best to treat workers, Ford implemented worker—and family-friendly policies that both enabled the Ford workers to buy the products they produced and also have more available time to spend with their families.

This is how *Time* magazine explains Ford's feud with the unions and its outcome:

Ford was adamantly against labor unions. He explained his views on unions in chapter 18 of *My Life and Work*. He thought they were too heavily influenced by some leaders who, despite their ostensible good motives, would end up doing more harm than good for workers.

Most wanted to restrict productivity as a means to foster employment, but Ford saw this as self-defeating, because in his view, productivity was necessary for any economic prosperity to exist. (January 14, 1935)

Not seeing the needs of workers, company, and society as necessarily at odds and feeling gracious for all they provided him, Ford also believed that productivity gains that obviated certain jobs would nevertheless stimulate the larger economy and thus grow new jobs elsewhere, whether within the same corporation or in others. His plan worked: Ford's Model A was the first car affordable to workers—his workers in particular, who also had more time to enjoy them, effectively bringing the country into the automobile age, which spurred a whole host of new businesses, and catapulting Ford into one of the most profitable companies of its time. Everybody profited.

Obviously, very few of us will reach the benchmark set by Henry Ford, but whatever you do for anyone, feel and visualize the community as the recipient of your deeds. By doing this, you will rarely be victim of ingratitude and you will be grateful for all the privileges life has given you to serve others. This will keep your magnetic leadership shining and radiating like a bright star.

Evidently, Henry Ford had a much bigger nest and more eggs to care for than most of us will ever have. He was able to master these laws, still you can learn from him to care for your nest and eggs not matter how minimal they are. Tearing off a page from a master's playbook and running away with it for worthy ends is perfectly legal under law both above and below.

Gratitude is the real backbone of magnetic leadership; people must feel your appreciation for what they have done for you, and you must show it in deeds and words. You can realize your most productive and useful relations not by profit sharing or offering a forty-hour workweek as Ford did, but by sincerely considering the needs and interests of communities even at the risk of annoying powerful special-interest groups. Special interests, of course, will try to revile you, but community will reward you by pouring the everlasting fuel of gratitude into your engine to keep you going and going and going.

Self-Control

Before proceeding, let's take a look at these words of Ernest Holmes, the founder of Religious Science:

> Mental hygiene is just as real as physical hygiene, and equally necessary. To be well, one must be happy. To be happy, one must have a sense of security. One must have confidence in himself, in those around him, and in the universe itself. He must be unified with himself and with life. (*The Art of Life*, p. 100)

In many ways, man is just an animal, but a unique animal indeed based on one major characteristic: the power of man's inner self. The inner self of man comprises intelligence, wisdom, love, and most of all, self-confidence, which manifests itself as a strong faith in one's ability to be and to do, as well as the expression of free will. All other living beings on Earth act on their natural instincts alone, but in addition to instinct, man acts on the power of the will, the voluntary power, the power to make the choice between good and bad, action or inaction.

This power of free will is fundamentally put into the service of self-control—over and above the effort to control events and other people—in the person committed to magnetic leadership. Self-control enhances magnetic leadership. It is only possible to continuously attract other people for the purpose of multiplying power by acting together if one has the power to control oneself. Usually the most powerful barriers to our joy and success, which we all face on a regular basis, are not our daily outer struggles but our ongoing inner weaknesses. Self-control is an incredible attribute that few people understand and use effectively

There is absolutely nothing, above or below, that can hinder the triumph of a person who has effectively overcome his inner weakness. For centuries, long before the temples of Apollo had engraved on its entrance the words *know thyself*, it was taught in ancient Egyptian temples that self-knowledge was the only true knowledge that man needed; with this, he could achieve anything that he set his mind to. Pythagoras, a great thinker of ancient Greece, is credited to have said, "No man is free who cannot command himself," and the

Roman philosopher Lucius Annaeus Seneca said, "most powerful is he who has himself in his power."

Italian Renaissance poet and playwright Pietro Aretino and seventeenth century British poet and scholar John Milton go even further in emphasizing the power of self-knowledge. In May 1537, Aretino proclaimed himself a monarch, saying, "I am indeed a king, because I know how to rule myself." Milton, describing a super monarch, said, "He, who reigns within himself and rules passions, desires, and fears, is more than a king."

Self-knowledge is important because it is the source of self-control., Self-control is a big deal because it is the only inner force that prompts courage, controls passion, and wipes out fear and doubt. Louis XIV, one of the most powerful kings of France, unambiguously stated that "there is little that can withstand a man who can conquer himself."

Haven't we been told that the biggest victory a man can achieve is self-conquest? Self-control does just that. Magnetic leadership is absolutely irrelevant without thinking about self-control, without which passions, anger, fear, and doubt will run rampant. That is just an inescapable truth. No matter how charming one is, a display of anger or fear in public may effectively destroy one's power to attract followers. Some public figures have not only lost the respect of loved ones and admirers, but they have also lost their careers for simply showing an incapacity for self-control publicly. Development of self-control is a central prerequisite of magnetic leadership. The obvious question is how to develop it.

One of the most effective methods of building self-control is bringing the power of the attention under control by focusing it on only desired objectives. The power of attention is one of the strongest power man has; it is referred to by masters of life as *the golden key*, because what man focuses his attention on, he becomes. Those who focus their attention on religion become saints, those who focus on the art of healing become doctors, those who focus on politics become politicians, and those who focus on teaching become teachers, and so on. A man who focuses on nothing becomes nothing; it is that simple.

Philip Massinger, English dramatist, once said, "He that would govern others first should be master of himself," and Dennis Johnson, Masonic Past Grand Master of Oregon, would later add, "The toughest person a leader ever leads is himself. Hold yourself to higher standards of conduct, performance, and behavior. If you wouldn't follow yourself, how can you expect anyone to follow you?"

That is the magic key to magnetic leadership. Focusing attention on something is easy when it is always about the desire you want to materialize. A magnetic leader has his thoughts always on the greater good of those he hopes to lead. By constantly thinking or mentally solving a social problem in advance, a leader becomes magnetic, because when the time of action comes, he will be calm, unafraid, and positive, thus radiating self-control and exhibiting magnetic leadership.

The world is not run by money or guns, it is run by self-controlled people, and it has been like that since the dawn of time. This is how an Italian boy named Napoleon became emperor of France and how the son of an African immigrant named Obama became president of the most powerful country on Earth. Those among us who have more control over our passions and emotions control and rule the world.

Savvy business, political, religious, and artistic leaders all have this one characteristic in common. They focus their attention and thoughts on their preoccupations; consequently they understand the best way to proceed and lead the rest of us. Life distributes success and happiness proportionally based solely on this principle. No one can help but become a magnetic leader by keeping his/her own emotions and passions under strict control. Now let's get more into the specifics of self-control in order to become masters of our own emotions.

Thought

Physicist Albert Einstein once said that imagination is more important than knowledge. *The Oxford American Desk Dictionary and Thesaurus* (2nd edition) defines imagination as the "mental faculty of forming images or concepts of external objects not present to the senses." Just like a house is made of stones or bricks, imagination is made of thoughts. Thoughts are those details that constitute imagination. Man is a creation of his thoughts. What a man thinks about constantly, he becomes; what a man focuses his attention on, he becomes.

Thought is the basic material of creation. Nothing can be created unless it is thought of first. The power of thought is fundamental to magnetic leadership. With thought, we can build and we can destroy; we can kill or give life; we can overcome low emotions; we can acquire courage or fear; faith or doubt; success or failure; love or indifference; strength or weakness; determination or discouragement; resilience or hopelessness; forgiveness or revenge; and so on. Magnetic personality development depends on what kinds of thoughts we decide to entertain. The best kinds of thoughts are the ones that make one a good or better person, and those are the thoughts that make society a better place, a positive and constructive environment.

By continuously thinking positive thoughts, you become a personification of those qualities by charging yourself with their powers, which will literally radiate through you and attract likeminded people who will make your magnetic leadership a reality. How to control thought? People certainly have unequal abilities to control thought, but wherever they are on the spectrum, they have the same ability to distinguish good from bad thoughts. Right and wrong may be matters of law, and most of us do not know right from wrong until we are in the situation, because what is right here May be wrong somewhere else.

For instance, polygamy is wrong in the West but not so in Africa or in some Islamic countries. On the other hand, murder is bad and wrong almost everywhere.

Knowledge of what is good and right on one hand, and bad and wrong on the other leads the way to controlling thought. The more you understand about these things, the easier it is to maintain control. Thought is controlled by always thinking about what is good universally and right locally—when the mind suddenly brings bad and wrong thoughts, immediately reverse the course and force your mind back to the opposite of the invading negative thought.

When you feel fear, purge it out with thoughts of courage; if in doubt, starve it to death with thoughts of faith; if in anger, quickly choke it off with thoughts of joy. That discipline of expelling negative thoughts from your mind is the power to control thoughts. I do not know any other. This must be done swiftly to keep negative thoughts from growing stronger, after which it may be difficult to deter them. If you are thinking about a fearful idea, switch to an idea of courage; if you are thinking about hate or finding yourself indifferent, think love; if you are thinking about discouragement, think about persistence.

When an unwanted idea persists from leaving your mind use your voice and repeat out loud in a low breath, the thoughts you want to occupy your mental universe. When overwhelmed by fear, switch to courage or repeat to yourself a courage-inspiring affirmation like, *I am fearless; I am invincible . . .* and mean it, until fear gives up; if you are gripped by thoughts of discouragement, say to yourself, *I am a winner and a winner never quits* . . . until your inner compass kicks in and indicates the true north of your actions.

Switching from negative ideas to positive ideas *unconsciously* is not as effective as switching ideas and sustaining them effectively with conscious will. That is why not all who switch thoughts become magnetic, but those who do so voluntarily become magnetic. The key word here is *attention*, the golden key that unleashes power. Thoughts must be controlled by attention to radiate magnetism, not instinct; mindfulness, not accident; focus, not daydreaming. Thoughts are like cows—you must guide them and never let them control you, or you will find chaos. You become what you think—by switching from negative to positive willingly and continuously you increase your personal magnetism.

It is important to note that going voluntarily from negative to positive thought is a fabulous accomplishment, but it is not enough. The new thought must become the object of concentration, the focus, in order for the process to reach its full potential. Concentration is the magic key of achievement, just like Dumont would put it:

> Read the life of any great man, and you will find that the dominant quality that made him successful was the ability to concentrate. Study those that have been failures and you will often find that lack of concentration was the cause. One thing at a time and that done well is a good rule as I can tell . . . You are aided by both

visible and invisible forces when you concentrate on either *to do* or *to be*. (*The Power of Concentration*, p. 103-104)

Passion

If you want to achieve something very important to you, you must love it deeply; you must love it to the point of accepting the pain and suffering that may come with it. Prophets and philosophers throughout history and tradition have taught that love is the greatest power there is in the universe. Intense love with minimal action has enough power to bring success. Love is what makes the difference between two people working on the same project with identical means and methods achieving different outcomes. Love is what makes the difference when two salesmen with the same capital and knowledge achieve two opposite outcomes—one fails and the other succeeds.

Deep love of your desires or dreams to the near exclusion of everything else is called passion. When a passion is uncontrolled, it is called obsession and becomes harmful to life, but this is beyond the scope of this chapter. The passion we are talking about here is the *controlled* passion—the one we always hear people saying: Follow your passions! Follow your bliss!

This is the reason why real happy people usually make up between one and two percent of the population in every society. In the United States, only 5 percent of the population controls more than 80 percent of the wealth. Many of us love pleasure and hate the pain that precedes success and happiness, which is why our dreams go with us to our graves. Life has a pyramid-shaped figure—those who love pleasure and hate pain are the masses that occupy the base, and those who love their dreams regardless of the pain that stands in the way are at the top. Passion (not obsession) or deep love of ambition is the energy that determines one's place on the pyramid of life. According to your passion, so will your leadership be magnetizing.

If you examine some of the great historical figures from various walks of life—religious, political, military, scientific, exploration, and business—you will find that deep-seated passion of their ambitions is a common trait. Take a look at personalities like Moses, Jesus, Alexander the Great, Christopher Columbus, Napoleon, Marie Curie, John D. Rockefeller, Mother Theresa, and many more: you will realize that these people were willing to give up their own lives for the sake of accomplishing what they believed in. It is so because the so-called law of attraction is simple passion or deep love of what you want. Only love attracts; only love brings together two forces; only love harmonizes; only love brings about happiness. It is practically impossible for two people who do not love each other at some point to get married. Even arranged marriages must be based on at least a mild love or attraction that will grow, otherwise disaster will be the outcome, sooner or later. It is not that poor people do not love money; they do not have a passion for it or love for it as rich people do.

"Nothing great in the world has ever been accomplished without passion," said German philosopher Georg W.F. Hegel.

The American abolitionist Harriet Tubman concurred: "Every great dream begins with a dreamer. Always remember, you have within you the strength, the patience, and the passion to reach for the stars to change the world."

Passion alone is responsible for great achievements; passion alone is the true power that ignites the light of success. Man is truly the presence of his inner self only when he passionately manifests the seed of creativity that all men are bred with, but few comprehend; only then can we all cease to be the sleeping forces. All the powers, including attention, love, courage, persistence, etc., that enable man to achieve greatness are all inside and mostly dormant, but they can all be awakened by the power of passion. Passion is such an incredible power; it enables man to step out of the world without making a free fall into the nothingness of the universe. It is a great key that unlocks all the godliness of man, if used wisely. History is a mere record of passionate men and women; it is an account of their successes and failures. No one can ever achieve magnetic leadership without true and sincere passion for their dreams. So, if you really seek magnetic leadership, think greatly about passion.

Passion is nothing less than a bomb; it must be handled with care. It can destroy your enemies just as easily as it can destroy you, if misused. Reckless use of passion is so dangerous that it cannot only destroy the man himself, but also those he had intended to help. When someone is addicted to forbidden substances, he will definitely destroy himself, and his loved ones may also pay a heavy price. Politics and religion are the breeding grounds where misguided passion can easily turn into fanaticism and extremism. For instance, some leaders have led their followers, societies, and even countries to mass murder and ruin. The example of the Khmer Rouge regime and its massacre of millions in "the killing fields," of Cambodia, as well as the Jonestown forced mass suicide in Guyana of the congregation led by Rev. Jim Jones are still too fresh in the minds of many.

In business, the foolish passion (or, more correctly, obsession) for profit blinds leaders frequently, causing the loss of investors' notes, pensions, and other nest eggs. The collapse of Enron, MCI-Worldcom, the housing market, the banking industry, and many more economic disasters in recent years have all been blamed on a few ill-advised men who held too much power.

Aesop of ancient Greece warned of the danger of passion. He said, "It is with our passion as it is with fire and water: they are good servants, but bad masters." As Aesop's metaphor implies, passion is indeed like fire; we need fire to warm ourselves during cold weather, to cook our meals, to light our homes; we need fire in the form of electricity or batteries to run our modern machines. But without its strict control, fire destroys man and the environment. Passion is also like water. Water, one of the bases of life, nourishes our bodies; it cleans us and everything around us. It nurtures our crops. But just like fire, without strict control, water destroys man and civilizations as it did in Louisiana with Hurricane Katrina, and in the tsunamis in Indian Ocean and Fukushima, Japan of 2004 and 2011, respectively.

Passion must be restrained. The only time passion is useful is when it is the servant of man; it is toxic when passion itself is the master. Philip Sydney, English poet, notes: "He whom passion rules is bent to meet his death." Passion is the mother of all success but also the source of some of the most monstrous vices; therefore, it must be contained and wisely commanded, in order to be valuable. A truly magnetic leader must possess passion, but more importantly, must learn—and succeed—to strictly control it or he will be a danger to himself and to society. Passions must be loved and cherished wholeheartedly—like children. Unlike children, they must be handled with a much tougher clutch; like children, they must be taught to obey parents and not vice versa.

The question, of course, is how do you do that? How do you let yourself be passionately driven and also protect yourself against its controlling influence? Of this dilemma, William Shakespeare tells us, "Let the sap of reason quench the fire of passion," to which Benjamin Franklin adds, "If passion drives you, let reason hold the reins." An old French proverb says, "The passions act as winds to propel our vessel, our reason is the pilot that steers her: without winds she would not move, without the pilot she would be lost." Finally, British statesman Benjamin Disraeli asserted that "Man is only truly great when he acts from the passions; never irresistible but when he appeals to the imagination."

The wisdom of the past not only sees the great potential in passion, but also the danger when allowed to run amok, understanding that passion must be controlled by the power of reason. When used under the control of reason, passions can take man to the height of greatness. But when used by an irrational man, he becomes a danger to both himself and society at large. Passions must serve the individual and society, not vice versa. To paraphrase the French mathematician and writer Blaise Pascal, when passions become masters, they are vices; they must be balanced with reason.

Life is about balance and, without balance, there is chaos. Passion and reason are for success what two hydrogen atoms (H2) and one oxygen (O) atom are for water. Unless you have H2O, you never produce water. But knowledge, the library of reason, alone can never produce success, otherwise all the MBAs from prestigious colleges would be all millionaires, but coupled with passion, the engine of persistence, it works wonders. Persistence with ignorance offers a fruitless and hazardous search in a darkened room.

Nature consists of so many examples of balance; magnetism itself is based on positive and negative poles. Electricity is a product of negative and positive energies. The universe itself is made up of scores of dual principles: good and bad, right and wrong, light and darkness, left and right, life and death, male and female, strong and weak. The balance of two principles is the sustaining balance that makes possible the existence of everything on Earth. Your magnetic leadership will be well-served if, and only if, it is a balance of passion and reason.

Another way to control the burning fire of passion is to avoid self-glorification, but rather always glory in the greater good.

Once they become popular, some people start entertaining the idea that they are unique; they think they are *all that* and different from the rest of us. That is when their ears grow beyond their heads and they start drowning in the flood of passion. And before they know it, they become outcasts and spend the rest of their lives apologizing—if they are strong enough—or simply hiding forever.

But some celebrities, on the other hand, use their popularity for selfless causes. They use their popularity to uplift the weak or bring attention to neglected issues in society. For these people, magnetic leadership never stops growing.

Those who are blinded by passion rarely find the true joy of life; if they do, it is usually for a very short period of time. Nothing is more detrimental than passion or desire without a noble cause. When the heart provides a worthy passion and the head provides a good rationale, the potential for the greatness of man is almost unlimited and the energy released by such a man knows no time or space.

Passions can make you great or destroy your life and the lives of others. If you want to be a truly magnetic leader, square your actions, circumscribe your desires, and keep your passions within due bounds and toward all mankind. By mastering your passions, you will rise above an average successful man, and you will build a truly magnetic leadership that will shine and attract all those who are looking for salvation.

Alignment of Body and Mind

None of us can be constructively magnetic by letting his/her sexual appetites overpower his/her willpower. Passion, the energy that drives a magnetic leadership, like any other energy, is more productive when controlled and used for proper causes. As we move into this segment, make the Detroit sports writer Mitch Albom's words your own and see how your personal magnetism will grow:

> The way you get meaning in your life is to devote yourself to loving others, devote yourself to your community around you, and devote yourself to creating something that gives you purpose and meaning.

Man is the center of his own universe. All the needs and desires of man—material, intellectual and spiritual—must be satisfied from where he is. Thus, our bodies are the truest schoolrooms from where we master the laws of nature and the universe. All intellectual and spiritual mastery is achieved from the physical body. From this schoolroom we learn the laws of Heaven and Earth; we are true students of life, capable of making free choice.

We live in what many call the Temple of the Highest. Destroying and abusing the body through substance abuse, prostitution, or suicide is considered the lowest point of immorality in many cultures. Many religions teach that those who commit suicide go to hell. In any country, murderers are either put to death or imprisoned for life; a few are locked up for several years.

Whatever your opinion, your body is the most important asset you have. Thus, taking care of your body is the most sacred duty you can perform. Taking care of the body does not just mean treating it well; it also means consciously and properly using the senses that connect the body with the outside world. Make sure your body is not an instrument or a servant of the senses, but instead their master. The more control our body has over our senses, the more successful we will be in the expansion of our magnetic leadership.

The reason for controlling the senses is a basic and simple one. The senses are the *entries and outlets* through which our spiritual powers may be wasted. You can become a powerful dynamite of magnetic leadership if you are able to effectively control your sexual appetites (using them constructively only), watch only positive images, engage only in positive conversations, and consume only constructive substances. Strictly controlled and constructively used, senses are very helpful in opening channels of communication with our Higher Self, our mind, or to God.

To give you an idea, imagine a car with an exhaust system with many holes as opposed to a car with only one opening. The car with many holes in its exhaust system will not run, while the car with only one will, of course, run efficiently. A harmonious alignment of our bodies and our minds is a great secret of success of magnetic power.

To be a magnetic leader, you must believe in the existence of positive, invisible powers and accommodate them by controlling physical senses. Even though invisible powers are stronger than senses, senses win every time there is a confrontation, not because of their strength but because they (invisible powers) respect man's birthright to make decisions based on his free will. But if you allow them to act through you, they bring you the near magic power that enabled the young David to kill Goliath, that allowed Alexander the Great to conquer the known world, that helped George Washington defeat the mightiest power in the world, and that allowed Napoleon to conquer Europe. All it takes is to first control the senses and then pay attention to the Higher Self within. This is one of the great secrets of magnetic leadership.

All magnetic leaders have utilized this secret, from Jesus to our modern day successful religious, scientific, business, political, athletic, and artistic leaders; the most successful have been those who understood this law, and closely aligned their bodies with their minds.

The construction of the Seven Wonders of the World was led by those who knew how to keep their senses in check and aligned their bodies with the mind of God. It does not matter whether you are the heir to a fortune or a self-made success, the cause is the same: better alignment of the mind and the body.

Once this alignment becomes dysfunctional, success crumbles. The alignment is what Jesus referred to when He said, "Seek first the kingdom of Heaven and everything will be given you." Those historical giants who aligned their bodies the closest with their minds have walked on water; taught timeless philosophies; discovered new continents and scientific laws; and founded religious schools, laws, and political systems that have made modern civilizations more in tune with peace, prosperity, and justice.

No stupid unbeliever can do that, none. There is no word in the vocabulary of man that can precisely describe the wonders you can achieve if you properly control your senses and align your body with the mind.

This is the most complex subject to learn and to pass on to others. From the *Know Thyself* of ancient Greek temples; the *Shekinah*, the Majestic Presence or manifestation of God of the **Kabbalah** and Jews; the *Kingdom of Heaven* of the Christian Church to the *I AM Presence* of the metaphysical schools of the late nineteenth and early twentieth centuries, there is no magical key, shortcut, or simple and easily understood practical explanation. Maybe we should just say, for the lack of better words, seek and thou shall find, then keep seeking and seeking and seeking throughout space and time endlessly even after physical life.

In light of the complex and daunting nature of the subject, we will try our best to lay out two different and simple ways to control our bodies for better alignment with our minds, making it possible to better develop a strong magnetic personality.

Time

The question of the existence of time is an ancient one. Some have argued that there is only present time; therefore, the past and the future are only illusions of our senses. Others argue in favor of past, present, and future. The former point of view is based on the motionlessness of the sun, the source of life. The latter is based on how our senses are affected by the Earth's yearly revolution around the sun while turning on its own axis. We will not get into that; whether it exists as a measure of something or does not exist at all, we will not take sides.

For the purposes of this discussion, we will simply define time as an energy that transforms life as it goes through different stages from birth to death, from childhood to adulthood to motherhood, fatherhood, grandparenthood, and all the way through to our ancestors. Time alone holds used, recycled, and usable energy that appears to our senses as past, present, and future. Time is thus a central element in all achievements. Unless one uses time wisely, nothing can be achieved. Wallace D. Wattles III, one of the early teachers of metaphysics in the twentieth century, writes:

> To be strong and wise is to be able to use time well; and to use them well is to become continuously stronger and wiser.

Success, growth, and development are only attained by the right use of time; and we are failures today in exact proportion as we have erred in our use of time past. To know the right use of the present moment is therefore of immense importance; and to have the will to make the right use of it is more important still. If man can, and will, make the right use of every moment of time, he must certainly become a being of marvelous power and wholeness. (*The Wisdom of W. D. Wattles III*, p. 72)

Magnetic leadership is diametrically opposed to the misuse of time. An effective use of time will make people attracted to you like a needle is attracted to a magnet. This is no exaggeration. Try misusing time and then see what happens to your leadership. A person who misuses time is labeled unreliable, and reliability is what leadership is all about. No one will follow you if they cannot depend on you. Failure and success are mirrors of how you have used your time in the past.

Those who have spent much of their time doing better and bigger things in their callings are leaders in their lines of work. There are certainly no better words in my opinion to express the magnitude of time than those of Wattles. Just as it is stupid to fight the wind, it is foolish to fight time. Ask anyone who tried to swim against the current and then ask a sailor how pleasant it is to adjust the sail and let the wind drive you to your destination. A magnetic leader must never let time pass and then try to catch up.

Working against time makes it possible for the body to work against the forces of nature as well as the universal mind and infinity; working with it brings the same elements in harmony with your desires and efforts. Working with time is the right use of energy. By failing to prepare your mind or give it sufficient time to digest your schedule and inquiries, you keep it from setting you up for success.

Lack of time puts the body in an unnecessary hurry to process your demands, and that inspires panic, anger, and doubt, making you practically ineffective in everything you do. When we are in a hurry, we fail to inform the universal mind or give it adequate time to gather all the elements and circumstances that will make our success possible. By rushing, we confuse our minds by giving contradictory instructions for the same wanted outcomes.

No wonder so many road accidents are caused by those in a hurry. These tragedies are caused by those who failed to leave on time and want to cover more distance in less time, and those who think their programs are more important than those of others because they failed to allocate sufficient time to the preparation. Just as a swimmer must swim with the current and a sailor must sail with the wind, you must work with time and not against it if you want to develop a strong magnetic leadership.

You must always schedule everything ahead of time, you must allow ample time for the fulfillment of every task, and you must be patient but prompt. Always start an activity on time in order to finish on time, never run the danger of starting late and hoping to finish on time. Continually trying to beat time will eventually become a lost battle. Always tell your mind when you want to sleep and when you want to wake up, and your mind will prepare you for a peaceful sleep and wake you up at the right time, whether you set an alarm clock or not. Always tell your mind what you want to do and when you want to do it; do it mentally, verbally, or in writing, and your mind will assemble the circumstances for your success, including some you did not or could not anticipate.

Make your mind your best partner; communicate with it frequently on all issues, just like you communicate with your earthly partners, and success will be assured. In fact, the alignment of the three dimensions of man-body (consciousness), subconscious (mind), and universal mind (the infinite)—by way of a strong inner communication through proper use of time and reflection or meditation makes the difference between the lucky and chosen ones, failure and success. If you have something to do, take some time to think about, do not rush, sleep on it if necessary, until you develop your intuitive power. Engineers and architects do this all the time; why shouldn't you? Archimedes did it; why shouldn't you?

Completing the proper preparation will give you plenty of time to visualize what Einstein referred to as imagination, which he said is more important than knowledge. Rushing increases blood pressure; drains precious energy; and inspires fear, frustration, and doubt, which in turn destroy self-confidence, a fundamental factor of success. The more preparation and thought you put into actions, the stronger the magnetic leadership you will develop.

The alignment of the body or consciousness, the mind or the subconscious, and the universal mind or infinity is what is referred to in the scriptures as communion with *the Father*.

Of this alignment and its wonders, Ralph Waldo Trine, the author of *In Tune with the Infinite*, writes:

> The true secret of power lies in keeping one's connection with God who worketh all things; and in the degree that we keep this connection are we able literally to rise above every conceivable limitation . . . There is but one source of power in the universe. Whatever then you are, painter, orator, musician, religious teacher, or whatever it may be, know that to catch and take captive the secret of power is so to work in conjunction with the Infinite Power, in order that it may continually work and manifest through you. If you fail in doing this, you fail in everything. (p.123 and p.139)

No one can work with the power of the infinite, as Trine suggests, unless he takes moment to plan, reflect, and execute everything at the right time. Rushing breaks the connection with the unseen helpers and sets you up for failure in building a magnetic leadership and every other thing you want to do. Unless you have a clear understanding of the past and present of a situation and specific scenarios of how it might develop in the future, you are better off as a leader not taking position. But learn how to use time effectively and wait and see how your inner and outer power will grow.

Body Movement

Stop and go; stop and go; stop and go; or just go until your reach the destination. It is a proven fact that when a vehicle stops frequently, not only will it take longer to reach its destination, but it will also consume more energy. Our bodies are no different. We work better and faster when we concentrate on one task from beginning to end without distractions or unnecessary interferences. Automobiles have to be refueled at gas stations to accumulate energy that makes it possible for them to run. Like automobiles, human bodies also have to refuel, rest, and engage in pastimes that help them operate at their peak; they have to sleep at night and take daytime naps to accumulate energy.

This energy is used wisely when used consciously; it burns out faster when used unconsciously. Yes, the most vital activities in life are unconscious. Digestion of our food, blood circulation, and breathing are all unconscious activities, but these should not concern us. When man makes the most of the movement of his body, subjecting it to his will, he conserves an inconceivable amount of energy that, when released for a specific purpose, is powerful enough to complete most of his daily duties. Conservation of energy is like building a hydroelectric dam: when water is released, it lights cities.

Your body doesn't need to be static or hyperactive, but it conserves more energy when small, precise movements of the hands, feet, fingers, neck, and head are more voluntarily initiated and less involuntarily activated. The ability to effectively control your body movement makes it possible to connect with the higher or inner self. It is just as important to control the legs, hands, and head movements as it is to control what to watch and what to listen to. Restlessness of the legs, hands, and head is just as consuming and detrimental as restlessness of the eyes and ears, that are not disciplined enough to choose what to watch and what to hear. The ability to control body parts as well as breathing and the eyelids makes a man truly a dynamic force.

Efficient body control combined with excellent thought control creates an enormous source of greatness in almost every endeavor. Body control does not just happen accidentally; it is the result of sustained thought, effort, and will.

The control of the body at will is called concentration, which is at the root of all triumphs. Dumont equates concentration with success. In *The Power of Concentration* he writes: "Concentration means success, because you are better able to govern yourself and centralize your mind; you become more earnest in what you do and this almost improves your chances of success," (p. 15).

Efficient body control is for a potentially successful person what practice is for an athlete. Unless an athlete practices well, his chances of winning against well-prepared opponents are very slim.

The disciplining of body must always precede that of the mind if success is to be obtained—that is why children are first trained to sit still and only then to read. Without delving into this deeper, it is essential to understand that as powerful as the mind is over the body, it is still crucial to discipline the body first before successfully disciplining the mind.

A disciplined body receives more inspiration from the mind, but when both are well trained, the magic happens. So, the more disciplined the body, the more cooperative the mind. As we said earlier, athletes and artists are usually more magnetic than most people, because they discipline their bodies, and their minds consequently serve them accordingly.

A restless body accomplishes very little at the end of the day, because it confuses the mind; it releases energy through multiple escape pathways, and it consequently retains very little information from the mind or the universal reservoir of energy, without which no one can do much of anything.

Control of the body and of the mind strengthens attention and focus. Attention is an incredible force about which we still know very little. The French have a proverb that says, "When you talk about the lion, you see its tail," meaning that when you focus your attention on something, that thing ends up happening directly or indirectly to you.

Nobody knows why this happens, and what is most likely true but hard to prove is that there are invisible forces beyond our comprehension that are always ready to come to our rescue, if we can just keep the way unobstructed.

The invisible forces are said to be very liberal; we must welcome them, because they never will intrude their way into our affairs or coerce our free will. Developing a magnetic personality means developing an ability to attract or surround oneself with like-minded fellows and like-hearted invisible forces—these must be lured with mental incentives.

This task is almost impossible if the leader confuses followers by changing his positions so often that he appears to lack command of his own body. A person who is not calm and concentrated cannot attract followers. Excessive body movement diffuses attention, confusing people as well as invisible forces. Changing positions frequently will drain your personal magnetism like water from a cracked tank. The reason why tomorrow is always worrisome is because we do not know much about it. Everything we plan for tomorrow is always an assumption. For that reason, people appreciate leaders who can provide some assurances or peace of mind; they dislike people who simply second guess what is coming up.

A magnetic leader is like Mother Nature: predictable 85 percent of the time and maybe less so 15 percent—these are those occasional or accidental moments. Since the dawn of time, seasons have never traded months, and we have prepared accordingly because of their consistency. The day announces itself with sunrise, and the night with a sunset. Even the rain does not fall out of a blue sky; it makes itself known through clouds. On the rare occasions when we have earthquakes, tornadoes, cyclones, heavy rain, excessive heat, or other severe changes in the weather, we weep for our pain and suffering but we are never disappointed; we dust off the hurt and move on with our lives.

But if you behave like nature, your magnetic leadership will know no bounds, because people will always give you a second chance when a really unpredictable situation occurs. So, before taking a position on any issue, it is imperative to thoroughly study and analyze the subject, and convince your intellect with objective facts before trying to convince anyone else. This mental labor is made easy by enabling both your intellect and intuition to contribute equally, and nothing supplies both faculties with raw materials better than concentration, which begins with disciplining the body.

Wisdom Joseph Ombe Ya Makano, the author.

Wisdom Joseph Ombe Ya Makano, the author.

Mwajuma, my companion for life

L to R Joseph Jr., Laliya, Wisdom Jr., and their baby brother Malaika, my beloved children.

The last picture of my mother, Laliya Abala Makano "Namkyoku." Thank you mom for the unconditional love that Inspired me to be the man "I AM" and I ever hope to be.

Author with six-year-old son, Wisdom Jr.

Author with life best friend, Mwajuma Yvette Makano

Author with life companion, Mwajuma Yvette Makano

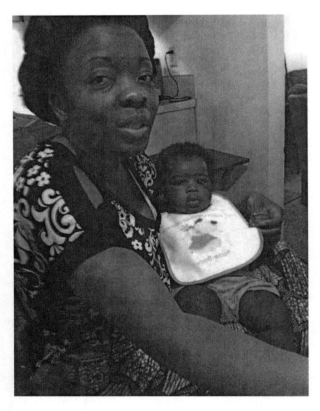

My best friend and life companion, Mwajuma Yvette Makano with our son Malaika Lusambya Makano. Thank you my friend. Without you this work would have been unthinkable.

With those I tightly hold near and dear from left to right: my wife Mwajuma, our sons Malaika, Joseph Jr., our daughter Laliya Nada, our son Wisdom Jr. and me.

The author, 2014

Author with those he holds near and dear; L to R: sons Joseph Jr., Alimasi and daughter Laliya

Enjoying the pleasure of life through fatherhood with son Malaika

Staring at life in the eyes with joy and admiration beyond words

Chapter Seven

The Art of Living

The Oxford American Desk Dictionary and Thesaurus (2nd edition) defines art as "a human creative skill or its application." It is called a skill because it is learned; it involves creativity, imagination, craft, technique, and so on. It may sound awkward to many, but living a good life is really an art, and no one is required to live a more creative life than a magnetic leader. Everything else in life may not be an art, but craftsmanship in human relationships and how to utilize human resources are truly artistic and compose a strong base for magnetic leadership.

Let's begin with a few words from Jesus. Long before Jesus uttered these words in public, they were taught in ancient schools in Egypt, India, Persia, Rome, and Greece. They were considered central instruction to the development of a strong magnetic personality for a few chosen who were expected to assume leading roles in their lines of work. It was knowledge reserved for high priests and the holders of high offices. Writers of the Gospels of Jesus called these words "The Sermon on the Mount," and here is the potion that interests us:

Judge not, that ye be not judged. For with what judgment ye judge, ye shall be judged: and with what measure ye mete, it shall be measured to you again. Again why beholdest thou the mote that is in thy brother's eye, but considerest not the beam that is in thine own eye? Or how wilt thou say to thy brother, Let me pull out the mote out of thine eye; and, behold, a beam is in thine own eye? Thou hypocrite, first cast out the beam out of thine own eye; and then shalt thou see clearly to cast out the mote out of thy brother's eye. (Matthew 7:1-5, KJV)

Emmet Fox, a New Thought spiritual leader of the twentieth century, called these five verses *the art of living*, and about them, he writes:

> This section of the "Sermon on the Mount" consists of five short verses, and only about one hundred words, yet it is hardly too much to say that, at its simple face value, it is the most staggering document ever presented to mankind. In these five verses we are told more about the nature of man and the meaning of life, and the importance of conduct, and the art of life, and the secret of happiness and success, and the way out of trouble, and the approach to God, and the emancipation of soul, and the salvation of the world, than all the philosophers and the theologians and savants put together have told us—for it explains the Great Law . . . .

There is nothing to be learned in any library, or in any laboratory, that is one-millionth part as important as the information contained herein. If it were ever possible to justify the fanatical saying, "Burn the rest of the book, for it is all in this one," it would be in reference to those words . . . . If the average man understood for a single moment the meaning of these words, and really believed them to be true, they would immediately revolutionize his whole life from the top to the bottom; turn his everyday conduct inside out, and so change him that, in a comparatively short space of time, his closest friends would hardly know him. Whether he were the Prime Minister in the Cabinet or the man on the street, this understanding would turn the world upside down for him, and, because the thing is infectious beyond computing, it would turn the world upside down for many, many other as well. (p. 108)

In the Bible, it is said that only God has the power to judge. Even in societies where the Bible is not widely read, people are restrained from judging one another. In ancient times, only kings and the highest ranking members of society had the right to judge the conduct of others. You will recall the wise judgments King Solomon rendered in his court.

In our modern world, kings and the powerful have lost the privilege to judge. Instead, we have professional judges who, after years of education and meticulous learning under the wings of experienced senior craftsmen of the art, are carefully chosen for the judge's bench. Even though they have been endowed with much power, crossing the boundaries of their power can easily put them in very hot water. They are paid handsomely and given a lot of prestige. Few careers come with higher esteem.

Indeed, judgment by God, kings, or judges is not the object of our discussion; we are interested in the type of judgment that hinders the development of a magnetic leadership. You, like the rest of us, are human and inherently erroneous from time to time. *"Errare humanum est,"* it is said in Latin: to err is human. Judging people is considered very anti-magnetic because most of us do not judge others based on knowledge, but rather on appearances or incomplete facts. Judging based on appearance or incomplete knowledge is exactly what sets people against one another in the first place. Judging people based on the color of their skin, religion, language, and physical traits is one of the most despicable crimes against humanity.

Unfortunately, discrimination has been occurring all over the world throughout history. The Holocaust is an example of what happens when we judge others based on their supposed external traits rather than their internal ones. To build a strong magnetic leadership, it is prudent to see your fellow man with inner eyes, see their inner qualities and avoid being judgmental.

You will always find faults in people with whom you work. If you are too picky, you will push people away and have no one to work with. Whether you know it or not, each human being has some qualities that may complement yours. They may not be necessarily obvious to a biased observer, but if fairly investigated and given a chance to flourish, they can immensely contribute to your leadership.

If you think this is more fiction than reality, look what happened to the now-famous British writer, J. K. Rowling, the author of the *Harry Potter* series of books. Before she penned the stories about the boy wizard, known simply as Joanne Rowling, she was an unemployed single mother, living on state benefits, member of a much maligned group of people thought to be freeloaders, in the US vernacular, *welfare queens,* who don't know "the dignity of work," in a certain politician's assessment. The story of Rowling is one of the best examples of how judgment based on superficial factors and incomplete facts has wasted some of the best minds.

Due to the discrimination she suffered, early on in her writing career, solely based on her gender and her social status, the world would have been denied the wonderful stories of Harry Porter, had she shared those negative judgments about herself; her publishing houses, their paper mills, a multitude of bookstores, movie studios, and theaters would have been far less profitable; and England would have been denied the prestige, taxes, and tourism revenue that it has earned for being the land of Harry Potter.

Rowling herself would have been denied a fortune and her neighbors would have been denied the happiness of living on a street that has twenty-four-hour security. This is the benefit that the world has gained with just one J. K. Rowling; how many millions of silently misjudged Joanne Rowlings do you think the world is undermining? How much money do you think has been lost as a result of the millions of J. K. Rowlings who were misjudged, their ample gifts turned away, because of external appearances?

It was discrimination at best for the publishers of Bloomsbury to think that boys would never read a book written by a female writer, and it was insane to think that in an age as technologically advanced as ours that Harry Potter readers would never discover the truth. It was beyond belief for the publisher to force Rowling to endure similar treatment to that endured by Amandine Aurore Lucile Dupin, the nineteenth century French writer who was forced by the social codes of the time to change her name to George Sand, smoke heavily like a man, and wear male clothing in public to hide the fact that a woman had the audacity to write.

One of the abilities of a magnetic leader is to bring obscure talent to light; to awaken the sleeping giant in each of us that is waiting for an opportunity to come out; to trigger the genius that is dormant and the skill that is neglected in the untried. How many times have we seen inappropriate or incompetent people given jobs while upstanding or qualified people are denied just because they were poorly dressed or lacked the right family background? These are the real life experiences through which people suffer on a daily basis, yet a magnetic leader does not let dogma or traditions obscure his vision. Anyone who has been to job-search training will tell you that, above everything else, your look, not your resume, is the way to open the door to your next job.

In the sports world, excellent athletes have been traded before they are given a chance to prove their skills. Many skillful players are drafted after the less skillful ones have been picked. Michael Jordan and Kobe Bryan were drafted third and thirteenth, respectively, and traded from their original teams. But both have led their teams to multiple national championships, they have received multiple Most Valuable Player awards and placed themselves as two of the best basketball players of all time.

A leader who judges others on the basis of appearance will always be prey to the con artists. Like Master Crow, he will always be taken advantage of by the well-spoken master fox; he will frequently be victim of sweet talk or flattery that have brought down princesses, kings, and the powerful throughout history. He will also deny himself the advantage of surrounding himself with the best minds possible.

No one advised more strongly against this vice than E. H. Chapin, the American preacher and editor of the *Christian Leader*, in these words: "Do not judge men by mere appearances; for the light laughter that bubbles on the lip often mantles over the depths of sadness, and the serious look may be the sober veil that covers a divine peace and joy."

Judging people from appearance stems from hate, and you cannot build a magnetic leadership by way of hate. Mother Teresa, one of the most magnetic leaders the world has ever known, put it in a blunter way: "If you judge people, you have no time to love them." Love is magnetic, but judging is not.

This is not to say that a magnetic leader should be a saint or an angel, far from it; we simply want to imply that if you want to acquire magnetic leadership, you must be open minded enough to be able to recognize the potential of others to make *you* magnetic in the end. Magnetic leadership is well built when it is done on the strength and efforts of many and diverse people.

As imperfect as democracy is, it stands above other forms of government because it gives people a pool of morally and professionally talented people from which to choose. Because voters have many choices to make, they usually have an opportunity to correct past mistakes and shape future candidates. If you are serious about building magnetic leadership, you should practice making decisions based on what is the best constructive outcome morally and socially rather what is good for you, in order to keep the shadows of prejudice from hindering your view. You should welcome and elevate people based on their virtues and knowledge—based on objective assessment.

"Remember, I'm human. Before you judge me or decide how you'll deal with me, walk awhile in my shoes. If you do, I think you'll find with more understanding we can meet in the middle and walk the rest of the way together," said Harvey and Ventura, authors of *Walk the Talk*.

In the middle, indeed; that is where all man's negative vibes end and the positive begins. Once you understand that all of us have negative and positive traits and tendencies, and conclude that the positive outweighs the negative, don't be too hard on your fellow man.

Yes, it is good to remember that the negative can be infectious, and the positive contagious. Keep an eye on the negative, so it does not spoil the positive, so you can forge ahead with what is constructive. The art of living does not discard the importance of evaluating the character, wisdom, intellect, and sociability of acquaintances; it emphasizes the necessity of looking for the constructive side in all men while shielding yourself from the negative side, if it is not poisonous or mortal to your magnetism. The art of living rejects the pursuit of perfect men; instead, it advocates the ability to work with people whose total balance of good outweighs the mass of their bad.

Before judging your fellow man, remember that you are also human and have faults that may be even greater than theirs. Thus, the harsher you are toward them, the harsher they can be toward you, and the less magnetic you will become. Support people for the same reasons that they support the insignificance of your flaws. Forgiveness has magic in it. The more you forgive people, the more magnetic will you be; the less you forgive, the less magnetic you will be.

Magnetic leadership is a give-and-take process. Just imagine who would care enough to pray to God if He was an unforgiving *person?* All religions agree that He is merciful and forgiving, and that is why over 99 percent of the seven billion people living on Earth desire to deal with Him in one way or another. If you want people to be softer on you, with a degree of tough love, you must passionately let people know about your understanding and appreciation of their virtues and, compassionately, your disapproval of their shortcomings. By so doing, you will enable people to feel comfortable around you and encourage them to bring out more openly the happy side of their lives.

A magnetic person does not have to be the most knowledgeable person in the world. Sometimes, all it takes is to assemble a team of talented people, put the right people in the right places, inspire them, play the role of a lubricant in a well-oiled machine, and let them happily do their jobs, stay on top so that the team functions well, and then take the credit as well as the responsibility for the outcome. As a magnetic leader, you will have to learn how to speak like an expert even on matters you know very little about by listening carefully to the experts on your team.

Magnetic political leaders learn this art well early on. They recruit the right people, apply the right laws, project an image of confidence to the public, and then they take responsibility for failure or credit for a job well done by their aids at various levels, even if all they did was to step out of the way.

Except in rare instances, to be magnetic you must be a cheerleader. Cheerleaders don't just applaud because the team is faultless; cheerleaders cheer because they see the errors made by the team, they know and understand the qualities of the team; and they know that if they cheer, they can bring out the best in the players and give them the confidence to know that victory is within reach.

This is why even a mediocre team or athlete plays better at home than away from home. By nature, men perform better when their virtues are acknowledged and encouraged. At home, the hometown crowd knows our weaknesses but sees and cheers only our best qualities; out of town or in a foreign land, the crowd knows our qualities but sees and cheers only our weaknesses. The crowds or the cheerleaders, mindful of both our qualities and our weaknesses, influence what we should display to the world.

On this point, American novelist Eleanor Porter once said, "Instead of always harping on a man's faults, tell him of his virtues. Try to pull him out of his rut of bad habits. Hold up to him his better self, his real self that can dare and do and win out." People are as trainable as Pavlov's dogs. Train people to bring out their virtues and they will respond amazingly, train them to be cynical and they will respond with equal force. Magnetic leaders make a choice on what they want people to offer the world; you must do the same if you want to be magnetic.

Until early in the twentieth century, psychology was defined as a science of the soul, and so the understanding of human abilities remained murky, if not elusive, at best for a long time of theorizing. This ended when John B. Watson came to the rescue at the outset of the last century. Watson stated that "scientific psychology focuses on the relationship between environmental contingencies and behavior rather than on the presumed content of consciousness." With that theory, the study of psychology has never been the same and the understanding of human beings has been clearer.

Why behavior instead of consciousness? Not just because the human eye is perfectly incapable of seeing the consciousness, but mostly because behavior is the reflection of the inner and dormant human abilities.

Unless you have a better understanding of the actions of others, your judgment of people's motives will always be erroneous and your own personal magnetism will suffer for it. "I am not judging people, I am judging their actions," said Jeff Melvoin. Actions alone reveal the inner world of human beings.

You cannot tell an honest or dishonest person by just looking at them. To identify a dishonest person, you must have proof of the wrongdoing. Disassociate people with problems but link actions to problems. That is the magic of a magnetic personality. It does not require a genius to tell whether or not someone knows how to swim if he drowns in a pool of average depth. Judge his ability to swim, not his worth as a person.

Those who judge based on exterior characteristics are sooner or later victims of the same deception. Judging people's actions as a means of understanding them is not a perfect method. However, it increases or keeps your personal magnetism intact and decreases the chances of making significant errors.

Human beings are very complex subjects. As invisible as they are, laws of nature are easier to understand than human behavior. If scientists had the level of understanding of human behavior as that of chemistry or physics today, the world would be a different place. In the last 150 years, not only have we greatly increased the ability of the human eye to see beyond millions of miles of space and into the infinitesimal nanometers of particles, we have almost decimated the notion of time and space here at home on Earth.

Today, you can almost talk to anyone anywhere on the planet as if you were sitting next to him; you can send and receive instant messages to and from anyone anywhere on Earth; and you can walk on three continents within the space of half a day. Amazing, isn't it? Yet we cannot pretend to know who we are with certainty, much less how someone else is. Humans are very complex and mysterious at best. What you see is not always what you get.

Questioning this characteristic of human nature, the inspirational author of *Jonathon Livingston Seagull* Richard Bach writes, "All we see of someone at any moment is a snapshot of their life, there in riches or poverty, in joy or despair. Snapshots don't show the million decisions that led to the moment."

Snapshots do not show much of anything. They help make a way that leads to understanding. The more snapshots you have of someone, the more likely you will understand him. Thus, it is in the best interest of anyone who is in the business of building a magnetic leadership to always give people the benefit of the doubt, always give people a second chance, give them the opportunity to prove you wrong. No one can hide his real intentions forever.

"Thoughts are things," according to the New Thought pioneer Prentice Mulford. Sooner or later, they will come out to reveal themselves. Life is a series of repetitive actions. What you think repetitively, will eventually come out. You hear people saying, "I do not like repetitive work." This is obviously nonsense. What they call experience is simply a level of comfortable repetition, nothing less; nothing more. Language, science, logic, and faith are all about repetition. The world has not rejected the formula that helped invent the wheel, because it has been repeated countless times.

Imagine if you had to learn a new skill or new things every day at work, not only would you never be proficient at doing anything, but nothing would ever be performed. Regardless of how smart or advanced our contemporaries think they are, all major and basic things are still carried out the same way the so-called primitive man carried them out. We are still walking on two feet, eating with our hands and mouth, sleeping at night, waking in the daytime, and having sexual intercourse in the same positions we have done since the dawn of time.

Life is repetition because the laws of nature are changeless and no respecter of human beings. So, we react to these changes in pretty much the same way day in day out, year in year out, for the survival of the human race.

In the clandestine profession, where this law is very much on the minds of everyone, spies are rarely given the same mission multiple times in the same location. When tracking a suspect, different agents are used at different times and locations to keep the subject clueless; otherwise, the mission's potential for failure will increase.

So, by judging people's actions rather than appearances, the possibilities of building a strong magnetic personality will multiply and the chances of creating hostility will lessen. Actions alone are the strongest measure of merit, know-how, and effectiveness, which are the foundation of personal magnetism. Society will always side with anyone based on meritorious criteria, and if society fails to do so, history will sooner or later correct the injustice against the hero by immortalizing him as it has done for many others. Wait for people to repeat the same action, good or bad, a number of times before judging them, and you will have the respect of your so-called enemies.

Compliments

I will open this segment with a few words from one of greatest teachers of the twentieth century, Ernest Holmes:

> Can you imagine a power so great that it is both an infinite presence and a limitless law? If you can, you are drawing close to a better idea of the way Life works. Most of the bibles of the world have said that all things are formed by Its word. This word

has been called the Secret Word, the Lost Word. It is said some of the ancients had a holy scroll upon which was inscribed the sacred and the secret name of Life. This scroll was supposed to have been put in an ark, in a chest, and laid away in a place which was called the Holy of Holies, the innermost room of the temple.

What do you suppose was inscribed upon this sacred scroll? Just this: the words "I AM." Here is a concept of the pure, simple, and direct affirmation of Life making everything out of itself. This is why most of the scriptures have stated that all things are made by the Word of God." (*The Art of Life*, p. 37)

The words *I AM* and their meaning have been the subject of study at esoteric schools of wisdom long before it was communicated to Moses on Mount Sinai by God that "I AM THAT I AM" was His name and they have continued to this day. For the Greek, I AM meant *know thyself*, just as it was inscribed on their ancient temples. Descartes' *Cogito ergo sum*, "I think, therefore I AM," became the principle component of Western philosophy for the same rationale.

What is it that makes those few words the most powerful words in the vocabulary of man? Because every time you describe how you are feeling—audibly, silently, frequently and deeply—you become that which you say you are.

For instance, keep saying "I am good," "I am strong" and "I am a winner," and you will eventually become good, strong, and a winner with considerable effort. But if you keep repeating the notions that "I am bad," "I am weak," and "I am a loser," you will eventually become bad, weak, and a loser, regardless of your efforts.

The universe makes sure you are what you say and feel you are; it brings angels to make sure you are the constructive quality you say and feel you are and sends demons to make sure you are the destructive qualities you say and feel you are. That is the secret of the ages. That is the magic that allowed a peasant girl, Joan of Arc, to lead the French army to several important victories during the Hundred Years' War against the British. It is also the magic that turned two slight men, Napoleon and Hitler, into giants and monsters.

The same power of I AM can be used to bring power to others and boost your own personal magnetism by simply substituting those words with "you are." People like compliments more than anything else you can give them. Compliments are to the personality, effort, and desire what gas is to fire, and water to the production of electricity. When you tell someone "you are good, you are strong, you are a winner," that person feels the same thrill you feel when you say "I AM this and I AM that." The thrill that the person feels doesn't end there, it comes back to you, because you are the source of the whole excitement, and the law of life is *what goes around comes around*. When you send joy, you will receive joy, and when you send sorrow, you will receive sorrow in return.

Magnetic leadership is the art of transferring the feeling of *I* to *you* and vice versa. Making people feel what you feel or wish them to feel takes personal magnetism to a higher dimension. "Only You," a poem by Dan Coppersmith, was used for this same purpose by a group in Seattle who changed the words slightly to build the power of it within themselves.

I was familiar with the poem, which teaches incredible and wonderful lessons, and while considering the inspiration for it, I came across a slightly modified version one day on the Internet along with this story about the Seattle event. At a workshop there in October, 2006, a participant recited "Only You" to the group and was asked to substitute "you" with "I" or "Me." The website reported that the narrator and everyone there was visibly "raised to a much higher place."

Adopt it for yourself in your conversations with others and see if it changes your life and those around you. Use it as an affirmation for yourself and a compliment for others; it will transform life around you. Here are both versions of the same poem "Only You" and "Only Me" as written by the Dan Coppersmith, who gave me permission to reprint them here for you:

ONLY YOU

No one on Earth

Exists quite like you

And no one is able

To do what you do

The person you are

The talents you bear

Gifts that only

You can share

Only you have learned

From the things you've done

Gaining prospective

From the battles you've won

The times when you've lost

Have been priceless too

The lessons contribute

To what makes you you

The rest of the world

Can't see through your eyes

Which is why your insight

Is such a prize

Because you are you

There are lives you affect

Much more than

You would ever expect

The things you do
The things you say
Send ripples throughout
The Milky Way
You're unique, amazing
Like no one else
You have the exclusive
On being you.
—Dan Coppersmith 2008

Only Me

No one on Earth

Exists quite like me

An original blend

Only I can be

The person I am

The talents I bear

Gifts that only

I Can share

Only I have learned

From the things I've done

Gaining perspective

From the battles I've won

Times when I've lost

Have been priceless too

Both contribute

To my point of view

The rest of the world

Can't see through my eyes

Which is why my insight

Is such a prize

Because I am me

There are lives I affect

Much more than I

Would ever expect

The things I do
The things I say
Send ripples throughout
The Milky Way
I'm unique, amazing
Like no one else
I have the exclusive
On being myself.
—Dan Coppersmith[1]

More on Compliments

The real nature of man is the state of mind in which he exists in early childhood, probably prior to the age of seven. Prior to that age, man is an incredible and magnificent creature; he is honest, happy, playful, authentic, and sweet, but very fragile. It only takes a little bit of annoyance to get him upset and screaming on the top of his lungs; however, it also takes equally few sweet words and things to instill an abrupt 180-degree change from sadness to happiness. The older man grows; the more shy, fearful, and stubborn he becomes. That is human nature. Growing older may seem like getting wiser, but it does not necessarily make man more in tune with higher feelings, feelings that make life what it was really meant to be: worry-free, fearless, anger-free, and pain-free.

But despite the loss of our childhood dreamland, a truly heartfelt compliment performs wonders in the mind of man. Compliments remind people of their actual and potential worthiness, power, and greatness. Compliments truly feed the mind of man just like food feeds his body. They have been used by the best and brightest among us throughout history to get people to eagerly serve causes with which they may or may not agree. The sixteenth United States president, Abraham Lincoln, who championed the unpopular but moral cause of the emancipation of the slaves, is said to have been a master at complimenting people and has been quoted as saying, "Everybody likes a compliment."

Writer and lecturer Mark Twain went so far as to say that he could sustain life for months just on a compliment. "I can live for two months on a good compliment," he said.

In a battle of hearts, nothing is more powerful at disarming and demanding the joyful surrender to an enemy than an honest compliment. All the armies in the world put together and the best trained personnel on Earth will not come close to winning the hearts of people as a single, masterfully expressed compliment.

Magnetic leaders use compliments to the fullest extent in their quest to win people's hearts. A sincere heartfelt compliment is like perfume spread in the atmosphere of someone—it affects both physical nerves and the spirit of man. It sweetens thoughts, romanticizes feelings, and beautifies language.

Even animals are susceptible to the power of compliments. A dog becomes more playful and obedient for patting after a job well done. Lions and many unlikely wild animals become domesticated and submissive when they are constantly complimented. Describing the splendor of the compliment, inspirational columnist, Leo F. Buscaglia said, "too often we underestimate the power of a touch, a smile, a kind word, a listening ear, an honest compliment, or the smallest act of caring, all of which have the potential to turn a life around."

Personal magnetism, the art of attracting people, is the equivalent of the work of an artist who paints an ocean in which the artist swims with sharks in total peace and harmony. Compliments have the power to not only rouse and excite its proponents, but also to weaken and ultimately extinguish the flame of rage from enemies and skeptics.

You may not be able to turn anger into joy in an adult as quickly as you could with a seven-year-old child, but with an honest compliment, you can certainly teach old dogs new tricks; you can help him feel important again. Virtually every human being is the center of his own universe; you cannot change that truth, but you can use it to advance your cause. People want to be at the center of universe, the center of positive attention, so help make their wishes come true, at least in their minds, by complimenting them. It is easy, priceless, and will cost you nothing.

People crave for the feeling of being recognized for their importance. A smile, a kind word, a listening ear, or an honest compliment goes a long way in building strong social bridges that last a lifetime. Dale Carnegie, the author of *How to Win Friends and Influence People*, the seminal work on personal magnetism, compares friendship to a commodity, and its price is the compliment. Carnegie advises all those who are in the business of winning friends, which is what personal magnetism is all about, to "make it a point to remember them [friends]. If you remember my name," he proceeded, "you pay a subtle compliment; you indicate that I have made an impression on you. Remember my name, and you will add to my feeling of importance."

Women are generally considered to be the most vulnerable to compliments. They succumb more easily to compliments than they do to wealth or power. They want to be told how exceptional they are, they want the unmatched compliment to quench the thirst of their love, and kindle the fire of their pride. It is common to live a hellish life with a woman who appreciates your money or power, but rare to live an unhappy life with a woman who appreciates your compliments. The French writer Jules Renard writes: "Don't tell a woman she's pretty; tell her there's no other woman like her, and all roads will open to you."

If you have noticed, both the Lord's Prayer and De la Fontaine's fable, "Master Crow and Master Fox," start with some sort of compliment. That is not an accident; it is based on the fact that spirits' hearts are little different from those of men—the only difference is the size, not the fabric. They are essentially the same, just as a drop of water is made of the same elements as the oceans. What is appealing to the spirits is most certainly appealing to men.

Revisiting the example we gave previously, the Gospels say that of the two criminals who were crucified alongside Jesus, only one was promised a place in Heaven. Guess who? The one who praised His innocence and power. We invoke the spirit and Jesus here not to be religious or anti-religious, but simply to try to explain how compliments can help your efforts to build personal magnetism with the meek and almighty alike.

It may seem a stretch to invoke religion, but the truth is that man practiced faith long before he practiced logic or reason (science); faith guides better than both logic and reason. This truth is well known among assiduous students of life—that even the most skillful and powerful political, business, or religious leaders consolidate and keep their power by complimenting people. You hear time and time again about all those who owe their livelihood to public sentiment saying: "the American people are magnificent . . . the American people are this, and they are that . . . The people of our great state are this, and they are that."

No one dares to mention the flaws of the people, at least not in public. In the last US election campaign, the Republican candidate, John McCain, disowned a close friend and a trusted advisor in a matter of minutes after it was broadcast that the advisor, former Texas senator Phil Graham, called America a nation of whiners. Many economists, TV commentators, and newspaper columnists, including those of the *Washington Post*, basically agreed with the comments made by the former senator. But McCain excluded him from his circle of advisors because telling people that they were in a "mental recession" might irk the voters, who make their decisions based on feelings, not facts.

"A compliment is verbal sunshine," American comedy writer Robert Orben said. It can shine on your professional, marital, or any other part of your life; if you ignore it, get ready for all the clouds and storms its absence may bring into your life.

Compliments are worthless, however, if they are offered merely to please others. To be effective, compliments must gratify you first. You must feel good to compliment someone for it to do its magic. If you compliment someone who has just done you ill, that person will know that you are being hypocritical. Your compliment will be worthless, because it goes against the laws of nature and even the laws of science.

One of the most clearly defined formulas of life is that "we harvest what we sowed." If you sow hypocrisy, you will reap hypocrisy. If you are truly interested in driving your life on a personal magnetism highway, you should carefully watch complimenting traffic signs if you want to reach your destination safely. You should never forget that compliments are a two-way road. Whenever you compliment people, always remind yourself you are not just enlightening their hearts, you are enlightening yours as well, and this will be impossible unless you have a good feeling and a good reason to compliment. If you have such a good feeling, rest assured, your compliment will never go unanswered.

Every time you compliment a decent and well-mannered person, he or she will most certainly return the favor, wholeheartedly thank you, and open his or her heart to your influence. Many animals stand their ears and keep quiet when they perceive a danger. Men mysteriously open all their senses and heart when complimented and are ready to fire back likewise. What do you think happens when someone wants to attract a member of the opposite sex? They pay that person a compliment, and because we are all vulnerable to the power of compliments, we fire back.

It goes like this among total strangers: "You look nice." "Oh, well you look nice too." "I like your hair." "I like your smile." This conversation may go on to open all the senses and the heart, and before you know it, they are boyfriend and girlfriend, and then fiancé and fiancée, and then husband and wife, and they have children and grandchildren, and the rest is history.

It reminds me of a famous seventeenth century French writer, Francois de la Rouchefoucauld, who whispered, "Usually we praise only to be praised." Think about it: the more compliments given to more people, the more magnetic the personality.

It would be wrong to conclude this segment about compliments without suggesting the best way, or at least, the most effective way of complimenting another. If you have been paying attention, you will notice that in almost every conversation, people want to talk about themselves; they want to tell you about their worries, fears, hopes, and joys; they want to discharge their emotions to someone else so that they can feel good, they can have a new start, or at least a new breath to carry on with their lives. They want to be about "I am this, I am that . . . I have this, I have that . . . I would, I will, I did . . ." This may indeed give them some temporary relief and pseudo energy to reach the next finish line, but it hardly makes them magnetic.

Frankly speaking, very few people are interested in you. They want you to either listen to what they have to tell you or they want you to tell them something good you know about them that makes them feel great—"Enough about me, now . . . what do *you* think of me? But most of all, they want to talk and keep talking.

This is the mystery of personal magnetism. If you want to acquire this incredible power, you must be a good listener, thereafter igniting a conversation. You must speak strategically and only when necessary. The password or code of personal magnetism is a three-letter word spelled Y-O-U. Use "you" more often than "I." The more the speaker utilizes the word "you" preceded by an honest and uplifting adjective, the more the speaker will be attractive to the listener and the stronger the magnetic personality he will acquire. Don't tell people about their weaknesses unless it is absolutely necessary, otherwise it will not do any good to your personal magnetism.

Nothing is more boring to your listeners than having to listen to you telling them how great you are or how much trouble you are in. Even if you are the greatest star in Hollywood, your power to keep the audience listening to anecdotes about yourself can have an unintended effect on your magnetism. If you are a star, your fans want to know how much you appreciate *their* support, how much you love *them*, how insignificant you are without them, how they inspire you, and how much you think of them. They aren't as concerned with how much money or property you have, or how great or skillful you are.

To get a better idea of the magic of the word "you," imagine two campaigners from out of town fighting for your vote. One tells you how many bills he has sponsored in Congress, how respected he is in Washington, and how much he knows about legislation, national security, the economy; and the other tells how he will work for you, how he will represent your interests, how he will ease your pain, how he will make your children's education affordable, make healthcare accessible, make the government serve you instead of the other way around. Be honest and answer this question: who would you vote for? Ponder the question until the answer satisfies you.

Why do you think politicians, who can be clueless about the hardships of an average citizen, go out to meet voters before Election Day, and listen to their painful stories, only to turn them into campaign examples of how much in touch they are with voters? Most of the politicians who make election campaigns about themselves, their experience, or their heroism usually have their careers cut short by voters; whereas those who make it about the voters have their careers extended as far as the law permits.

In the United States, the most recent presidential elections have gone like this: George H. W. Bush (incumbent, WWII hero) versus Bill Clinton (feeling voters' pain, draft dodger); Bill Clinton (people's bridge to the twenty-first century) versus Bob Dole (WWII hero, experience); Al Gore (experience, Vietnam veteran) versus George W. Bush (compassionate conservatism, Vietnam War dodger); George W. Bush (people's security) versus John Kerry (experience, Vietnam War hero); Barak Obama (hope, change you can believe in) versus John McCain (experience, Vietnam War hero). Experience does not get self-proclaimed heroes elected; instead, those who present themselves as defending people's interests—whether it's true or pretense—got themselves elected into the presidency. That is the *power of you.*

To understand the YOU-power, you need look no further than the previously-mentioned "Only You" poem by Dan Coppersmith. In every paragraph, Coppersmith makes the listener feel he is a big deal, he is so important, without him the universe might be in serious trouble. Even though most of us are always uneasy listeners, his words make us so comfortable that we want to listen to him all day long. His words do more than just rekindle the spirit; they give life and hope to the listener. Why? They play with human nature. Deceit may be common, but it is against human nature. You may have noticed in almost every society, liars have very few friends but, paradoxically, the truth can be frightening. Throughout history, people have lost their lives for telling the truth. Nothing is costlier and more dangerous than the truth. The truth may get you respect but not without a high price. Lies buy unnecessary trouble and must be avoided at all costs. The truth, which may bring trouble and respect, must be told creatively in order for it to help you make the friends you need, obtain the respect you want, and eliminate the danger that may come with it. Use parables, allegories, or proverbs if necessary; reveal it to as few people as possible, and never to the masses. This is the secret of seers, prophets, truth-seekers; this is the secret of great souls; and this is one of the secrets of personal magnetism.

Like Coppersmith, when you choose to break the silence in the conversation, use the second person most of the time; tell the *you* in front of you the truth he needs to know about himself, praise him whenever he is right, tell him about his uniqueness, his natural gifts, how privileged you are for being his friend; above all, tell him in the most creative way. Go beyond Coppersmith's words: "you are unique, amazing, like no one else; you have the exclusive on being you." The sky is the limit as far you want to take your magnetic personality.

Most of us are so resistant to the idea of praising others, and here is where we miss the train. Jesus once said, "But I say unto you, that ye resist no evil: but whosoever shall smite thee on thy right cheek, turn to him the other also," (Matthew 5:39). This is the second cheek: be not defiant in praising friends and foes alike in a creative manner, because it is the best way to get their attention and drop their guard against your influence. As we will see later on, giving is more positive and powerful than receiving. Give to the soil a few seeds of rice and water, and you will harvest countless grains of rice. Praise first, and in the end, you will be influential. It is that simple.

It would be incomplete and quite frankly disingenuous to close this segment without elaborating on the side effects of compliments. It would be like claiming that the construction of a house has been completed without finishing the roof. Compliments are useful depending on the level of their sincerity; otherwise, they would be like biting the hand that feeds you. Compliments can be interchangeable with flattery but should never be used for that purpose. As persuasive as flattery may be, it is a killer for personal magnetism. Flattery is deceptive, but compliments are inspiring; they are birds of a different feather; they are two different species and can never mate.

You can get everything else you want, but you can never build personal magnetism on sweet-talk. Sweet talk has short-lived persuasive power. Not so with compliments, which are like a loyal servant who is on your side and ready when you need him. Flatterers are listened to a few times, but a compliment turns casual friends into confidants.

The villain of flattery has been denounced for it does more harm than good to a relationship. It causes unnecessary humiliation to one party and a sense of guilt to the other. Aesop's previously-mentioned fable retold by French poet Jean de la Fontaine is a good lesson for anyone who might be looking to flattery as a way of building personal magnetisms. As much as people want to feel good, an honorable person would hardly welcome a phony compliment. Be gentle when complimenting people, do not force the compliment with a misleading expression of praise when deep inside your heart lies another truth. The fruit of compliment comes sooner or later, but when it comes, it is gratifying and lasting. "The Crow and the Fox" fable is more of a lesson for the flatterer than for his victim. If you are seeking person magnetism, study it carefully.

Chapter Eight

Thoughts, Feelings, and Mental Sight

Of all the discoveries or inventions with which science has enriched our lives, nothing represents the function of the human body better than the radio. Humans are like radios because we receive and emit at long and short waves.

At long waves, man emits and receives sounds, better known as language. The power of this human radio is very limited to time and space. The receiver has to be at a reasonable distance to receive and emit efficiently. Unless aided by technology, receiving and emitting the past or future can be a quagmire.

At short waves, man emits and receives thoughts, feelings, and inner sight or mental pictures. When proficiently developed, this power is basically limitless. With thoughts and feelings, man can think and feel joy and pain of and about the past and the future; man can basically travel to infinity and back to the center of his universe instantly. And with inner sight, man can see love, hope, and joy, not merely as intangibles or principles, but as real meanings or essences of life, without which life is either meaningless or nothingness.

Communication at long waves takes place in the outer level, or the world without, whereas communication at short waves takes place at the inner level, or the world within. These two worlds, without and within, may be different, but they are not opposite to one another; they may not be totally complementary, but they positively or negatively stimulate each other. The world without is the world of free will, resistance, and stubbornness, while the world within is the world of obedience, readiness, love, and joyful service. The world without is the world of the students; the world within is the world of the Masters. Thus, the expression "when the student is ready, the master appears"—pure and simple.

The world without stimulates or sets off the world within, and the world within inspires, empowers, and cleanses the world without. But rather than talking about the dimensional nature of man, this work will instead focus on the worlds in which man truly lives, the only worlds in which man truly exists simultaneously, and the worlds that have reciprocal impacts on each other. These are the worlds that impact the alpha and omega of the life of man and, subsequently, the development of a strong magnetic personality. And those two worlds are the world without and the world within.

The world without is the seat of consciousness, whereas the world within is the seat of the subconscious. Of these two worlds, Charles F. Haanel writes in *The Master Key System*:

There is a world within—a world of thought and feelings and power; of light and life and beauty, and although invisible, its forces are mighty. The world within is governed by mind. When we discover this world, we shall find the solution for every problem, the cause for every effect, and since the world within is subject to our control, all laws of power and possession are also within our control. The world without is a reflection of the world within. What appears without is what has been found within. In the world within may be found infinite Wisdom, infinite Power, and infinite Supply of all that is necessary, waiting for unfoldment, development, and expression. If we recognize these potentialities in the world within, they will take form in the world without. Harmony in the world within will be reflected in the world without by harmonious conditions, agreeable surroundings, the best of everything. It is the foundation of health and a necessary essential to all greatness, all power, all attainment, all achievement and all success . . . .

The world within is the practical world in which the men and women of power generate courage, hope, enthusiasm, confidence, trust, and faith, by which they are given the fine intelligence to see the vision and the practical skill to make vision real . . . . We are related to the world within by the subconscious mind. (pp. 3-5)

The world within supplies life to the world without. It is the world of inspiration and information, while the world without is the world of actions and transformations. The world without is a world in which man transforms the pure energy received from the world within into good or bad actions; he transforms this energy by qualifying it with courage or fear, confidence or doubt, belief or discouragement.

The world without is a reflection of the good use or misuse of the supply from the world within. The world within is the world of laws and trust, and the world without is the domain of responsibility and consequences. The world within respects the free will of man and supplies the energy to the world without; the latter takes the responsibility for and the consequences of misuse of the energy provided.

The energy received from the world within can be transformed into machine guns, science, and logic. It simply gives us what we ask for, whether positive or negative. Since the energy is always used as the man "thinkth" or pleases, usefully or otherwise, man is 100 percent responsible of all the consequences as well the benefits. On a daily basis, man crosses these two worlds, back and forth, countless times by way of unbreakable bridges called words, thoughts, feelings, sights, and actions.

If you started asking some deep questions about the mysteries of science and scientists early on in your life, along the way, you might have heard that our modern scientists mysteriously travelled to Atlantis, an ancient mythical continent, first revealed by the Greek philosopher Plato. Atlantis is a continent that reputedly submerged under the Atlantic Ocean just when it reached the apex of its scientific and technological development.

On their journey, these scientists retrieved and brought back to life the inventions of that mythical civilization. For decades, I subscribed to that theory and still do, except now I know that the so-called lost continent from where the inventions came was not Atlantis (as we have been led to believe by those who want to keep man ignorant miserable, poor, submissive, and suffering), but the world within. Rather than going there mysteriously, they travelled there naturally, just as all of us do, by way of thought, feeling, and sight.

Thoughts, feelings and inner sights alone are what Jesus implied when He said, "No one comes to the Father but by me"—meaning right thinking, good feeling, and accurate sight. When thoughts, feelings, and inner sight are harmonized, wonders happen anywhere and anyhow. The world within has everything that outer man will ever need or think of. It has castles, amusement parks, and technological wonders that have not been built or imagined yet and many other objects that cannot be expressed in human language now or ever.

Thoughts, feelings, and inner sight are man's sole bridges to the world within; they are man's sole links between Heaven and Earth. Man becomes whatever he thinks and feels consciously or otherwise on a regular basis. We don't have to look further for the evidence than the bestselling book of all time, the Bible. Proverbs 23:7 states,

"As a man thinketh in his heart, so he is." Later (Matthew 9:29), Jesus clarifies adding, "According to your faith be it unto you."

Outside the Bible, one of the most successful men who ever lived, Henry Ford, for his part conceded to this truth, acknowledging that, "if you think you can do a thing or can't do a thing, either way you are right." Because if you think you can do something, and then you can—the world within will provide you with energy to do it, and if you think you cannot do anything, then you cannot, because your inner world will not provide you with the energy to do it. Thus, your thought, feelings, and inner sight are the only power for *or* against you.

It is practically impossible to do something of which you did not think or have a feeling or a mental image or sight. Thoughts, feelings, and mental pictures are not manmade. They come to us from the world within after stimulation by the world without. Due to apparent life pressure, you often find yourself in a situation you have not given much thought or feeling, but because your choices are very limited and sometimes you have no choice at all, you accept the responsibility of doing something for which you have neither the practical experience nor the educational training—just faith in your ability to learn and act to the best of your power.

Pioneers frequently find themselves in this kind of situation, and who better than Isaac Newton and Albert Einstein to illustrate the case? Newton, the British physicist, had a need to understand and explain the functioning of the universe, which became a sudden preoccupation. Without any prior theories, he was prompted by those who came before him, through thoughts, feelings, and mental sight to rely on the apple to understand and explain the functioning of the universe, how and why planets orbit the sun, and the theory of gravity. The German physicist, Einstein, *rejected* all previous theories, including those of Newton, and relied on time and space, but through the same process of thoughts, feelings, and mental sight constructed his initially controversial "Relativity Theory" to explain how the universe works. Thoughts, feelings, and mental sight are the true basis of faith; they empower man to face and conquer new realities.

When your way of thinking, feeling, and mentally picturing things changes, and you depend solely on your inner powers rather than your outer ones, you will perform the extraordinary by seeking solutions from the world within, where everything originates, where the greatest of men retrieved solutions to their problems.

We all have this same power, but for many of us it comes only when we face a difficult situation of life and death. Disabled people have been known to escape fires and other dangers when the alternative was death or serious injury. Some elderly people have overpowered armed assailants half their age when waiting for the help of the outside world would mean their total annihilation.

The so-called heroes and brave people are those who utilize their inner power to successfully carry out an action under very difficult circumstances. The energy used by disabled people to escape danger, elderly people to overpower attackers, or that used by heroes and brave people is always there and ready for use for all of us. We have the right and power to use it anytime and anywhere to get shocking results. All it takes is a strong faith (thinking, feeling, and mental picturing) in our inner, higher and truer self.

Many of us are living saints to a certain degree, and many of us are honorable or potentially so, and that is a good thing. But what do we do if our subconscious does not lead anyone to mastery? What we do in our consciousness is what counts most. The subconscious is always subject to free will. In other words, free will holds veto power over the suggestions of our subconscious; however, even though consciousness may still be subject to the power of free will to some degree, consciousness has the power to mold it to a large degree. Consciousness transforms doing into habit, and habit transforms doing into perfection at both the conscious and the subconscious levels.

In many schools of wisdom, it has been taught that feelings and thoughts are two major activities of the mind—one being feminine and the other masculine—brought together consciously for a constructive cause, they form two great forces of positive and dynamic creation.

The feeling of the feminine side of our consciousness can be irritated by such negative forces as hate, anger, fear, and jealousy; and it can be illuminated by love, joy, courage, enthusiasm, humility, or faith. Thought, by the same token, can be misguided by pride, arrogance, stubbornness, and condemnation, but it can be illuminated by knowledge, humility, light, and a relentless search for understanding.

An important key to the art of personal magnetism is the conscious translation of one of the following *languages,* if you will, into the two others:

- Feeling language into thought and mental picturing languages
- Thought language into feeling and mental picturing languages
- Thought language into feeling language

For instance, conscious consistency of thought transforms love or makes love radiate happiness or hatred into sadness. Sincere or deceitful feelings of love of something inspire constructive or destructive means to attain it. The conscious translation of one of these languages into the other is best done simply by observing the principle that is known to the world as the Golden Rule.

For instance, if you *feel* teaching people is a good art, just *think* and *mentally picture* yourself in the shoes of a pupil, and then draw your conclusion. If you *think* shooting people is a good sport, try to *feel* and *mentally picture* yourself in the shoes of the victim; then make up your mind about shooting people. By so doing, your thoughts, feelings, and mental pictures will contact similar thoughts, feelings, and mental pictures and, thus, the fate of your personal magnetism will be decided.

Affirmations

The question now is how to consciously start the circle of translations of thought, feeling, and mental picturing to help build a strong belief as a basis for personal magnetism. Faith helps, of course, but the application of the law fortifies faith. The law in this case is simple and straightforward. If you want to go inside, you must do it from the outside; if you want to go into a dwelling, you must open the door from the outside. If you want to see the invisible, you must see the visible first. We know the atmosphere contains water because we see water evaporate into vapor and then into the air as it comes back to us in form of rain. If you want to communicate in short waves, you must do it with long-wave communication tools. To broadcast an idea to all who can listen, the broadcaster uses the human voice, a long-wave communication tool at best, which unaided can hardly be heard half a mile away. But with the assistance of technology, the long waves are shortened and spread through the cosmos more or less instantaneously.

To consciously and accurately speed up the three-dimensional translation of thought, feeling, and mental picturing, or short-wave communication, you must use a long-wave communication in the form of sounds or words. The sounds or words that perform this process with great success are called affirmations. For affirmations to work, you must possess courage, persistence, self-confidence, and constructive intentions.

The translation of thoughts, feelings, and mental picturing is powerful because as short-wave communication, they travel as far as the ends of infinity and bring their equivalent to the center of the universe, which is right where you are. Open your inner eyes to see better, your inner ears to hear better, your intellect to understand better, your heart to feel better, and most importantly, pay close attention to your instincts and open yourself to divine inspiration that will lead to trust and strong belief in yourself. A steady belief in yourself and a strong will are the true magnets that will attract people to you.

Very few sane people are attracted to a man of frail will and doubtful mind. No magic pill exists that will make you strongly believe in yourself, besides your conviction in your own effort to do so and a strong will to keep going despite the inevitable setbacks that are part of the learning experience. These convictions and efforts are acquired by affirmations. Earlier, it was explained that the world without stimulates the world within. Affirmations are long waves or sound-based communication. They are language or words based on communication intended to arouse the inner world.

Affirmations are long-wave communication to be stirred into short waves and sent to the ends of infinity, bringing with them corresponding thoughts, feelings, and mental pictures. They are the expression of the will. They signal the readiness of the world without to receive the pristine energy from the world within. They inform the Higher Self (Our Father in heaven) that fears, doubts, and selfishness have been consumed—now let flow your energy ("your will be done on earth as it is in heaven . . .") down here below (on earth) for the manifestation of your majesty. Analyze the Lord's Prayer here, and you will see how everything falls into place almost perfectly.

If stimulation of the higher world by the lower world seems strange to you, think about this: energy that sustains life comes from the sun, yet no one jumps up to catch and store it; we plow the soil and then place grain in the ground, where sunrays have no direct access. From the planted grains, we get plants that provide us the vegetables and fruit that we eat and store for future use.

The sun provides life to the earth because of the earth's readiness and desire to receive it. Awakening below causes awakening above, it is said, not otherwise, else realms above which are all intelligence, all love, all wisdom and all power would have awakened realms below in no time at all and the word *suffering* would not have existed. The law has never changed, then and now. As Jesus, in Matthew 18:18 according to the King James Bible, put it,: "Verily I say unto you, Whatsoever ye shall bind on earth shall be bound in heaven: and whatsoever ye shall loose on earth shall be loosed in heaven."

What do grains, vegetables, and fruit contain? The sun gives energy to sustain life. Affirmations play exactly the same role. They place desires or *seeds* in our minds, mental and feeling bodies, thus stimulating our thoughts, feelings, and mental sight for the achievement of our intentions. The better seeds or desires we sow in our mind, mental and feeling bodies, the more constructive the results.

Affirmations spread the seeds or desires in the mind, mental and feeling bodies by repetitively evoking quality or qualities you want to acquire. For instance, if you keep repeating to yourself silently or audibly "I am honest; I am healthy; I am happy; I am a winner," you will be honest, healthy, happy, and successful. It is the law. By so evoking, the world without will stimulate the world within to supply you with honest, healthy, happy, and winning thoughts, feelings and mental pictures that will manifest in your world or the world around you. If you evoke the opposite, so the opposite will manifest sooner or later.

It is a changeless law to be obeyed above and below. You know how hard it is to get rid of a habit learned over a long period of time. Habits are great tools of life; they can make life easier or a burden. Habits are not merely powerful tools for the physical body; they are also for our inner bodies. Affirmations have been in use by wise and learned men and women for eons. One of the most famous is the Lord's Prayer, or Our Father, which Jesus gave to the outer world, and it has for the last two thousand years performed wonders for those who have devoted necessary effort.

He, the Lord Jesus, devoted thirty-three years of His life constantly affirming "I am the resurrection and the life," and Scriptures say that he achieved just that. To get a slight feeling of the power of affirmation, go back and reread the second Dan

Coppersmith poem in chapter seven; think about it, feel it, mentally picture what images are described in it, and then carefully watch the reaction in your body. If you read it with all your attention focused, you will feel humbled, relaxed yet empowered and strengthened like steel by the true power of words radiated from inside out.

Forming a habit of repeating the quality or qualities you want to show to the outer world, while accompanying them with thoughts, feelings, and mental pictures of the same is truly a magical way of becoming what you want to be and accomplishing what you want to do.

The author of *The Magic of Believing*, Claude M. Bristol, says the following about affirmation, belief, and performance: "It's repetition of affirmations that leads to belief. And once that belief becomes a deep conviction, things begin to happen."

Florence Scovel Shinn, popular writer of practical self-help books, adds: "We cannot always control our thoughts, but we can control our words, and repetition impresses the subconscious, and we are then master of the situation."

And in these words, the founder of the Science of Success, Napoleon Hill, concurs, "Any idea, plan, or purpose may be placed in the mind through repetition of thoughts."

These three giants of metaphysics enlighten the secret of affirmations. By repeating the qualities you aspire to, your subconscious or inner world, which is the supplier of your conscious or outer world, delivers everything it has and is, as far as your demands are concerned.

It is practically impossible to act courageously when your consciousness is filled with fear, or vice versa. It is against nature to believe and doubt at the same time, and whoever goes against this law of nature never acquires personal magnetism. He will be better off being a follower, rather than trying to lead others.

First Things First: Affirmation

Life is basically an exercise of two kinds of battles that we must face if we want to live a life worth living. These are the battle against the outside and the battle against the inside. You may have heard people telling you to choose your battles carefully. This is a true word of wisdom, indeed. Both battles have to be dealt with, no question about it. But choosing to start with the wrong battle is what weakens and exhausts us, and guarantees our miseries and eventual failure.

First Things First is a title of a book by Stephen Covey. As the title says, the book beautifully shows its readers where to start for a successful outcome in every undertaking. Unfortunately, many people start with the last battle first. People commit heinous crimes against themselves and blame others for their own mistakes. Would it not be a crime to feed pizza to a child who's a few days old, instead of milk? And is there a teacher who would keep his job if he was caught teaching algebra, philosophy, or geometry to a kindergarten child instead of the alphabet, counting, or respect for others? Yet, many of us adults often do the same kinds of things to ourselves with impunity, or so we hope.

People choose easier, less ferocious, and more popular battles against outside forces day in and day out at the expense of the more difficult and more important battles against our inner demons, whose conquest would make the battle against outside forces significantly easier. Ninety-five to 98 percent of us lose these battles against outside forces, because we simply take up the wrong battles at the wrong time. It is like a team or an athlete who chooses to compete first and then practice later. Because it hardly works with teams and athletes, it hardly works with at least 99.99 percent of the population.

We often hear that the wealth of most nations is controlled by less than 2 percent of the people, simply because a vast majority of the successful people chose inner battles before confronting outer ones. Of course, I am illustrating the point here using a financial analogy, but the reader can transpose it into almost every life endeavor: politics, academia, science etc . . . . There is never enough room at the top for many people. In religion, it is even worse. Can you count how many Jesus-like or Virgin Mary folks have we had in the last two thousand years?

Wrong battles are fought unsuccessfully to the last breath and many pass away not even trying to stand up to their inner demons. The reason this battle is wrong is because we make it the first battle rather than the second. It is like when climbing up on the roof, one must first step on the lowest step of the ladder instead of the highest step if the job is to be performed safely.

To be clear, we are not suggesting "believe, then relax, and world will open up." Far from that. Belief and action always go hand in hand, as we are told by James (2:14–26), "Faith without works is dead." For a more detailed analysis on the marvels of belief in conjunction with actions, I strongly advise the reader to study my next book, *Exalted Secrets of Brilliant Minds*, which is the second work in the *Hints of Wisdom* series. Action is the externalization of belief. Faith and action are two pages of the same paper; there is no one without the other. Nobody strengthens his muscles by believing in his ability to do so.

No one becomes a victorious athlete by practicing and playing alone; but also believing in their ability to win games. No one becomes a skilled politician, public speaker, or community leader by acting like a politician, public speaker, or community leader; he/she can only do it in conjunction with faith in his/her ability to succeed in politics, public speaking, or community leadership. Aren't there teams with very talented and skilled players that end up losing to less skilled and talented teams who simply have more faith and confidence in themselves?

In fables, the fox is rarely portrayed as a strong animal, but it is known to bring birds, lions, elephants, and stronger animals to their knees because of its balanced faith in itself and actions. The size, strength or wings of an opponent does not scare the fox. How does the fox do that? It fights its first battle first. It wins its first battles first before taking on a rival. It submits its fears, doubts, anger, and discouragement to its courage, faith, self-confidence, persistence, and other positive inner qualities before talking to a crow, lion, or any other inwardly confused foe.

Observing these two battles that man fights, John Addison writes, "You've got to win your mind before you win your life." This brings us to the second battle, which in fact should be the first battle, the battle that makes the battle against the environment easier and winnable. This battle is to simply convince our mind about what we can do or be.

"Yes, we can." These three words and the seed they implant in the mind of a strong will to win enabled a little known, racially mixed, former Illinois state senator and a first-term US senator to become the president of the United States.

It is amazing what man can conquer after conquering himself. Once you are convinced of who you are, once you think, feel, and picture your faith, self-confidence, and strength surmounting any obstacle in your way, then your battles in life are made less vicious. Muhammad Ali, the most famous man of his time, did not jump in the ring before convincing himself first, his opponent next, and finally the world that he was the greatest, and he was the greatest because he believed it. "I figured that if I said it enough, I would convince the world that I really was the greatest," Ali once said.

The power of affirmations is only ignored by ignorant minds. But those who have their inner eyes open know the incredible wonders that are accomplished through the use of affirmations. Affirmations help saturate the mind of man with qualities that burst into the outer world to the astonishment of the unguarded. The great souls not only use affirmations as they breathe, they teach their students to do the same. Jesus taught his disciples the Lord's Prayer, one of the most powerful affirmations of them all. As short as it is, if repeated as frequently as possible and accompanied with a thought, feeling, and a picture of what it calls upon, it performs marvels. Try it and see.

Even though the Lord's Prayer is an excellent weapon in your fight against inner foes, it is a bit too long to be conveniently utilized on short notice or in case of emergency. After all, Jesus Himself used only short but powerful and forceful statements such as those quoted in the St. Germain Foundation's *The "I AM" Discourses, vol. III:* "I AM the Open Door that no man can shut," "I AM the way, the life and the truth," "I AM the Light that lighteth every man that cometh in the world," and the most powerful of them all, which propelled Him like an arrow in the heart of Heaven, "I AM the resurrection and the life."

In "The I AM Discourses", volume #3 of the Saint Germain Series of the Saint Germain Foundation, the Mighty Glorious Ascended Master Saint Germain (about whom enough will be said in the #2 book of "Hints of Wisdom" Series: "Exalted Secrets of

Brilliant Minds", to give ample clues to earnest seekers who wish to know more about this Extraordinary Being) says this about this Jesus' Mighty Statement:

All through the ages there have been certain standards of conduct necessary for the student who desires to reach beyond certain attainments. This is the conserving and governing of the Life Force, through the sex.

For an individual who has been using this energy without any thought of governing it to suddenly say, "I will cease this," cut it off as it were, without understanding the correct attitude of consciousness, would be simply suppressing a flow of energy, which he has caused to flow in the wrong direction. Any student who wishes to govern this will find this simple Statement the most efficient – **if used understandingly** *– of any one particular thing that can be given. This will normally and naturally govern the flow of the Life Energy and bring it back into its natural channels. It is the Mighty Statement of Jesus:* **"I AM' the Resurrection and the Life."**

This Statement will not only purify thought, but is the most powerful, lifting, adjusting force that can be used for correction of this greatest of barriers to the Full Height of Spiritual Attainment. Anyone who begins to feel the Inner Impulse to correct this condition and will use this Statement earnestly and continually will raise this marvelous current of energy to the highest center of the brain, as was originally intended.

He will find his mind flooded with the most marvelous ideas – with the abundant, sustaining Power and ability coming into expression and use for blessing of all mankind…

Feel deeply this Statement of Jesus: **"I AM' the Resurrection and the Life.** *" Repeat it three times, either silently or audibly, and notice the lifting of consciousness, which you will experience. There may be some who will need to try this several times in order to feel the amazing uplifting that others will experience at first trial. This will show you what can be done by it continued use.* Page 19-20

And in the *Masks of God: Occidental Mythology,* Joseph Campbell writes:

In one of the recently discovered Gnostic codices of the jar of Nag-Hamadi we find the following, attributed to Jesus: I am the Light that is above all; I am the all. The all came from Me and the All attained me. Cleaver a piece of wood, I am there: Lift up the Stone, you will find Me there, page 367.

Because of the frequency, intensity, and the strength of the desire of the fulfillment, the result was . . . well, make your own description.

So many affirmations exist that it is practically impossible to tell which one is more effective. It may not be easy or possible to tell the best affirmation, but the formula for the most effective affirmations is the same, and it is matched by the one used by Jesus. The length of the affirmation is relative to personal needs and feelings, but the first two words used by Jesus—and believed to be of central magnitude by serious students of self-knowledge and truth, well before God revealed His name to Moses as being I AM THAT I AM, are I AM followed by any quality you long to acquire.

Introducing any and all positive statements with the words I AM is the best kept secret of an effective affirmation, known only to the chosen and the blessed few. "I am fearless; I am strong; I am loveable; I am love; I am healthy; I am confident." It is important to note that a good affirmation does *not* contain the word NOT, even if it is used to mean a negative quality that you are not. The word *not* troubles the mind since it is the expression of negativity, thus an affirmation of destruction. *Not*, by itself, is like a wall through which light does not pass. When you say *not* in most cases you intend to express something negative or destructive. "I am not sick; I am not weak; I am not sad" may just mean I *am* sick; I *am* weak, I *am* sad." On the other hand, "I am not happy; I am not healthy; I am not fearless," will not mean I *am* happy, healthy, or fearless, because *not* only acts as a wall that keeps light away. It also sends confusing and inappropriate commands to the mind.

Many experts of positive thinking believe that the mind does not think in terms of negative or repulsion. Instead, it is an instrument of the law of attraction; it understands and interprets the instructions of attraction better and faster than those of repulsion. So, when you say, "I am sick; I am weak; I am sad," or "I am not sick; I am not weak; I am not sad," the mind may not differentiate between the two; thus it can give you sickness, weakness, and sadness in both cases.

Thus, rather than giving your mind the instruction of repulsion, it is advisable to give the instruction of attraction. When you are healthy, say, "I am healthy" rather than "I am not sick." A simple trick is to always remember to order what you want, not what you do not want. Ask life what you want, and waste no time or energy telling life what you do not want. Imagine how fast you would drive McDonald's employees crazy if you drove into their drive-thru and told them what parts of the menu you did *not* want, rather than just telling them what you want?

That is the real world, and it is not different from the world of the mind; actually, it is its perfect reflection. The mind cares less about what you do not want, and if you could care to listen, you could hear it begging you to please not waste its time and energy sorting out what you do not want. Your mind wants you to demand

and command it to bring you what you do want; supplying your needs is what it does best, not your no-needs or your unwanted.

As mentioned earlier, it is perfectly acceptable above and below to tear off a page from a master's playbook and use it for your own good. The Master asked His mind to attract for him the "resurrection and the life," and He got no less than His demands. You cannot go wrong; either use the same words of the Master or substitute them with similarly and positively charged qualities, and the result will equal the intensity of your desire. You cannot go wrong by literally cloning the Master's affirmation to suit your own needs. Remember—He never said, "I am not death, I am not darkness, and I am not gone astray"; instead, He said, "I am the life; I am the light; I am the way." So, anyone who wants to build a strong, personal magnetism would be better off imitating or copying the Master's code words.

Visualization: Affirmation's Empowering Sister

Affirmations are so important because they help in the growth of faith, the kind of faith that sustains self-confidence without fear and doubt, which will scatter the energy that is vital for success in every endeavor. Affirmation, on the other hand, has a twin sister that makes it ever more powerful if effectively used, and that is visualization. To illustrate what visualization is to affirmation, consider how our hands or legs accomplish much by working together.

Yes, you can achieve a lot with one hand; yes, you go some distance with one leg; but you are more efficient and agile when using both hands and both legs. If you understand how easy it is to perform a task with both hands or walk some distance with both legs, then you know how easy it is to hasten manifestations from the world within to the world without. Just like the left and the right hands and legs support each other, so do affirmation and visualization.

A softly voiced but forcefully toned affirmation brings power to your vision, but visualization brings speed to any manifestation, because it focuses the attention. As you add to the equation by controlling and stilling the senses to form and hold a picture in your mind, you will be led through the canal that connects man with the limitless source of visions, feelings, and thoughts. Affirmation by itself is like a scattered force, but coupled with visualization, it is like a concentrated force, dropped consistently at a single focal point.

We talked about visualization earlier, but it is imperative that we emphasize it here because the power of affirmation when used along with visualization can never be overstated. The major role of affirmation is to gather the aspired qualities of the world within, but visualization serves an equally important role of delivering your requests with precision. One of the secrets of success is, therefore, the frequency of affirmations for a fast materialization of desired qualities, and focused visualization efficiently paves the way for a swift delivery. Affirmation and visualization brought the wise men and seers of the ancient world in tune with the infinite, and these tools are readily available to do the same for anyone in the present world, as long as proper effort and applications are utilized.

On this point, in *The Superbeings*, John R. Price states, "The Superbeings put great emphasis on meditation, affirmations—speaking the word of truth until it is firmly etched in the consciousness—and the technique of creative imagination. All insist 'right thinking' is absolutely necessary . . ." (p. 68).

Charles Haanel in *The Master Key System* adds:

> Make the Mental Image; make it clear, distinct, perfect; hold it firmly; the ways and means will develop; supply will follow the demand; you will be led to do the right thing at the right time and in the right place. Earnest Desire will bring about Confident Expectation, and this in turn must be reinforced by a Firm Demand. (p. 77.)

It is an unfair demand and practically impossible to sing like a parrot all day long, "I am healthy; I am happy; I am strength; I am authority; I am magnetic." It is even more hopeless singing this or that while picturing yourself unhealthy, sad, and weak or at least complaining about your health and showing your sadness and weakness to the world and then expecting positive results from the request.

Nature linked language and mental power for a good and purposeful end. A person who speaks what he does not think scares society, but a person whose mouth puts into words only what he feels, thinks, and most importantly, sees distinctly in great detail is a master not only of those whose words are empty and feelings and thoughts are blind, but also a master of the forces of nature.

There is a reason why Jesus refers to those who pray loudly in public as hypocrites—while this might impress people, it does not impress the mind effectively, and it does not enable visualization of what you want delivered. He recommends that prayers (affirmations) be offered in private, because this will not only make one feel the true meaning of the words being uttered, but most importantly, it will allow one to be undisturbed as one visualizes a picture of what one wants the messenger from the inner world to deliver in a timely fashion. In private and in silence, you will undoubtedly create the channel and the attention, which is the only way the infinite communicates with us.

Thoughts and feelings are kept secret for a reason—they are the sole power of creation and destruction. When expressed imaginatively and in an orderly fashion, they bring happiness and joy, but when expressed unimaginably and in disarray, they bring chaos and pain.

The importance of making affirmations while picturing the desired demand is beyond description. In fact, some of the best works of art in existence are not housed in museums; they are displayed in houses of prayer such as churches, temples, pagodas, synagogues, and mosques. It is not just by accident that houses of worship are decorated with marvelous images, some understood by the masses and others not understood; either way, the reason for this may be found in what the renowned preacher and theologian Jonathan Edwards described almost three centuries ago, "Temples have their sacred images, and we see what influence they have always had over a great part of mankind; but, in truth, the ideas and images in men's minds are invisible powers that consistently govern them; and to these they all pay universally a ready submission."

The technique of making affirmations while visualizing the outcome is as old as human knowledge or feeling of God. Images have always been at the center of worship in every society. Many societies have erected symbolic statues of the good and the ideal. Those who have used these statues to stimulate their imagination and mold a pure image in their mind have found happiness. Those who have used the inspiration from sacred images and statues to conquer the world within can never have any other outcome but that of touching joy, the highest vibrating feeling in the universe.

On the other hand, those who literally interpret sacred images or statues, those who fail to get inspiration from these same sources to inner and pure images of their own and those who take them for reality rather than a springboard to a higher purpose, will hopelessly envelop themselves in a cloak of the lowest vibrating feeling of the universe, which only brings misery and suffering. For this reason alone, for fear of misleading the weak, major religions are reluctant to create or present an image or statue of God.

The art of personal magnetism is not different from developing any other art: it gets better with practice. If you desire to sharpen the art of personal magnetism, you must constantly and forcefully repeat the qualities that you believe will make you the magnetic person you want to be. You must do this in a hushed breath or in the sacred silence of your heart wherever you are. But in addition to affirmations, you must imagine or visualize yourself acting as a magnetic individual attracting the right people. This will make people love you and enjoy your presence not for what you have, but for just being you. The more details of personal magnetism you visualize for yourself, the more magnetic you will be. It is no different than inventing something.

The person who invented the car, for instance, did not just see a box of metal speeding down the road. He saw in his mental world a metal box, yes, but he also saw the wheels, engine, seats, the factory where the box would be assembled, and the mine where the raw materials would come from, the mold of the raw materials, and the workers who would assemble the car. So, visualize yourself with all the qualities of a magnetic personality you would like to embody. See yourself serving others, thanking those who helped you along the way, and encouraging the heartbroken. And here shines this key. Affirmations by themselves are like starting a car engine;

visualization is like stepping on the gas paddle to get the car moving in the right direction.

The Secret of Conquering the Ego

Nothing brings down a successful or powerful person faster and more disastrously than ego. *The Oxford American Desk Dictionary and Thesaurus* (2nd edition) defines ego as "part of the mind that has self-awareness." I respect that Freudian definition, but in reality, the ego is the feeling of self-centeredness and self-aggrandizement that renders man incapable of seeing life or the world through the lenses of another or walking in the shoes of fellowmen. The ego is the author of that bigheaded gospel according to "I", "my", or "mine." Ego is the most skillfully hidden and destructive inner enemy or demon of any living person. It has brought down kings, empires, kingmakers, generals, armies, athletes, businessmen, priests, beauty queens, and even civilizations. Though all human beings have egos, it is more heightened and powerful in the hearts of those who believe they have reached the apex of their dreams—the rich and the famous. When former US senator John Edwards, the 2004 US Democratic Party vice-presidential candidate and 2008 Democratic Party presidential candidate was revealed by the media to have fathered a child out of wedlock while his wife was suffering with a terminal illness, he blamed his ego, which he said led him to think he could do whatever he pleased, having reached the zenith of the social ladder.

Former US president Bill Clinton's ego prompted him to have sexual relations with impunity as well. His folly or ego led him to believe he could have a sexual relationship with an indiscrete intern, Monica Lewinski, in the Oval Office and keep it hidden from the invisible yet watchful eye of the law, or so he thought. As always, his ego was misleading and wrong at best, consequently, the result was catastrophic and his presidency almost came to an untimely and disastrous end.

The ego expresses itself in different shapes and forms. Its exposure is usually short but strong; it only extends for a long period of time when its victim senses the potential shame and then tries to cover it up. It could be seen as a mental breakdown that leads to unintended consequences; lawyers and legal experts have discovered a better yet deceptive term—*temporary insanity*—to make it admissible in court and make a case for the innocence of their clients. The website of legal experts, wisegeek.com defines temporary insanity in these terms:

> A temporary insanity plea is a plea submitted by someone accused of a crime that suggests the person was not guilty for several reasons. First, the defendant was diminished in mental capacity and could not understand the nature or quality of his behavior. Second, the defendant could not differentiate between basic ideas of right or wrong when he acted in a criminal manner. Since this condition was temporary, it means the person is no longer

insane, but was at the time a crime took place. Should a person be judged not guilty because of a temporary condition, he or she may be released without incarceration of any type, whether at a mental hospital or prison. (http://www.wisegeek.com/what-is-atemporary-insanity-plea.htm. Accessed 03/29/2009)

Indeed, ego really is temporary insanity. Just because someone is a president, a US senator, or a pastor of a church, it does not preclude him from suffering mental illness, but whether a man is not responsible for the acts performed under *temporary folly* to legal experts is a chicken-and-egg question. Although it might be a legal ambiguity, nature certainly does not treat it that way, since it rewards and punishes equally everything—conscious or unconscious, ill or sane.

No one is immune to this negative inner force. Any man who ever lived has faced this seemingly negative foe of man, and that includes Jesus of Nazareth when he walked the face of the Earth more than two thousand years ago. According to the Bible (New International Version online) Matthew 4:1-11 says:

> Then Jesus was led by the Spirit into the desert to be tempted by the devil. After fasting forty days and forty nights, he was hungry. The tempter came to him and said, "If you are the Son of God, tell these stones to become bread.

Jesus answered, "It is written: 'Man cannot live on bread alone, but lives on every word that comes from the mouth of the Lord.'"

Then the devil took him to the holy city and had him stand on the highest point of the temple. "If you are the Son of God," he said, "throw yourself down. For it is written: 'He will command his angels concerning you, and they will lift you up in their hands, so that you will not strike your foot against a stone."

Jesus answered him, "It is also written: 'Do not put the Lord your God to the test.'"

Again, the devil took him to a very high mountain and showed him all the kingdoms of the world and their splendor. "All this I will give you," he said, "if you will bow down and worship me."

Jesus said to him, "Away from me, Satan! For it is written: 'Worship the Lord your God, and serve him only.

Then the devil left him, and angels came and attended him. (www.biblegateway.com/passage/?search=Matthew% 204:1-11. *Accessed* 03/22/2009)

This illustration is solely intended to illuminate readers on how they can overcome their inner foes, which are the biggest obstacles to the development of personal magnetism. It is not our intention whatsoever to put any belief for or against the divinity of Jesus

Christ under the microscope. Thus, it is perfectly logical to agree or disagree with the idea that Jesus was a man like the rest of us, who happened to understand the laws of nature better than anyone who ever lived, and performed superhuman manifestations, or was the embodiment of God.

Regardless of one's opinion on Jesus—divinity or manhood—we can at least tentatively agree that there was something in Him that resembled the rest of mankind, and by that, we mean His inner weaknesses or ego that had to be conquered first—we repeat—*first* to allow Him to be victorious and eventually become Christ and Savior. Recall first things first?

His followers believe He is today, and ego was one of those weaknesses and challenges He absolutely had to deal with to be victorious, not just the agony of the cross. Before moving on, we would like to add that like many other undesirable life experiences or unrecognized life opportunities, ego is not necessarily a bad thing. In many cases, when positively understood, it is a blessing in disguise; it can be a useful stimulant that motivates you to turn to the Light of God that never fails to provide poise, inspiration, and glory.

Religious beliefs aside, people can argue about what really brought Jesus to the edge of disaster and almost pushed Him over the cliff. The answers would definitely be numerous and varied, but I would not rule out His own ego. His ego seems to have been skillfully described in the Gospel as the devil, which used all the traps at its disposal to bring down Jesus. But the Master knew that to fight a bull you have to catch it by the horns, not the tail.

The so-called devil does not seem to be anything other than ego, because as the saying goes, if it walks like a duck, quacks like a duck, looks like a duck, it must be a duck.

The ego awakens at a time of serious physical weakness. For Jesus, it was after forty days of fasting. For Clinton, it was after long hours of work on the federal budget and frustrating negotiations with the Republican opposition. A flirtatious intern who brought him pizza was caught in a net by Clinton's inner spider.

Ego incites pride and promises fake dominion. For Jesus, it pressed to prove His divine uniqueness and promised "kingdoms of the world." Ego blinds people by showing them how successful they are and how high above the law they have climbed. For Edwards, the son of a millworker who never dreamed of becoming a US senator, much less a presidential candidate, his material success was too much to believe; it was an incredibly blinding light that drove him over the edge to his moral and political ruin.

Ego can be described in different ways, but the bottom line is that it interferes with rational thinking and is poisonous to personal magnetism; you must fight it with the sharpest and deadliest weapon there is. The question, of course, is what is that weapon? Clinton and Edwards fell powerlessly to the arrow of their egos, thus there is nothing to be learned from the Clintons and Edwards of this world. Jesus, on the other hand, fought, shamed, defeated, and expelled his ego with a powerful yet simple weapon: words. As previously mentioned, when correctly understood, ego can be a camouflaged opportunity, Jesus knew it and used it to the best of his knowledge and, as a result, He had his personal magnetism attract angels from Heaven.

You do not have to call angels to your visible world, but by defeating ego, you can attract joy and harmony in your heart, in addition to drawing or magnetizing the hearts of your fellowmen. A good student is he who steals a page from a master's playbook, expands it, and uses it to the best of his ability. How did Jesus do it? It is not the Biblical Jesus we are talking about from here on, but Jesus as the philosophical, constructive force, the power of good. Even when you think it is about the INRI * it is not; it is about the power of good that is in all of us. Jesus did not subdue his ego by anger or physical means but by persistence and a powerful command or affirmation in a masterful tone: "Away from me!" He ordered, and his command was scrupulously obeyed.

Personal magnetism can take a lifetime of assiduous work; it is always at risk, not only from outside enemies but from inner forces to which most of us fall with little resistance. Its only protector and defender is an educated and disciplined mind. No army or

---

* Latin initials for *Iesvs Nazarenvs Rex Ivdaeorvm*, meaning Jesus of Nazareth, King of the Jews, so called by Pontius Pilate, the Roman governor, and placed over the cross.

intelligence service can guard you from this double-edged, inner, and potentially poisonous sword.

If you see its positive and illuminating side and use it appropriately, joy will flood your heart; enlightenment will brighten your mind; inspiration will sharpen your intellect; clarity will lead your thoughts; truth will impregnate your words; virtues will spring from your actions; knowledge will perfect your wisdom; enthusiasm will heighten your feelings; opportunities will sprout on your path; poise will fill your air; confidence will guide your vision; silence will bring you closer to the one whose name is neither printable nor pronounceable by the lips of men; your breath will exhale health and inhale faith; you will be among the chosen few; fire will consume your *miscreations*; you will seek supreme good; your body will radiate energy; your attention will be focused on the light; your shell of ignorance will be broken; your faith will open the door of enlightenment; your victory will come on the wings of desire and determination; your persistence and strong self-control will discourage your enemies; strength and courage will conquer your doubt and fears; the wand of fire will blaze in the heart of your consciousness; knowledge will be brought to you in a golden platter; you will learn by reflection and not by memory; love will be the prince of your feelings; faith and joyous enthusiasm will sustain your will; the pen of light shall engrave your name in the heart of eternity; infinity will act through you; you will shine like a branch of the *tree of life*; your eyes will see the golden link; your ears will hear the music of the spheres; your feet will climb the golden steps; freedom will make you self luminous; you will become a disciple of true faith; angels will lift you up beyond the stars; they will sit you in the heart of the light of a thousand suns; they will reveal the truth to you; they will glorify your inner and higher self and make you the voice of infinity forever; and your presence will bring peace, love and harmony to your fellowmen. This will be your proof over ego and other lower feelings, and your personal magnetism will be invincible forever.

Ego, which at its strongest manifests itself as an impulse, is restrained by taking exile in the heart of silence. When an inexplicable urge to take action suddenly invades your thoughts, feelings, and mental picturing ability, it is advisable to run as fast as you can in the heart of silence by slowly and silently counting from one to any number that you feel comfortable with, back and forth, until you can take control of your senses again and, most of all, your will.

This process usually does not take a long time; depending on your inner growth, anything between sixty seconds to five minutes can be enough time to shut down a strong impulse and all its operations. Ancient generals knew this principle; therefore, they would send their bickering soldiers to prison for no more than three days in order to solve a conflict between soldiers peacefully and many times without even a trial.

In prison, bickering soldiers were forced to embrace the heart of silence to clear their minds, receive inspiration, and judge themselves. So, when they came out, they convinced themselves that their anger was not only not justified, it was foolish and childish, and peaceful reconciliation with their fellow warriors was a more rational solution.

Ego is more dangerous when it is slow and heavy on the processes of feeling and thought; it is like volcano lava, less predictable than impulse but more destructive. It destroys everything in its path, including rock and water, but it can be overcome by air and time. This is the ego that Jesus faced, and it was only subdued by powerful and sincere commands expressed in an unambiguous tone. This ego is really a replica of man inside the man; it is a man in a man. It has almost literally all five senses that man has. Fortunately, it has no will of its own. It listens and obeys the commands of the man outside or the conscious man if ambushed before the spread of deadly poison. It loves man's sympathy, fears and compassion.

When INRI thought He could persuade His foe with some sympathetic words—"Man cannot live on bread alone . . . . Do not put the Lord your God to the test"—it kept coming, looking for an opening to strike a fatal blow. It was not until INRI spoke powerfully in a truly masterful tone—"Away from me!"—that it got the message. To defeat your ego and grow your personal magnetism, you must learn not just to talk to it but *to command* it to submit to your will. It has ears to hear your command, eyes to see its way out, feet to walk, heart to fear for its life, and a brain to think twice before making another attempt.

Commands are your 9-1-1 emergency line—it takes care of both the insured and the uninsured—but affirmations are your insurance policy. You can ignore the health insurance and risk losing everything you have worked for or file bankruptcy should you need expensive medical care down the road. To help the growth of your personal magnetism, it is advisable to develop affirmations and use them constantly to keep your inner foes from influencing you negatively. All wise and magnetic people in history have done this, and you must do it too if you want to count yourself among them.

Giving and Receiving

The most important activity in the universe that most people know very little about—or at least only pretend to know about—and which is the basis of existence is the activity of creation. Creation is the first principle of everything. It is the first principle of the universe. It is the first principle of life. Creation, in its truest sense, means giving. Giving precedes receiving as creation precedes existence.

Before something can exist, there must be a giver of life, energy, and substance to it. A farmer must give something to the soil before he can plant fruit and food. The giver is always more powerful. Before the invasion of the world by modern religions, people in most cultures adored the sun for its generosity of giving its free gifts of love, light, energy, and life. Creation, or the expansion of existence, is the highest activity of God and the sole purpose of human life, plant life, and everything in between. God finds more joy in expanding His kingdom to the next imaginable frontier of infinity.

Man has no greater physical pleasure than sex and food, the two main activities of the creation and expansion of life. Those who give the most hold the most power. In all human societies, the rich—or those who have the ability to give the most to people and governments—have the most influence on people and governments.

To keep the wheel of creation ever turning, the needs of every species must cycle and recycle as a wheel, enabling species to rejuvenate endlessly, and thus keeping creation indefinite. At the very center of creation, though, there exists an engine and the fuel that makes it run without end—and that is best described by the principle of giving and receiving.

St. Paul had better words to describe this principle in his letter to the Galatians 6:7-9: "For whatever a man soweth, that shall he also reap . . . And let us not weary in well doing: for in due season we shall reap, if we faint not."

Everything is based on this principle, including your physical, mental, and spiritual universes. We know both our friends and our enemies by what they give us or do not give us; we associate ourselves with people or groups of people according to what we are able to give to them and receive from them.

There is no exception to this rule at any level of life. On a physical level, man will never associate as closely with other animals as he would with fellow human beings. Regardless of the affection between man and other creatures, bonds will never be stronger than the one that exists between men, because only man can give another man a sense of security, protection, and hope for tomorrow. Of all creatures, only man can provide his fellowmen with physical, mental, and spiritual satisfaction. On a mental level, a wise man will never befriend a fool, because the give-and-take activity would be absent at that dimension. And on a spiritual level, light and darkness will never cohabitate, for obvious reasons. Yes! I can hear you, my reader, saying: "How dare you? Isn't it true, in fact, that the brighter the light, the darker the shadow?" And I concur, but it's also true that it is always sunny above the clouds even when it is raining down here. In a well-lighted and unobstructed room, light and darkness never see one another face to face now or in eternity, here or in the infinite.

Naturally and unavoidably, kings and commoners, the rich and the poor, regardless of health or wealth, wisdom or intelligence, power or security, all of us have gaps and needs in our lives that we cannot fill without the association with others. Giving and receiving for mutual benefit is the strongest bond of all relationships in the universe.

No one will be either the giver or the receiver all the time, but if you are not both at the same time, you will be neither. It is always a good thing to move, quite often, from the giver's seat to the receiver's seat and vice versa. Assuming the sacred Scriptures of our modern religions are true, God gives life or existence to His creatures and, in return, expects or explicitly demands gratitude and praise . . . or else.

Unless the magic of giving is clearly understood, effective personal magnetism will never be achieved. The secret of building a strong magnetic personality is thus the ability to know how to fill and satisfy the gaps and needs of others *before* they can fill and satisfy yours. Anyone who will understand and employ the art of giving and receiving well will have an unmatchable positive personal magnetism.

We sympathize with some of our readers here. We confess this point may not be as clear as we would like to make it. However, this is one of those subjects where the vocabulary of man will always fall short in conveying the meaning intended. Should this be your experience, fear not. Go straight to the great teacher within and all will be plainly explained to you better than the most skillful writer could.

The art of giving and receiving, well performed, makes one a sweetheart of the heavens, a manipulator of the rich, a friend of the wise, and a demigod of the poor and the weak, nothing less nothing more. Skillful giving and receiving is the only act and the sole motivation that prompts people to "worship" their fellow human beings.

People don't worship other human beings because of wealth or power, but because of the understanding and satisfaction of their material, mental, and spiritual emptiness that is weakening their lives. The true magic of personal magnetism is attained when you acquire the ability to satisfy not each need one by one, but to satisfy all of them through the satisfaction of just one.

Sometimes, all people need from you is just to give them hope and faith in the power within themselves and the infinite opportunities that life will spread around them if they only feel happy and ready to believe in themselves again. Sometimes, all people need is for you to tell them that the golden key is not at the top of the hill but inside themselves and that alone will fulfill their material, psychological, and spiritual needs—and of course, their attraction to you too.

Seers and wise men have used these techniques to build myths and legends around their personalities. You may never be like the seers and wise men of ancient times, but by skillfully giving and receiving you can make a giant leap forward, you can bring out your irresistible, magnetic personality and make it an object of admiration for your fellowmen. Giving and receiving is, in fact, the law of balance that harmonizes the universe.

By giving to others and receiving from them, electrons, atoms, and molecules find perfectly compatible teammates to fill the universe harmoniously. They unfailingly place themselves at the right place at the right time and happily contribute to the synchronization that stabilizes stars, planets, seas, and life in general.

Without this principle, happiness, the highest-vibration feeling in the universe, would be unachievable, and chaos would be the fill of the cosmos.

When a human life is first born here on Earth (through our mother's wombs), the first thing you get—breath from the open air—is given free of charge. You bring nothing material with you, not even food for your own survival. And from then on to your last breath, every material thing you ever have in life comes from someone else, regardless of your wealth or power. As a child, the only thing you are given from your loved ones is joy—through joy, your needs are provided for adequately. Philosophers and seers give nothing but hope, faith, and enlightenment. Many of them were poor in monetary wealth, but to this day they are worshiped by kings and the richest of the rich.

Even though everything you have or will ever have in your lifetime comes through the channel of others, giving is the master key that opens its doors. Giving creates independence and power, while receiving creates dependence and powerlessness. Giving is harder than receiving but more rewarding. Giving and receiving are twin sisters, joined at the hip. They are forever connected like two ends of an electrical battery, giving being the positive side, while receiving is the negative side; like two sexual partners that give birth to a child, giving is the male and receiving is the female partner.

It is essential to note that the giver is partially receiver and vice versa. In a solar system relationship, the sun is the giver and the planets receivers, but one half of the earth is governed by the sun while the other is governed by the moon and stars. But overall, the whole earth is bathed in the ocean of light and that of darkness every twenty-four hours. Similarly, females become givers and males become receivers. The name of the game is knowing the right time and place to be giver or receiver. Life is full of illustrations to inspire you; just keep calm and move on.

Few lessons can illustrate how receiving breeds greatness. On the other hand, an inexhaustible wealth of information can explain how giving courteously swells one's personal magnetism. Anyone who has ever thought of building a powerful magnetic personality must master the art of giving, just as the farmer must know how to give to the soil before the soil can generously give back in quality and quantity what was given to it in the first place. Though both the rider and the driver enjoy the ride, the driver enjoys it twice; in addition to the ride, he enjoys the privilege of the being in command. In the same way the driver is responsible for his own happiness as well as that of his passengers.

It is the same law of old—we reap what we sow, and we cannot sow a handful of grains of corn and then expect to reap tons of corn or sow a mediocre quantity of seeds and expect excellent returns. The laws of nature are irresistible, inescapable, and unbreakable; only compliance guarantees satisfactory results. Otherwise, no results will occur.

You may have heard the expression "there is no such thing as a free lunch," meaning there is nothing for nothing. Giving for the sake of giving is counterproductive; it's against the law of nature and may earn the giver disrespect and condemnation from society. No one should give because they have more than others, but giving should always be done for the belief in a greater good. You get what you give. You cannot sow corn and reap beans.

If you give for a belief in the greater good, greatness will be given to you in return. Only an ingrate will bite the hand that feeds him, and such an ingrate has no place in the heart of man or God. Give no mind from where the greater good will come, but have faith in its coming sooner or later. Nature gets nothing for free; it pays back but in its own currency at the time and place of its own choosing.

Unless giving will result in making the returns of the giver worthwhile, at least mentally, otherwise giving is meaningless. To give and then regret tortures the body and kills the soul, but to give and then celebrate in the silence of the heart, regardless of the attitude of the receiver, invigorates life and illumines the soul. Done strategically, nothing bears more dividends than giving.

Jeffrey K. Wilson once said:

> Giving pays the highest interest rate, and has the longest term of any investment available. There is nothing wrong with lending a hand to individuals we may come across in our daily lives, but the hand that we lend to individuals is not the one that produces the highest interest rate or the longest term; it is the

hand that we lend [to] worthy causes that transforms mankind." Though giving to individuals is praiseworthy, it is usually, and unfortunately, based on discriminatory criteria.

Giving to your child, relative, friend, or fraternity member is not extraordinary; it is a natural basic human inclination and makes no one a historical figure. Therefore, it makes no one truly magnetic.

The Good Samaritan would not have been such a mythical personality, his story would not have been told by the Great Teacher had he helped a child, a brother, or a long-time acquaintance thrown sideways by burglars. Jesus chose to use this particular parable in order to demonstrate how giving is an indispensable characteristic of personal magnetism, and generations after generations have been told about the Good Samaritan for the last two thousand years. Centuries have passed and the Good Samaritan, metaphorically speaking, still profits from his investment at the highest interest, and there does not seem to be an end in sight as to when the investment will collapse or the interest be cut down. He still inspires nations that go to the rescue of other nations in times of unexpected and calamitous natural disasters such as tsunamis, earthquakes, floods, hurricanes, tornadoes, and other catastrophic events that are beyond human power.

To this day, the Good Samaritan still inspires the most successful men and women who have dedicated their fortunes to fight poverty, diseases, illiteracy, homelessness, injustice, environmental abuse, and other human ills around the world. He still inspires benefactors to invest their money in research and development for a better world for all of us, including human, animals living in the forest, water, or air, and even the Earth itself. No wonder the Good Samaritan continues to exist in the minds and hearts of everyone who hears his story and wants to emulate him. Giving toughens personal magnetism by touching and affecting the lives of not just those who are dear and near to us, but also those dear and near to the community, society, the nation, and the world.

Few acts in life are more mysterious than giving. Eliphas Levi, the inspiration of my fourth book, *Emancipated Intelligence,* writes the following about charity in his book *The Key of the Mysteries,* translated by Aleister Crowley:

> Before Charity, faith prostrates itself, and conquered science bows. There is here evidently something greater than humanity; charity proves itself by its works that it is not a dream. It is stronger than all the passions; it triumphs over suffering and over death; it makes God understood by every heart . . .
>
> Charity! Word divine, sole word which makes God understood, word which contains a universal revelation! Spirit of Charity, alliance of two words which are a complete solution and a complete promise! To what question, in fine, do these two words not find an answer? What is God for us, if not the spirit of charity? . . . Is it not the Spirit of Charity which refuses

to discuss faith lest it should trouble the confidence of simple souls, and disturb the peace of universal communion? And the universal Church, is it any other thing than a communion in the Spirit of Charity? It is by the Spirit of Charity that the Church is infallible. It is the Spirit of Charity which is the divine virtue of the priesthood . . . It is by charity that twelve Galilean artisans conquered the word; they loved truth more than life, and they went without followers to speak it to people and to kings; tested by torture, they were found faithful . . . God is the absolute object of human faith. In the infinite, He is the supreme creative intelligence of order. In the world, He is the Spirit of Charity . . . To be rich is to give, to give nothing is to be poor; to live is to love, to love nothing is to be dead; to be happy is to devote oneself; to exist only for oneself is to cast away oneself, and to exile oneself in hell. Heaven is the harmony of generous thoughts; hell is the conflict of cowardly instincts . . . **To understand the Spirit of Charity is to understand all mysteries**; pages 17, 18, 20, 29, 68.

The law of multiplication works best when giving than in receiving. Very few poor people get relief from poverty by receiving help from others, except in a few cases of inheritance, and sometimes this also slips away without warning. Anyone who banks on donations will most likely cling to the lowest ladder of society for a long time. Just as it is hard to make wealth by receiving, it's also difficult to self-impoverish by giving happily. The universe has its fair way of compensating the needs of its people; it does a good job of draining the case of the receiver to replenish those of the giver so the former can keep receiving and the latter giving.

Givers sometimes find themselves in a position where they are incapable of keeping pace with the law of multiplication, because the more they give, the more they get, making the coffers of joy in their hearts practically impossible to deplete. They find it an extremely pleasurable game, and they keep doing it until they drop; many go to their graves leaving their wealth in trust funds to keep giving to worthy causes. In the eyes of the poor at heart, nothing is more rewarding than receiving, but in the mind of an educated soul, nothing is better than giving. As the Bible bluntly states, "It is more blessed to give than to receive," (Acts 20:35). Life is about debit and credit, and the laws of accounting work perfectly in the game of giving and receiving.

The more you give, the more credits, thanks, praise, admiration, eulogies, gratitude, happiness, and, yes, personal magnetism you get; the more debit you take, the more freedom you lose, the more debts you accrue, the more deductions you get to your stock of happiness. Both giving and receiving add something to your life; giving adds to your credit, and receiving adds to your debit. Make a choice, what do you want? More credit or more debits?

On the other hand, giving can be a curse if not properly dispensed. Many people will not take even gold or diamonds if these are given in a manner that ridicules or humiliates. We should not be disrespectful to the receiver.

French writer Pierre Corneille agrees: "The manner of giving is worth more than the gift." People in need are rarely lazy or stupid; usually they are at a roadblock of life that requires them to bend their chins down before they can push their chest forward, raise their heads and shoulders, and proudly walk to a much better and safer road ahead. Life is full of stories of people who were at some time of their human experience bowed to their knees, never giving up their dreams and eventually rising to glory and happiness untold. It must be a humbling and appreciated experience when life offers you opportunities to extend a hand down to pull up a fallen fellow. Those who exhibit their best nature in these circumstances never have regrets, but those who do not are usually taught a hard lesson by life that it doesn't pay to bend or break the law.

There is no universal manner of giving that is acceptable to all. The culture usually dictates how to behave when giving. The only way of giving that comes the closest to being most universally admired is giving anonymously whenever possible.

Of giving anonymously, the founder of Collegiate Empowerment, Anthony J. D'Angelo writes, "Giving is most blessed and most acceptable when the donor remains completely anonymous." What makes giving pleasurable is not so much what is given as it is how it is given. If you give with pride, you will be ruined inside out, since you will attract parasites who will outfox you; they will reduce you to rubble, as all arrogant people find their downfall. Alternatively, if you give unenthusiastically, you will mourn your so called losses until your heart becomes resistant to the feeling of happiness, because rather than being a blessing, giving has been a curse. However, if you give joyfully, your heart, while expecting nothing at all in return, will be a harbor where ships of treasure seekers sailing troubling oceans of sorrow will find peace and comfort.

"He who cannot give anything away cannot feel anything either," philosopher Friedrich Nietzsche wrote. It must be an act—or a command—more from the heart than from the head, more feeling than reason, but a fair balance of both is usually the best mental solution. It does not make much sense to give to those who already have more than they need, or those who will simply misuse what you worked hard to obtain. Being wasteful has never been generous. And while it might be an easy decision to give, the road it presents can be noxious.

"To give away money . . ."—as frightening as it sometimes seems to be—as Aristotle observes, "is an easy matter and in any man's power. But to decide to whom to give it, and when, for what purpose and how, is neither in every man's power nor an easy matter."

Money, for that matter, does not solve all the problems in the world; if it did, the whole world would have by now an amusement park at least every fifty square miles for people to enjoy life. Plus, assuming all the governments of the world are well intentioned and dedicated to the wellbeing of their citizens, they could have just printed money and given it to people to make them happy.

Printing money is not as difficult as it was in Roman times or other ancient civilizations, since we have machines more advanced than those of Johannes Gutenberg and far more capable of printing paper money beyond our needs. Why don't governments just do that? Because not only will the money be as worthless as the paper on which it is printed, but also because money is not always the solution to all problems. In other words, as we will elaborate on later, not all solutions to all problems come from money. And sometimes, if not always, money is the elephant in the room and should be acknowledged and led out.

Let's contrast the thinking of writer PJ O'Rourke and definitions of money and poverty by two of the world's most respected publications. O'Rourke writes, "You can't get rid of poverty by giving people money." Why not? It is a perfectly logic question if you take time to ponder on the definitions of poor and poverty. *The Oxford American Dictionary and Thesaurus* defines poor, as "lacking of adequate money," and the online publication of *Merriam-Webster* defines poverty as "the state of one who lacks a usual or socially acceptable amount of money or material possessions."

So, if money cannot get rid of poverty according to O'Rourke, then what else will? Can we say that O'Rourke is crazy or may be from another planet? Here on Earth, in one form or the other, we have been using money for thousands of years as a way of building our comfort by acquiring what we need from our fellow man. The more money you have, the further removed from poverty you are, apparently.

What can we say of O'Rourke? Can he indeed be right? Not only does he have the knowledge, he also has a very good judgment in his thinking. Giving money to people will never assist them in getting rid of poverty, not a bit. Because as Andrew Bernstein said, "Nothing is given to man on Earth—struggle is built into the nature of life, conflict is possible—the hero is the man who lets no obstacle prevent him from pursuing the values he has chosen." Poverty has less to do with money or wealth distribution and more to do with self-knowledge, self-control, self-belief, and self-drive, which the effective handling of money requires. With these qualities, there is no amount of money that cannot be acquired, and there is no amount of money that can buy these qualities. Here is the problem and here is the answer.

Life was not meant to be easy, and it should not be. No matter what, man must be the main solver of his life challenges. Even if one was born a prince or from an aristocratic family, there are no guarantees: unless one makes one's own efforts, one will lose one's privileges. History is full of stories of princes who lost not only their power but the comforts of life after taking everything for granted.

Money helps get rid of poverty when it is handed out, not like fish to be eaten, but like a teaching tool to learn how to catch one's own fish for future needs, and in this spirit should one give tirelessly and joyfully. We have all heard stories about people who were born into wealth and died in poverty. If you haven't heard such a tale, keep chatting with friends and you will. And in this regard, O'Rourke's words may not necessarily be prophetic or reveal any mythical truth, but he certainly makes a strong point that is most likely from a wise man.

By now, you may have your our own opinion about whether or not money is the solution to all problems. But let's assume that the majority of us agrees that it is not. So, let's try to understand the relationship between money and poverty. If money is not the solution to poverty, what is?

We have already stated that poverty has less to do with money or wealth distribution and more to do self-knowledge, self-trust, self-belief, and self-drive or, better yet, the discovery of the inner self or the self-divine that enables man to move, see, hear, smell, feel, think, and connect the inner world, the universe around us, and the edge of infinity. If you are addicted to reading bumper stickers like many people are, it is most likely you have come across one that reads, "The best things in life aren't things." Whether you agree with it or not, there is a point to be carefully studied.

Many people would go as far as to give their lives, not for anything material, but for the best interest of others so the upright principles they believe in can guide the living. Anyone who can creatively inspire people to rely on the inner self, also known as the divine self, in order to find the knowledge they need, trust in their own ability to perform to the best of their knowledge, believe in perceived outcome and courage, and the persistence to overcome all obstacles, to this person only the sky will be the limit of personal magnetism he can build. How then to inspire people to turn to their inner self in order to successfully perform in the outer world? The answer to this question can be found in just one source, a source that manifests itself in several manners, a source known as the inner power. Let's look at some of the three expressions of inner power that motivates the hearts of men: love, self-confidence, and participation.

Chapter Nine

Love and Self Confidence

Love is said to be the greatest power in the universe. God is said to be love. Love keeps harmony in the universe. Planets, stars, and other celestial bodies are kept in harmony by the power of love. All other forces of nature such as life, light, peace, and perfection are thought to be both influences and different manifestations of love. Here on Earth, nothing is felt and no word is spoken more often than love. Families, communities, and nations thrive and live more peacefully due to love—not technology—among members. No two people can start a family without love.

In a single day, the feeling called "love" is spoken a gazillion times. We all go on saying love countless times in our lifetimes. Poets write about it imaginatively, artists paint it colorfully, musicians sing about it passionately, prophets allegorize it, and philosophers mystify it.

Of course, the love we are talking about is not necessarily the love of lovers, but more like the love expressed by artists, prophets, and philosophers. It is the love that makes people feel valued as a very important part of the organization. This is not the love that makes people feel dizzy or cuddled like a baby, but the one that makes them feel and know themselves to be a part of the puzzle as well as part of the solution, the love that makes them feel guilty when the organization underperforms and feel exuberant when the organization over performs, the love that makes people feel the failure of the organization as their own failure and the success of the organization as a personal success, the love that makes people self-blame for the failure of the group but congratulates everybody for success. It is called unselfish love.

This is possible not because of money or any material remuneration, not even because of promotion, but because of a culture of appreciating every person and his contribution to the cause throughout the organization, no matter how remote or central the impact of the role. This is the love that makes everyone feel and perform to the best of his ability and effectively contribute to the team effort, regardless of his position on the food chain.

Mother Teresa, one of the most magnetic personalities of the twentieth century, talked about this same love when she said: "Let us not be satisfied with just giving money. Money is not enough, money can be got, but they need your hearts to love them. So, spread your love everywhere you go." It takes a great skill to spread this kind of love throughout the organization. It takes a lot of affection. It takes actions both guided by unselfish motives and certainly not misguided by human sympathy. The kind of love that does not spoil but rather strengthens hearts and souls of men. The kind of love that teaches that life is not just about receiving but also, and most importantly, about giving something back to the community for its support and inspiration.

By giving this kind of love, you inspire people and build your own personal magnetism that not only contemporaries will adore and look up to, but also future generations. People love and adore those who inspire them by words and actions. It is no accident that artists, philosophers, and prophets are some of the most lovable and famous people in history. To this day, King Solomon, Prophet Samuel, philosophers Socrates, Plato, and Aristotle, as well as Jesus and Mohammed are still the darlings of today's thinkers, politicians, and millions of people the world over.

In the Gospels, Jesus says, "man cannot live on bread alone, but lives on every word that comes from the mouth of the Lord." It is, of course, not just any word but *the* word that inspires, that ignites a consuming flame in the hearts of men across time and space. Anyone who is in the serious business of building a strong personal magnetism cannot rely on physical nourishment alone, but must rely on psychological and spiritual nourishment as well.

Physical and metaphysical nourishment produces two unambiguously distinct outcomes. The first nourishment produces a static outcome—a following of fans that will disappear as soon as your influence wanes—but the second nourishes the mind and consciousness for a dynamic outcome that creates disciples whose conviction grows and strengthens as time goes on. Add to that a mixture of culture and tradition that helps to uphold their faith with the highest care and pass it down to the next generation and to thirsty souls of foreign lands.

Here is the difference between athletes and artists: Athletes touch people's hearts while their skills are at the highest performing level, but artists not only touch people's hearts, they also mold thinking itself for generations. Athletes earn people's admiration for the length of their careers, but their magnetism weakens and they eventually wear out as their muscles deflate; but artists' magnetism grows with time, going from generation to generation. Athletes' personal magnetism is like a sword—it is only sharp as long as someone takes the time to sharpen its edges, whereas artists' magnetism is like a serpent that casts off its old skin and revitalizes itself as needs dictate. Few people can recall famous athletes of even few decades ago, but Leonardo da Vinci and his *Mona Lisa* still puzzling us more than four hundred years later.

This is a jewel of the secrets of personal magnetism: that it is acquired through unselfish giving of the seed of love. Do not just satisfy or hold captive the physical; lock up the soul in the cage of unlimited joy and yours will be a personal magnetism that knows no limit of time or space. Plato, Jesus, and Michelangelo gained their immortality through the same method. For more than two thousand years, a young carpenter born in the poorest circumstances imaginable has been a subject of worship, and for more than four hundred years, we all still believe that the *Mona Lisa* is nothing but a cluster of hidden codes of secret societies, and everyone wants to gain fame trying to reveal whatever Leonardo da Vinci is suspected to have concealed from the world. That is the power of captivating the soul rather than the weak and mortal physical body, which is strong but for a limited battle and lives but for a limited time.

Loving someone is to know that that person also has goals of his own, and we all know that nothing makes man happier than accomplishing his aspirations. Obstacles are built in life, and a life without difficulties is not one that has ever been experienced on this planet. Impediments are always going to stand in the way of happiness. The most important impediments must be moved out of the way first by the person himself, and no one else, if he wants to taste the recipe for happiness. While our behaviors are mere expressions of our souls or mind, they are also the best tools at our disposal to show others our love and our appreciation of their positive sides.

By nature, the truth is so simple that it appears to so many as ridicule, and consequently, very few believe it when it is revealed to them. Perhaps this is why most spiritual scriptures are written in ambiguous language—to satisfy those with their inner eye open to clearly see the truth in all its simplicity, while those who think the truth is nothing but a mystery are left to wander from page to page until their souls come to terms with the candor of the truth.

Deeds through which people detect your love and forgiveness are not very complicated to observe. Let's explore some of them.

The list is intentionally designed to be short and incomplete for a simple reason. Its main purpose is to serve as a springboard to a more complete and deeper investigation. The hope is that it will help to stimulate the interest of the seeker to know, to dare, to do, to explore the kingdom within and to be silent.

No matter how much you love people you cannot control their thoughts, feelings, imaginations, you cannot self-discipline on their behalf. These and more man has to do himself. Even those who are "lucky" enough to be born into wealth or are princes who were handed power over the destiny of their nations, still have to, like the rest of us, overcome life's most important obstacles, and inner obstacles for themselves, if they want to manage and maintain wealth or power.

The consequences lived by one prince who thought everything had to be done for him was recently reported by the BBC:

> Nepal votes to abolish monarchy. The Himalayan nation of Nepal has become the world's newest republic, ending 240 years of monarchy. A constituent assembly meeting in the capital, Kathmandu, overwhelmingly voted to abolish royal rule. The Maoists, the largest party after laying down arms and standing in last month's elections, were committed to ousting King Gyanendra. People celebrated wildly in the streets of the capital after news of the assembly vote. The approved proposal states that Nepal is "an independent, indivisible, sovereign, secular and

an inclusive democratic republic nation." Only four members of the 601-seat assembly opposed the change. Royal privileges "will automatically come to an end," the declaration says. It also states that the king's main palace must be vacated within a fortnight, to be transformed into a museum. "I am overjoyed," student Rajesh Subedi, 21, told AFP news agency as Kathmandu celebrated. "This is the most important day of my life." The BBC's Charles Haviland in Kathmandu says it is not clear how soon King Gyanendra will leave. The Maoists and other politicians are being conciliatory about the monarch now being ousted and say he should live on in Nepal as a private citizen. (http://news.bbc.co.uk/2/hi/south_asia/7424302.stm)

After 240 years, the monarchy was dismantled, and the king became a private citizen subject to the same treatment as all Nepalese people. What happened? If you think any human being has it easy, think again. Of course, stories like this come only once in a very long time, because there are so many monarchies, but there are hundreds of stories about aristocratic families that bend their knees to the obstacles of life; in fact, overcoming those obstacles on a daily basis is what keeps them where they are.

No one can help us to remove thorns in our souls but ourselves. Life is indeed a combat; you must prove your ability to survive and save others if you want to move upward in the line of command. Thus providing the necessary mask, shield, and sword is the only thing you can give people for their own protection and victory in the battle of life, which no one can escape.

These elements of attack and protection are all comprised in just one arm of self-defense, and that is self-discipline. In order to survive all the struggles of life, the strong man of ancient times used a sword or an arrow; the smart man of modern times uses a pen and keyboard, but the wise man of all times employs self-knowledge, self-confidence, self-discipline, and self-motivation. Famed ancient schools never taught its students how to be magnificent soldiers of the battle field or wise men on the throne; they taught them how to conquer inner enemies before facing outer enemies, how to rule themselves before ruling the kingdom.

Anyone of average intelligence has a dream that can find its roots in his early childhood. Ask any child of six years of age, and he or she will tell you what he wants to be when he grows up; very few will tell you they want to be anything less than successful, no one will tell you he wants to be a sad and miserable person. Ask most people in their sixties whether they lived the life they dreamed of when they were six years old. The majority will tell you quite frankly, NO!

The question now is, why do we start by dreaming big dreams and better lives for ourselves but end up living a life of grief and unhappiness? The answer may just be a nasty, dirty and ugly four letter word spelled f-e-a-r. Fear of action. Fear is the opposite of love. Because we all want to conquer and rule the world before conquering and ruling ourselves first; we want to fight outer battles before fighting our inner battles. We want for ourselves that next thing first rather than that next quality first. Dreaming big is a very important characteristic for anyone who wants to build a very strong magnetic personality. Unless there is a dream first, nothing can ever materialize.

Just like an architect must first design the house before even buying the building materials, the invisible must precede the visible; thus, the dream must precede the action. As important as it is, dreaming is a given to all of us. The challenge is bridging the dream and the action. Here is where the rubber meets the road; here is where success and failure are determined. Most people believe taking action on their own, without guidance or supervision, is frightening; they cannot stand it. Initiative to them is the scariest monster they will ever face.

Some people would rather face death than take action and risk hearing the criticism of naysayers and dark angels of discouragement. They listen more to agents and voices of discouragement than to their own inner power, which is capable of not only moving mountains, but throwing them in the oceans. We forget that taking action toward a life goal may be frightening, but nothing is more destructive than inaction. Instead of overcoming fear by simply tuning our minds from fear to courage, we choose to give in to the destruction of inaction, which makes many of us go to our eternal resting place scratching our heads, unhappy, and *thinking* how much better we should have done. For this reason, the dream of having more things should never be bigger than the dream of being a better man. Acquisition of better qualities must precede acquisition of better things if personal magnetism is to be dynamic. Things do not immortalize man, but qualities do.

Many of us have undeveloped or barely developed inner qualities to shake off fear, doubt, and selfishness, and of those who do have well-developed qualities, the majority are unaware of them until they find themselves in a crisis. Consequently, people distrust themselves to the point that they spend time and effort seeking someone to think *for* them, defend them, and even tell them what to do. That is why those who value inner qualities such as courage, selflessness, and self-confidence usually rise as leaders; they take advantage of the opportunity and run with those qualities as far as they can go and as long as time allows—or until someone else in the crowd figures out how to stop them and confiscate the prize.

The wise, of course, do not wait for their downfall; they simply groom someone or facilitate the creation of an efficient system to carry on for them at the right time—usually when their star is still shining at its brightest, thus, leaving an everlasting legacy that neither time nor space will ever destroy.

Sporting goods manufacturer Nike knows a thing or two about competition; after all, it is named after the Greek goddess of victory. The world's biggest shoes and athletic apparel maker did not gain its position by delivering the best products on the market, but rather by simply preaching a philosophy of self-confidence through an easy, straightforward and catchy three-word sentence that reminded people of the secret of success: *Just do it.*

The company's logo inspires the approval of the high spirit of victory, and its creator was paid only thirty dollars. But with that alone, Nike became the undisputed king of the sportswear business, from the remotest village in the world to worldwide events such as the FIFA World Cup. Dressing prestigious national teams like the United States, Brazil, and Nigeria, to name but a few, it has left its much more experienced and older competitor, Adidas, to rethink how to make better shoes and also fight for its life.

Jack Welch, the highly regarded former CEO of General Electric, once said: "Giving people self-confidence is by far the most important thing that I can do. Because then they will act."

We are told by psychics that man uses less than 10 percent of his potential intelligence and the other 90 percent is simply unused. But with less than 10 percent of our potential intelligence performing, man has gone on missions to the moon and has shortened travel time and made real-time face-to-face communication around the world a virtual reality. Amazing, isn't it? There is no question that breakthroughs in communication during the twenty-first century would make contemporary man look like a god to the inhabitants of Earth just two hundred years ago; our airplanes and other means of transportation would make us look like messiahs to the Romans and to the Israelites that Moses led into the wilderness.

With more than 90 percent of our potential intelligence, of course, we could do wonders, but with more than 90 percent of self-confidence, we could make this planet, literally, a paradise. We could conquer most of the biggest challenges that man has faced thus far, including hunger, poverty, wars, and diseases and replace them with peace, harmony, and joy everywhere. Why do I say so? Self-confidence is what inspires intelligence. An intelligent but less-confident person has fewer chances of finding his way out in times of trouble; on the other hand, a self-confident person has a far better chance of making it out alive in the most complicated situations.

Before moving on let's make a point about the 10 percent-90 percent theory of human brain and mind. We said what we said fully aware of some who claim it to be simply a myth. We respect their opinion. Snopes.com, the myth-busters' website, argues against what they call "the 10 percent myth." It claims that there is no hard evidence that man uses only 10 percent of his brain and mind potential.*

What is amazing is that the website also fails to provide credible hard evidence to the contrary, except some shallow rhetoric. It does not disprove that, for instance, those who use a higher percentage of their brain and mind potentials such as disciplined, self-controlled, determined, fearless, self-confident, or self-possessed individuals

---

* See http://www.snopes.com/science/stats/10percent.asp (accessed 01/07/2012).

are more likely to be smarter, wiser, and ultimately more creative than undisciplined, weakling, fearful, worried, doubtful ones, who use less of their brain and mind potential. The website goes on to assert:

> Brain imaging research techniques such as PET scans (position emission temography) and fMRI (functional magnetic resonance imaging) clearly show that the vast majority of the brain does not lie fallow. Indeed, although certain minor functions may use only a small part of the brain at one time, sufficient complex set of activities or thought patterns will indeed use many parts of the brain. Just as people don't use all of their muscle groups at one time, they also don't use all of their brain at once . . .

This is clearly missing the point. The 10 percent-90 percent theory does not mean that only 10 percent is used at one time or the other, while the other 90 percent lies fallow. It is a matter of proficiency—quality rather than quantity—the level of intensity with which our inner qualities motivate the function of our intellects and emotions or thoughts and feelings.

Just like two joggers use 100 percent of their muscles, the one who uses his more efficiently at a higher percentage will definitely reach the finish line faster and easier than the one who uses his less.

That is what is meant by 10-90 percent theory, but we will let readers chew and digest what they will as it is for their minds to retain what is essential to their mental fitness and reject what is not, but remember this: "As is our confidence, so is our capacity;" said the nineteenth century British writer, William Hazlitt and the philosopher Eric Hoffer adds: "It sometimes seems that intense desire creates not only its own opportunities, but its own talents." Now let's carry on.

No enemy of man is more powerful than fear. Intelligence, sometimes, gives in to fear. On the other hand, self-confidence grounded in pure love of self (not selfishness,) surrender to own inner and higher self or consciousness of inner constructive qualities never gives in to fear; in fact, it destroys it. Self-confidence flavored with true love is the very demonstration of courage, the mortal enemy of fear, the essence of action, and the mother of all creations.

If you think I am just daydreaming by suggesting that predominance of self-confidence is more important than the predominance of intelligence, think again. Why do you think some of the smartest economists and MBAs are hired and managed by sometimes unschooled but more self-confident business owners? Why do you think some of the smartest political scientists would rather fill the shoes of advisers and policy analysts than become decision makers themselves? Why do you think these very people would rather play behind-the-scenes roles and let less intelligent business and political actors take the frontline? The answer is simple: their degree of self-confidence.

The most successful people are not necessarily the brainiest, but they are definitely the most confident. How many PhDs do you think a college drop-out like Bill Gates utilizes to multiply his billions of dollars and keep an eye on his philanthropic activities as they blossom? Intelligence does not necessarily make one the master of his own fate, but self-confidence does. Intelligence frees only the body, but self-confidence frees the body, the mind, and the spirit; it makes one see the invisible that exists in the mind and bring it vividly into the visible world for goodness sake. A recent article titled *Intelligence is Overrated: What you really need to succeed* appeared in the online version of Forbes Magazine, www.forbes.com, and published the following:

> Albert Einstein's was estimated at 160, Madonna's is 140, and John F. Kennedy's was only 119, but as it turns out, your IQ score pales in comparison with your EQ, MQ, and BQ scores when it comes to predicting your success and professional achievement... By itself, a high IQ does not guarantee that you will stand out and rise above everyone else. Research carried out by the Carnegie Institute of Technology shows that 85 percent of your financial success is due to skills in "human engineering," your personality and ability to communicate, negotiate, and lead.

The article goes on to say that only 15 percent person's success is due to technical knowledge. Thus, instead of entirely focusing on conventional intelligence performance, a person should make an effort in strengthening his/her EQ (Emotional Intelligence), MQ (Moral Intelligence), and BQ (Body Intelligence).

The article is loaded with rich and practical advices that cannot all be quoted here without infringement of copyright laws; hence, I will let you read for yourself the whole article here: http://www.forbes.com/sites/keldjensen/2012/04/12/intelligence-is-overrated-what-you-really-need-to-succeed/ (accessed May 10, 2012)

A very high degree of intelligence coupled with the same or a higher degree of self-confidence makes one become a true master in the eyes of his fellow human beings. Intelligence is manipulation of knowledge for a desired aim (sometimes positive, sometimes negative,) and it guides the senses; self-confidence, a product of self-discipline, is the wisdom of stirring intelligence in the right direction for a constructive goal. It keeps love and power from turning into forces of lethargy and destruction.

Not only must a magnetic personality be a self-confident person, he must also inspire self-confidence in those around him. As Jack Welch said in the quote above, when people are given self-confidence, they act, and when they act, they carry the load of the organization. And the more people carry the load, the more likely the organization is to achieve impressive goals. Inspiring self-confidence grows both parties' personal magnetism, because it is an act of love.

People lack self-confidence because of fear. Fear can sometimes be a vague subject to study and can be defined in more than one specific way. For the sake of necessity, I will talk about the cause of fear rather than fear itself. One of the major reasons why people lack self-confidence is because of the feelings of self-pity and self-blame due to ignorance of the true causes of the lack of life's fulfillments. Ignorant is how people come into this world. Everything we know we learn from others: our family members, teachers, books, and the public in general. When asked to do something they do not know the answer for or to do something they don't know how to do, people will naturally say, "I do not know, or I don't know how." While true, this response is a total surrender to ignorance and fear, and it consequently destroys self-confidence.

The right attitude would be to show a hunger for knowledge and a readiness to learn. The answer should thus be "How? I want to learn." This mental attitude of recognizing ignorance as a temporary obstacle while acknowledging the power to eradicate it is a surefire way to build self-confidence. Life by nature is a machine of many built-in chips, called *obstacles*. It would not be enjoyable if life was free of challenges. These obstacles are purposely built-in as a reminder for us to consult and use our inner power; they are simply spiritual roadblocks that ring a bell to remind us to go back inside and seek advice from our higher and divine self. But don't worry; it takes time to understand and patience to wait for inspiration and intuition.

A charismatic leader always leads his followers toward self-confidence. Jesus was the best example of this principle. With faith, "Verily, verily, I say unto you, He that believeth on me, the works I do, shall he do also; and greater works than these shall he do . . ." He told His disciples (John 14:12).

Another thing that sows self-mistrust in the hearts of people is the public. Our eyes are among the least harmful things on our bodies, but they are extremely frightening. In the whole history of the world, no instances have been reported in which someone was physically hurt as a result of a dirty look, and yet looking people directly in the eye frightens many to death. Even fables or legends in which someone got killed or injured as a result of eye contact are hard to find, except in the few instances of stories like Medusa's. Still, people are afraid to look others in the eyes as if they were avoiding wolves and some nasty dogs.

In a related vein, the entertainment world experiences some of the most tragic deaths by public performers who kill themselves overdosing on drugs that they had hoped would simply help them survive the "torture" of being in the public eye. We have seen bright teachers turn into idiots with the fear of standing in front of a class and looking students in the eyes. As innocent and docile as the human eye looks, it is also one of the most frightening things to some of the best and brightest people. This is a fact, and it is unfortunate that it is one of the biggest destroyers of self-confidence to so many people.

In his book, *Creative Mind and Success,* first published in 1919, Ernest Holmes writes:

> The man who has learned to love all people no matter who they may be will find plenty of people will return that love to him . . . . One of the first things to do is to learn to love everybody. If you have not done this, begin to do so at once. There is always more good than bad in people, and seeing the good tends to bring it forth.

It is not our intention to present here a religious book; there is already an extensive selection of better-written books on the religious aspect of love. Thus, we aim to purposely sidestep the discussion of love in religious terms and instead strive to bring out its psychological meaning and how to employ it in a way that if used effectively, it unfailingly strengthens personal magnetism.

Love is one of the most, if not *the* most, powerful qualities in the universe. It brings electrons, atoms, and species together and maintains harmony throughout space. Love inspires people more than any other quality. It is practically impossible to be inspired by something unless you have some kind of love for that thing. The first and most important quality of leadership since the dawn of time is love of the people one is privileged to serve. A leader who blinds people with sincere love is loved and admired in return by his fellowmen and easily forgiven for his shortcomings.

Love causes hate, fear, doubt, and discouragement simply to disappear while inspiring self-confidence, faith, determination, and action in the fulfillment of one's dreams. A leader who cloaks himself in an aura of true love effortlessly inspires confidence, success, and faith in his followers' abilities to achieve whatever they have long wished to accomplish.

It should be noted that overwhelming people with love is different from hypocrisy or misleading people. It is, in fact, tolerance and understanding of people's weaknesses and persistence in demonstrating a better way of doing things. When you forgive or are patient with the mistakes of your fellowmen who are making every effort to improve themselves, you overwhelm them with love and ultimately with happiness. In return, they will forgive your weaknesses and inspire you to be a better leader, as long as your love of them is felt to a consistent level if not higher intensity.

Overwhelming people with love or wholeheartedly loving is legal! It is safe! And it is the magic secret of a highly-developed magnetic personality. No one can be magnetic unless he/she has a heart that always finds excuses to love others and not excuse to hate anyone. Love is the secret behind the power of the famous law of attraction. There cannot be attraction without love.

Love expands the pool from which magnetic people choose loyal and competent associates with whom to work. Unless the concept of love is understood and applied effectively, the notion of personal magnetism is essentially a pipe dream.

To be truly successful in life, we are told to do something that we can do, love, and enjoy doing. Love is said to be the power behind success in every activity. You cannot fear and love someone simultaneously; therefore, where there is love, there is no fear or doubt; where there is understanding and faith, there is progress and happiness. Love breaks all kinds of barriers of communications between men of different backgrounds and even between men and animals. Legend has it that Rome was founded by Romulus and Remus, two orphaned brothers who were breast-fed by a wolf. How did that happen? Love between the angelic human babies and an affectionate beast of the jungle.

Pet shops sell incredible animals like snakes, turtles, and birds that are adopted by men. As love feelings travel between the animals and their owners back and forth for a long time, animals end up loving and recognizing their owners and people start considering these animals as family members and spending enormous amounts of money for their care, just as they would spend on the care of their human family members. We have seen lions, tigers, and leopards adopted and living in absolute peace with their owners for as long as the flow of love between them remains uninterrupted.

The point here is that humans are by far different from reptiles, lions, and fish, but all these are drawn to those who sincerely love them. If a leader sincerely loves people and does what demonstrates true love in the best interest of the people, he will get his love back manifold.

Showing love to people may not be as easy as we think. There is no Holy Grail-type secret of love, but there are techniques of exhibiting love that are very common, though often ignored, as a secret of personal magnetism. These techniques were taught in ancient schools of wisdom as the fundamental keys of love and joy.

Somewhere we learn that love does not hurt; elsewhere we hear people saying "tough" love is not always comforting. In the "book of all answers," the Bible, scriptures admonish us "to love your neighbor as you love yourself," or more specifically, "to treat others as we would like to be treated." Magnificent, but as promised, we will sidestep the religious meaning of love, since love works the same wonders regardless of religious affiliations.

Let's take a look at love through the lenses of Ernest Holmes, who defines it as "refusing to see the negative side of anyone . . . People are dying for real interest, for someone to tell them they are all right."

Chapter Ten

Loyalty

Charles Haanel, the author of *The Master Key System* and one of the most influential metaphysic writers of the late nineteenth and early twentieth centuries, is said to have influenced some of the richest people of the twentieth and twenty-first centuries: billionaires and millionaires of Silicon Valley; military, political, business and religious leaders around the world. He writes this about loyalty in his posthumously published *The Master Key Arcana*:

> Loyalty is one of the strongest links that bind men of strength and character. It is one that can never be broken with impunity. The man who would lose his right hand rather than betray a friend will never lack friends. The man who will stand in silent guard until death, if need be, beside the shrine of confidence or friendship of those who have allowed him to enter will find himself linked with a current of cosmic power which will attract desirable conditions only. It is inconceivable that such a one should ever meet with lack of any kind. (p. 82)

Any person who is in the business of building a strong personal magnetism and has not yet understood thoroughly the power of loyalty in his relationship with those on whom he will build his personal magnetism may be lost already before his journey has even begun. Few words in the vocabulary of man are potent enough to adequately define the significance of loyalty. Thomas Watson defined it thus, "Loyalty is the lubricant of life," and Confucius, one of the wisest men who ever lived, is quoted to have said, "The scholar does not consider gold and jade to be precious treasures but loyalty and good faith."

The truth is that life is a massive web of visible and invisible, physical and spiritual relationships, and among them, the sweetest and the deadliest are determined by loyalty or lack thereof. Loyalty gives flavor and essence to life, and the lack of it makes life uncertain, dangerous, and unbinding.

In ancient Greece, a student had to prove loyalty before being taken by a teacher. In ancient India, Egypt, China, and other civilizations, a vow of loyalty that contained promises of perilous consequences had to be taken before admitting anyone into certain brotherhoods. Loyalty is mostly demanded among the strong and the powerful. They know too much to let a child play with fire. The truth is protected with loyalty and life.

In life, we are always surrounded by people who are either our relatives or friends. Our relatives are those whose relationship is somewhat forced on us by nature or social contracts; we have little or no choice or freedom in committing ourselves in this relationship.

Our relatives constitute a relatively safer environment, and loyalty rarely has to be demanded; rather, it is mostly assumed. Any betrayal in this type of relationship is shocking. Friendship, on the other hand in most cases, is with people who are initially strangers that we end up trusting because of common interests and values. Friendship is no less important than blood relatives, since it provides us with our life partners, with whom we spend the best and sweetest parts of our lives, life mates who illumine our lives with laughter and play, colleagues we work with for the harmonious expansion of life, and total strangers we meet on the street or on the highways of life who come to our assistance selflessly in times of emergency or need.

Friendship, however, is a nonbinding contract; therefore, it is the more capricious and more perilous of these two types of relationships. Friendship has a built-in loyalty component, whose malfunction disintegrates the whole relationship apparatus. Let's see some of those components, how they work, and how to build a loyalty-based friendship that will be the cornerstone of your personal magnetism.

Be your own compass.

It is very easy to ask another for loyalty but harder to ask yourself the same. People sometimes like to ask more of their fellowmen than they can provide or do for themselves. People like free rides and free lunches, but they do not like the work that delivers those free services. All believers want to go to Heaven yet they despise the discipline and effort required for that important favor. Unfortunately, that is life. It is full of ambiguities and unfairness. Birds work for their meals and shelter without complaint, but humans love good stuff with less effort. It is understandable but inexplicable. People are usually quick to ask others to do better, while they are doing the exact opposite of what they preach. We hear this all the time: "Do as I say, not as I do."

We are all too eager to raise the bar for others but ready to lower them for ourselves. When people lower the bar for themselves, they think they are smarter. Ask disgraced, fallen leaders in politics, business, religion, art, and sports, and they will tell you that they let arrogance and pride overtake their reason. Those who are honest will say they thought they were above the law. Former US senator John Edwards, of whom we spoke earlier, cited this very reason when his extramarital affair was uncovered by a news organization while his wife was suffering with an incurable cancer disease. "I thought I was above the law," Edwards regretfully told *ABC News Nightline* August 8, 2008.

That arrogance and pride, or better yet, selfishness not only makes it impossible to build personal magnetism, it is the true poison of loyalty. You will go a long distance, if not many world tours, before finding someone who will be loyal to you if your character is like a flag that flies in any direction the wind takes it. Very few people, except flatterers, will stick with you in both times of pleasure and hardship because of what you have.

Trustworthy people stand by someone because of what that person stands for. For this simple reason, in countries with honest and fair systems, people who came from humble beginnings govern, because they rise through the ranks while unambiguously demonstrating what they stand for.

These rulers from humble beginnings reach the top of their mountains not because of their ability to accumulate material wealth, but because of their ability to accumulate inner wealth that lights the path of their lives, and this inner wealth is what attracts people who carry them to the top joyfully. With their inner wealth, they are capable of unequivocally defining and lighting their positions in a way that does not confuse people.

This inner wealth is not kept in a fortress, but it is a hundred percent priceless; no money is required for its acquisition, it is simply accessible to all at no charge. This inner wealth is a set of principles that must define you and your positions, since it is these principles for which most people, or at least those you want to attract, yearn.

A magnetic person is never like a ship to be taken anywhere, nor is he a passenger looking up to the captain for his safe arrival; he is the compass as well as the captain of his own ship. He is only at the mercy of his ability to steer the ship on the course of his preference. When conditions arrive that are beyond his control, he takes the ship in the direction of his choosing at the speed of his comfort without fear of revolt from his passengers; he holds in his heart a principle that guides all his actions and for which he is ready to give his life. He is his own compass; he acts with integrity and honor.

Loyalty is a product of many qualities, but none of them are more defining than integrity and honor. People will usually forgive a leader who made an honest mistake, but they will rarely forgive a leader who lies to them. In your quest for personal magnetism, you must be loyal to yourself first before expecting loyalty from others; you must first conquer lower instincts and emotions that keep you from acting honestly and honorably; then you must be truthful in your thinking and deeds. Integrity and loyalty are almost synonymous; one does not exist without the other. John Boyd once said: "If your boss demands loyalty, give him integrity, and if your boss demands integrity, give him loyalty."

Nothing makes it easier to demand and receive loyalty than constantly thinking about the truth, and acting truthfully to the best of your mental and moral capacity. Being loyal to yourself is essentially thinking and acting with integrity, choosing the high road over petty compromise, effective solutions over easy ones, regardless of consequences. Practice makes perfect—by going through this routine mentally, you will impress these qualities upon your subconscious, so that in times of need, your mind will supply your conscious with the readily prepared solutions.

The significance of being one's own compass cannot be overstated. Even though no wise person will seek to build a personal magnetism for the purpose of becoming a "semi god," integrity and honor are two things you should not give your advisors the privilege of reminding you about. Weakness is human, but never let your integrity and honor show signs of weakness.

You can and should seek advice about ethics and know-how, but integrity is about morality and truthfulness. Morals and truth are the foundations of trust—they should be assiduously learned, and every minor shortcoming be patched up with urgency and dedication before throwing yourself in the arena of public life.

The personality of a public figure starts to suffer when his moral fitness becomes subject to inquiries. Unethical behavior is usually censured and never forgiven; lack of knowledge is fixed by studies and advice, but moral failings are never without permanent injuries. People are always willing to put their lives in danger to follow an honest, honorable, and courageous leader. They are always looking for someone to think for them and tell them what to do. They even sometimes go to the extreme of almost worshiping a fellow man in the name of his integrity. However, when they find out that they were misled or lied to all along, the rupture in the relationship is damaged irreparably.

The damage to loyalty is irreparable because, as this anonymous quote says, "He that is false to his first oath will be false to his second as well." For this basis alone, it is extremely important to be a good and lifelong student of moral qualities, not only to learn how to act with integrity and honor, but also to know how to leave a little room for those around you to notice your *human* weaknesses. That way, they can easily forgive you in those times of honest shortcomings and still follow you whenever your action is unquestionably honorable. Thus, you become your own compass as well as that of those around you.

It is helpful to remember that in the exercise of loyalty, if people do not trust you, they will *mistrust* you. Moral failings can easily tarnish a man's reputation harsher than any other failings. Failing is human; no one is perfect; people are not interested in finding a perfect person to be their role model. They want to be led by an imperfect person, but they would rather listen to someone who is mistakenly wrong than someone who is consciously so.

This is the importance of leaving some room for those around you to notice some human weaknesses in you. It is a slow but certain suicide to give people the impression of being perfect or morally infallible. Those who judge others harshly are people of this type. Setting and holding high moral standards, while ready to understand the weaknesses of fellow human beings, is truly being one's own compass and also the group's point man. Tolerating acceptable moral standards, while keeping your own as high as possible, makes you appear fair, just, and strengthens your personal magnetism more than you can imagine.

Asking people for their best while striving to excel in your own task is what Lee Iacocca meant when he said, "Talk to people in their own language. If you do it well, they'll say 'God, he just said what I was thinking.' And when they begin to respect you, they will follow you to death."

Of course, most people don't like being asked to do their best, but as you ask their best, strive to perform your own very best in action, thus you will lure them into your trap of wanting them to exceed your expectations. People will always choose as a role model someone who strives to perform to the highest standards before asking others to do the same. This whole idea can be wrapped up in just one sentence once uttered by Eleanor Roosevelt: "It is not fair to ask of others what you are not willing to do yourself."

Walk on a two-way street.

Florence Scovel Shinn, in her little book *The Power of the Spoken Word*, writes, "The law of laws is to do unto others as you would be done by, for whatever you send out comes back and what you do to others will be done to you." This is what ancient wise men called the Golden Rule—made famous by the Lord Jesus but taught by all great teachers of the truth, among them Confucius, Buddha, and in all schools of wisdom from Egypt to India to China to Greece.

Nowhere is the explanation of the Golden Rule added by Shinn, included: "for whatever you send out comes back and what you do to others will be done to you." This is the very fundamental nature of loyalty. No one will ever be loyal to you because of your wealth, power, or beauty, but because of your loyalty to them. It is exactly how much loyalty you give to those around you that will be given you—no more, no less. You cannot give people 50 percent loyalty and expect them to give you 100 percent. If you want 100 percent loyalty, you must give 100 percent of it to others. A person who is not loyal to others should not expect loyalty from them, regardless of their position.

A leader who wants to be well-served by his followers must first begin by showing and acting loyally toward them before asking them for loyalty. Loyalty is a commodity bought and sold with a currency of its own, also called loyalty, not dollar, pound, franc, euro, or yen, but *loyalty*. Unless you are ready to give loyalty, you will never receive it. Power does not guarantee loyalty. In fact, the most powerful people are the most vulnerable as far as loyalty is concerned. The wise understand it, and they pay more attention to loyalty than to anything else they possess.

Successful businesses are never built on products but rather on customer loyalty, which is the only way to guarantee the future of a company. Customer loyalty, cleverly termed customer service, is the most important department of any business; only a business doomed to fail neglects this department.

The principle of giving loyalty first before receiving it back is tangible throughout Mother Nature. Let's consider one easy factor that may help us to understand how the law of *give first loyalty* *before receiving it back* works in nature. Take, for instance, the Atacama Desert and the Amazon jungle. The Atacama is deadly dry. According to NASA, *National Geographic,* and many other publications, Atacama is the driest desert in the world.* And according to Softpedia.com, "The average annual rainfall is about one inch (25mm), and at some mid-desert spots, rain has never been recorded, at least as long as humans have measured it."

On the other hand, the Amazon jungle is wet and receives more rain that it sometimes needs. Is nature unfair to the Atacama? The answer is obviously no! Nature simply returns what each of these areas gives first to its atmosphere. The Amazon jungle gives its atmosphere water in form of vapor, which it returns back in the same quantity; whereas, the Atacama Desert gives almost nothing resembling water, therefore it gets extremely little. Unless, there is change, the Amazon will always give and receive water from the atmosphere and the Atacama will keep crying endlessly for what the Amazon jungle takes for granted. We are, of course, not experts in planetary weather or world economic policies that may have consequences in climate change; this illustration is used here for metaphorical purpose only.

Loyalty is never demanded; it is exchanged. Grace M. Hopper, an American computer scientist and United States Navy officer, once said, "Leadership is a two-way street, loyalty up and loyalty down. Respect

---

* See http://news.softpedia.com/news/The-Driest-Place-on-Earth-Atacama-Desert-55456.shtm (accessed 01/04/12).

for one's superiors; care for one's crew." Loyalty cannot be instilled by fear, money, or bribes. It is earned through the consideration of others' esteem, happiness, personality, and well-being.

A boss who sends an employee a message of congratulations or condolences receives back more loyalty from that gesture than from the salary he pays him. Loyalty is no one's right by any means but everybody's privilege, so you must work for it assiduously. Peace, justice, and prosperity that are in the open may be regulated by sets of laws, but not loyalty, for this is in the hearts of people, which are elusive to regulations. Even a vow and contract do not guarantee loyalty. You may try to demand loyalty, but be mindful that no one owes it to you.

Take as an example the all-powerful US Secret Service, which protects the lives of the president and others associated with high office. Its business requires one hundred percent loyalty in every circumstance, including death, but before demanding such a precious quality as loyalty, it treats its agents with the highest respect possible to inspire them while they are alive and active, and it honors them after retirement or death to inspire those still operating in difficult situations.

Religions have a tough time teaching loyalty, because as magical as faith is, humans naturally want to see the rewards of their loyalty. The subject of religious teaching is invisible, and the sum of its rewards is never clear. You may not admit it, but all of us are disciples of St. Thomas: we want to see before believing.

Loyalty deals with faith, which gives one, as Shinn would say, "A sublime assurance of one's good." Giving a sublime assurance to a human being is never an easy thing, but going the extra mile oftentimes pays off handsomely.

The case of the Arab-Israeli conflict is a perfect example. It is strange that the State of Israel would consider releasing Palestinian and Lebanese prisoners, whom it considers to have committed some the most heinous crimes, in exchange for the remains of long-dead Israeli soldiers or citizens. Except for the moral and psychological obligation, the remains do not do much good. The true prize for the Israelis and all governments in this type of situation is the loyalty and commitment of the living, who are currently or will in the future defend national interests, and inspire faith in their sublime assurance that the country will be loyal to them no matter what.

The Volatility of Loyalty

As awesome as it is, loyalty is one of those things that too much or too little of which may never be a good thing. It is difficult or maybe risky to determine the right dose of loyalty that is enough to be an effective medicine. It is like a well-cooked and spicy food that when eaten too much of causes heartburn, and when eaten too little of leaves you unsatisfied, while just enough is hard to measure. It is a perfect case of damned if you do, and damned if you don't. No question about it, we all want very loyal friends, colleagues, or subordinates, and no one wants a blinding or misleading loyalty.

Neil Kinnock, the former leader of the British Labour Party, once said, "Loyalty is a fine quality, but in excess, it fills political graveyards." Can we add to Kinnock's idea that the excess of loyalty does not just fill political graveyards, but family and business graveyards as well? Why is it that in medicine it is not advisable for a doctor to treat his loved ones? This is because he would want to be too cautious for fear of causing too much pain to his loved ones and may end up either making a mistake or performing the unnecessary action and end up fatally hurting the patient, the very thing that he wanted to avoid in the first place.

Why is it in politics or in business that leaders who surround themselves with too many *yes-men* end up being the most ineffective leaders? In education, why is it that teachers who do not tolerate students to challenge them are some of the less competent teachers in schools? These questions relate directly to the question of what is the proper measure of loyalty.

The answer to this question is naturally ambiguous. No clear or straight answer is possible, but this I know to be self-evident: challenging or questioning the authority is not necessarily a sign of disloyalty. Loyalty is a balance of positive and negative; a mix of good and bad; a product of emotion and reason in the name of the greater good. A loyal friend must neither be just a fanatical yes-man, in this case he renders your vision sightless, nor a pessimistic no-man, and in this case he hinders your inspiration. He must be courageous enough to strike on the chord of balance between the two with the best interests of the whole first and his friend second.

A person who is devoted to acquiring personal magnetism should never allow himself to be patted on the back by those with whom he surrounds himself or those he hopes to attract. He should always question the sincerity of any gesture of approval as well as criticism. A leader may be smart, wise and well-intended, but he is still and will always be a human being; therefore, he is subject to error and limited knowledge.

Consequently, it may be a fatal mistake to eradicate advisers, friends, or colleagues who dare to challenge a point of view regardless of its popularity. Encouraging diverse points of view among supporters increases the likelihood of finding the best alternative, and its discouragement blinds the group and presents the surest way to failure.

Examples illustrating this point of view abound in life. Rather than giving an illustration that works negatively, I will cite one that works positively. 3M is a company that prides itself as a "company that has been blessed with generations of imaginative, industrious, talented and innovative individuals," and rightly so. But it was not always that way—at least, not until the company adopted a policy of tolerating mistakes.

When researchers were working on a certain type of glue, they made one type of glue by mistake that could not stick. The research was considered a loss until someone came up with an idea—rather than throwing away the product, he suggested it be used to make the now popular "Post-It." Post-Its proved to be a great success for 3M Corporation and it has ever since adopted the culture of both tolerating employees' mistakes and challenging common sense.*

One last point on the volatility of loyalty is an observation more than it is a warning. Giving and receiving loyalty too soon or too late may be as fatal as demanding or buying it. People can trust new friends with objects of small value without too much concern, but it can be a grave mistake to trust them with such worthwhile things as loyalty before or long after the relationship has endured effective tests. Many end up heartbroken; they feel cornered for entering into a marriage after knowing the mate for just a short time, or regardless of the outcome of the tests, hoping marriage would fix the differences. The mutual understanding is that each of you is actually asking or expecting the other to sacrifice his or her life if necessary for the good of the other. When you are loyal to someone, you want him or her to be loyal to you as well.

On the question of loyalty, William Shakespeare writes,

> The purest treasure mortal times afford is spotless reputation—that away, Men are but gilded loam, or painted clay. A jewel in a ten-times-barr'd-up chest Is a bold spirit in a loyal breast; Mine honor is my life, both grow in one; Take honor from me, and my life is done . . . (King Richard II, 1:i:127–133)

---

* See http://www.ideafinder.com/history/inventions/postit.htm.

Except in rare instances, loyalty should only be erected on a solid rock of pure friendship; anything softer than the stone of friendship should be unacceptable.

Principles and laws based on loyalty may be counted on, but they do not guarantee peace of mind—it is externally enforced and outer power supported; therefore it is not magnetic. Friendship-based loyalty is magnetic because it is voluntary and a pure expression of free will and inner power.

Of friendship, the ancient Greek philosopher Socrates advises, "Be slow with friendship, but when thou art in, continue firm and constant." Since friendship is the product wrapped in a package called loyalty, it must be developed at a moderate pace with unequivocal strong will.

Unlike goods we buy at department stores, loyalty is not a time-limited, satisfaction-guaranteed type of thing; it must be earned day by day, and satisfaction must be timelessly guaranteed. When it comes to loyalty, it is always in the best interest of each party to know one another well, and once you are comfortable with each other, never assume to know everything. It must be work in progress, on a daily and on a merit basis.

This should not come as a surprise to anyone, because, if you look at marriage, the strongest and best friendship-based relationship, people still get divorced, even after a strong and long expression of loyalty, frequently becoming mortal enemies afterward. This clearly makes the point about loyalty being an ongoing and merit-based type of thing, and when betrayed, leaving devastation in its wake.

The last and most important thing wise people since ancient times have warned truth seekers regarding loyalty is to give it and expect it from only a select few, and then go to sleep with the inner eyes and ears wide open and watching over you like cherubim in East of the garden of Eden with a flaming sword uncompromisingly protecting the tree of life.

In short, when dealing with those you believe to be loyal, stay alert, remain calm, always paying attention to your instincts, and most importantly, listen carefully to the innermost voice that only you can hear. Then act promptly and effectively, so you do not give loyalty to imposters, who would sell you out for a few pieces of silver. In addition, you should not give loyalty to the masses, which could easily turn on you with an order from a demagogue. Loyalty, like the gates of Heaven, is opened to a precious few.

Making decisions about loyalty involves some of the most thought-provoking dilemmas any potential or developing magnetic person must ponder. The choice of closest or first-ring allies must be an almost entirely loyalty-based mechanism, with strong consideration given to competence, but that of the second-ring allies must be a mix of both loyalty and competence. The further away from the center—or from you—the more competence must outweigh loyalty.

Competence, in fact, is the very seed of loyalty. For two reasons: First, no matter how powerful your personal magnetism may be, people hate to be run or served by those they believe to be your cronies. They love to be ruled or served by competent people, regardless of your relationship with them. People care about results and the satisfaction of their needs. Competence does just that. So, by assigning very competent individuals closest to the masses, the masses will not only trust you, they will start feeling a sense of obligation of loyalty to you. Assigning the most competent to serve those you cannot physically reach, you make them feel like you are looking out for their best interests, in return for which they will make sure they look after your best interests as well. Thus, the development of loyalty between you and the masses.

Second, when individuals feel that you trusted their competence, regardless of philosophical differences, you hit a strong blow to their egos, softening their resistance to your influence. They will start trusting your judgment, or at least they will give you the benefit of the doubt where philosophical differences are deep and require time and better understanding to change. With this strategy, in the end, former antagonists who are competent individuals will more likely than not become loyal to you over time, slowly but surely.

Chapter Eleven

Associates and Noble Characters

Associates

When thinking about the qualities that will make or increase your personal magnetism, never underestimate the impact your associates can have on the development of this incredible power. It is no accident that this point is discussed among the last. Although you must develop yourself to your fullest capacity, you can only go so far on your own, and the choice of associates you make can actually make or break your personal magnetism.

Birds of a Feather Flock Together

A wise man may walk with and teach the unwise, but he surrounds himself with likeminded people. Similarly, the drunkards are habitually in the company of fellow drinkers. As the saying goes, *you will be judged by the company you keep.* There is still much to say on personal magnetism, after all, the subject is an endless field of study, but by taking a look at our associates, we begin to round out the discussion of personal magnetism as well as seeing its horizon.

Like most qualities that characterize man, personal magnetism is an inner quality that no one can see, but its evidence is externalized by people who are drawn together around a person who possesses it. Much has been written about how to attract or make friends by some of the best minds that have ever lived. We honor and praise their work. As for this work, far from being original, it is in fact inspired by extensive research into many schools of life, including the writings of Dale Carnegie, Napoleon Hill, Ernest Holmes, William Walker Atkinson, G. W. Ballard, Charles Haanel, Professor Dumont, Robert Collier and the like, so we will focus not so much on friendship in general but on the specific, small group of associates—the inner circle—that will project your magnetic personality beyond the borders of your immediate world to the four corners of the Earth. These are the people who stand between the magnet personality and the masses of adoring supporters. We choose to limit ourselves to this small group of individuals, because they know the mysteries behind the personal magnetism of the leader at their center. The number and depth of secrets they hold are second only to the spouse, if not the leader himself.

The understanding that choosing an inner circle of associates is seriously strategic is of enormous importance. For the sake of better clarification on how one should go about choosing trusted collaborators, we will go from the general to the specific.

The Inner Circle

A loving heart is nothing but a priceless oasis of light in the darkness. As such, it attracts doves and eagles, wolves and sheep, spiders and flies, men and serpents. An individual who radiates impeccable qualities is truly the sun of his world and the world around him. Like the sun, he joyfully attracts the good and the bad and everything in between.

While attracting so many people is the principal goal of personal magnetism, it can be hazardous if not well managed. Like the physical sun gives perfectly energizing life to the healthy, less energizing life to the unhealthy, scarcely energizing life to the dying, and no energy at all to the dead other than decomposition and a faster return to Mother Earth, a wisely magnetic person does not waste time and energy trying to attract everybody, for he knows very well that regardless of the wisdom of his words or the preciousness of his offers and promises, there will always be some people who will be sympathetic and receptive, some will be reluctant, and many others may even be deadly resistant for any reason. Therefore, personal magnetism is not about attracting everybody but the sympathetic, the persuadable and the open-minded.

The sacred scriptures of most religions teach that in heaven there are an unlimited number of angels, all equally dear to God, yet only the cherubim are closest to God. If it is true that God has His closest associates, it must be imperative for a leader to have his closest associates as well. A magnetic person radiates his spiritual, mental, and even physical grace through his closest associates. For this reason alone, a leadership attitude more than anything else is perceived through the kinds of people a leader chooses as his closest partners to form the fortress of his inner circle. Choosing closest friends does not have an exact formula; otherwise there would be no such thing as disappointment.

Puritanism leads to extremism, tolerance leads to impunity, and both lead to the destruction of personal magnetism. There will always be wolves in sheep clothing as long as humans are human, and there is nothing a personal magnetism can do about it. The instances of facing wolves in sheep clothing may be rare, but those of dealing with sincerely imperfect people are far greater than dealing with perfect ones. Thus sincere, honest and prudent efforts in choosing allies will always help the expansion of personal magnetism, regardless of the personal shortcomings of those around the leader. Many magnetic people or leaders have been brought down through no fault of their own, but by the transgressions of their close advisers.

Those leaders who preserve their personal magnetism even as close associates show lapses in their behavior, do so because the public can see a transparent process of choosing inner circle members as a fair effort that is neither extreme nor *laissez-faire*.

The choice of the inner circle must be based on the qualities of the characters of the prospective candidates, in agreement with the best interests of the public or organization, and not necessarily the leader's principles or beliefs.

This is how; an already competency challenged leader, former US president George W. Bush even further tarnished his leadership image and legacy. He chose his vice president, most of his cabinet members, and many high-ranking officials based almost exclusively on loyalty. Those who showed slight disagreements were pushed out. Regardless of their popularity with the public, Secretary of State Colin Powell, Secretary of the Treasury Paul O'Neal, and Chief of Staff of the Army General Eric Shinseki were either fired or forced to retire. Additionally, a number of US attorneys were fired and replaced by more loyal—and allegedly less competent—replacements. Following their ousters, policies were shaped to conform to the president's principles rather than the nation's long-held ideals.

After Bush's departure from office, declassification of top-secret memos instructing lower level officials brought shame to the country worldwide and public opinion of the president's political party suffered severely. As these words were being written, debate was still raging about whether to investigate wrong-doing by the Bush Administration and prosecution of all involved at all levels. As we said in the chapter on love, if sincere praise can almost disarm a god, imagine what it can do to a human heart. Elevating people's good performance and understanding their weaknesses puts the heart of man on a fire of joy. A man who does not understand this simple but profound truth can never conquer the hearts of fellowmen and will never acquire personal magnetism.

Love, as defined by Holmes here, does not contradict the Golden Rule, but it is a more esoteric side of the rule of rules. Praise is an arrow that brings down the evasively flying heart of love. When you truly love others or show attention in the interests of someone else, even to a minimum degree, the love you receive in return will be at least equal to the amount you send out. However, like mirrors reflect the light of the sun back to the sun and in darkness, when you send out love to so many people, the amount you send out will be reflected back to you from each individual you loved as well as in the spheres of their influence. You become a focal point of love radiating extraordinary power that blinds the eyes of the involuntarily unloving, who fall joyfully and bend onto their knees to your soft but unswerving magnetic personality.

The power of forgiveness is one of the most attractive there is. Forgiveness is a twin quality of love. An unloving person is almost certainly an unforgiving one. The power of forgiveness in the name of the masses is so prestigious that it is left only to the highest ranking members of society. In many countries, only the president or the prime minister has the power to forgive a criminal in the name of society. A person, who knows how to forgive his fellow man, will over time wield unbelievable influence over them.

Forgiving is by no means an expression of giving in; instead it is a display of love and understanding. No one is perfect. So, by forgiving others you empower them to forgive *your* shortcomings.

No one is more repulsive than those who always see the negative side of life everywhere. Consciously or otherwise, we all try our best to improve ourselves as we try to be better people, and we are more attracted to the person who encourages even the smallest of our efforts toward our goal. Unconsciously or otherwise, we dislike anyone who just does not recognize even our desire for self-improvement. As Holmes asks, "Which person do we like better: the one who is always full of trouble and fault-finding or the one who looks at the world as his friend and loves it?"

In response to his own question, he adds, "The question does not need to be asked; we know that we want the company of a person who loves, and loving forgets all else." People will never love you because of who you are or what you have, at least not in the true sense of love; they will deeply and sincerely love you because they think that you have their best interests at heart.

Anyone who loves someone who does not have his best interests at heart will undoubtedly be heartbroken, sooner or later. Even the fanatical usually turn their backs on their idol if his attitude does not meet their expectations. Anyone who loves someone who does not have his best interests at heart is the best prototype of a hypocrite and is to be guarded against, because he would not hesitate to stab you in the back at the very first opportunity.

Animals smell love, but people feel it; they love those who love them and mistrust those who mistrust them. Faultfinding is the easiest way to push people away, whereas understanding people's lower sides will attract a pool of diverse and talented people who can help you to build your personal magnetism.

The majority of people are fearful of the world in front of them and doubtful of their abilities to overcome the obstacles life seems to present every time their goal of happiness seems within reach. This fear and doubt are perpetual for many people, who hunger for someone more inspiring and faithful, someone stronger than themselves, willing to encourage even the smallest steps they make out of their struggle. Take advantage of them by praising their smallest effort and forgiving their limitations. They will feel your strength, try to emulate you, and you will be their friend and their hero for life.

Let people know your pleasure and sincerity by helping them and having a heart-to-heart conversation with them, so they can feel your cordial friendship, and they will stick with you for better or for worse. Always visualize yourself helping, forgiving, and encouraging others whenever and wherever you are, so that when the opportunity to help comes, you will be ready like an athlete who has practiced for the game or the student who is waiting for the final exam with confidence. Consider the good deeds you render others as seeds you have purposely placed in the ground. Though they may let you go hungry for a while, they will germinate and eventually supply you with abundant food and life in the cold season when you need them most.

The greatest men in history did not do otherwise. Loving people and encouraging their positive sides provides an unlimited and rich pool of people from which to choose the most effective and useful as you look to spread your influence beyond your immediate circle. All great historical characters have used this same tactic to reach their goals, and the results have been nothing but wonderful.

You can still love people with all your heart and steadfastly refuse to be influenced by their negative sides. But love is meaningless unless it is felt. Many people end up disappointed when their best effort in loving others is paid back in "monkey currency" or ingratitude. Ingratitude disappoints everyone—men, as well as spirits. Disappointment breeds anger and hate. But nothing is more demagnetizing to personal magnetism than anger and hate. An angry and hateful man has less than zero magnetic power; he attracts no one including himself because he does not love himself either. That is why here on Earth there is a reason why modern scientists define psychology as a science of behavior and not a science of the soul.

Humor

It may come as a shock to many people to hear that humor is an inestimable tool of leadership and, therefore, of personal magnetism. No tool simplifies the work of a charismatic public speaker and an effective leader the way humor does. Logic feeds the reason, dogma feeds the heart, and humor is the seasoning, the spice that makes their tastes pleasant and smoothly digestible. Highly magnetic people have used humor to the fullest benefit in their quest for more influence. It is a well-known factor among assiduous students of leadership that to "develop your leadership," you must "develop your sense of humor," as the *Reader's Digest* says.

Former US president and four-star general Dwight D. Eisenhower, who led the United States to victory in World War II, once said, "A sense of humor is part of the art of leadership, of getting along with people, of getting things done." Life is already a very stressful experience by itself; humor takes some of the unnecessary heat out of it.

Explicably or otherwise, life is already full of fear, doubt, disbelief, anger, faultfinding, and self-condemnation, which burn the human heart greatly and constantly. Humor is an acid reducer of these heavy and negative chemicals. Rare people among us are immune to the torture of negative emotions, thus people are constantly searching for a leader who not only does the thinking for them and inspires them, but who also prescribes an adequate dose of mental and emotional therapy through humor.

The importance of humor in human life cannot be overstated and the proof is everywhere. Let's just take an obvious illustration. Look at television programming. The Discovery, History, and National Geographic channels have some of the most mind-stimulating programs that not only inspire us but also show the world the progress of human ingenuity and the wonders of nature. Compare these channels and their programs to comedy and movie programs on the USA network, Comedy Central, NBC, ABC, and CBS. Which of these channels do you think are more watched, and which one are paid the most? There is no question that humorists and comedians are paid the most and appear in the most watched programs on television. As Mark Twain writes, "Humor is the great thing, the saving thing. The minute it crops up, all our irritations and resentment slip away and a sunny spirit takes its place."

Good ideas are good things; they can be found in many places and perfected by time and silence, but good humor is a *strategic* thing; it is sudden, inspired by instinct and perfected by the desire to be happy and share happiness with others. Skillful use of both good ideas and good humor makes man literally adorable. Both the leader and his entourage must be efficient producers and consumers of humor; advisors must be able to take things with a grain of salt and keep their morale up with humor and without fear.

Life is paradoxical. For the majority of people, happiness comes with financial freedom. But as contradictory as it is, poor people commit suicide for financial hardship, and rich people kill themselves for the insecurity that comes with financial success. How can these two end? The negative and positive always cause an explosion. How can the depression of financial insecurity and the insecurity of financial success be cured by the same medicine? If there is such medicine, it is humor. Humor comforts all people across the spectrum if applied at the right time and right place. As long as fears, worries, and doubts enslave or perpetually threaten to enslave the heart of men, humorists will not only win their daily bread but they will delight and free the hearts of men as well.

Humor should not be left to professional comedians and movie stars alone to make huge fortunes; it must be used, as well, by those who are in the business of personal magnetism to attract the genius to form the aura of their personality and the masses to spread the myths and mysteries of their person and life story. No one is bulletproof against the right dose of humor administered at the right time. As Ralph Waldo Emerson once said, "Wit makes its own welcome, and levels all distinctions. No dignity, no learning, no force of character can make anyone stand against good wit."

A superb leader is an artful user of humor; those who ignore it do so at their own peril. A humorless leader is usually characterized as stiff, cold, or even angry. A magnetic person does not have to be a comedian, but he does have to be an emotional therapist who uses humor, a harmless chemical and addiction-free medicine, to comfort and excite those around him and the masses.

Laughter: the Best Medicine

We hear people all the time saying that "laughter is the best medicine." Writing about the magic of laughter, William W Atkinson writes, "Laughter is really a tonic, and for many things it is better than a doctor." It is not enough for the leader to simply employ humor to motivate his supporters; he himself must be the *smiler-in-chief*. "The pursuit of happiness" is a serious business.

People pursue happiness in all avenues of life, but it is really found in the hearts of others; it is discovered and distributed by facial expressions with smiles and laughter. No face is more attractive than a smiling one. Smiles and laughter are signals to others that one knows and holds the secret of happiness. The more you smile or laugh appropriately, the more personal magnetism you radiate. By nature, people do not follow an individual they perceive as insincere. Humor used without a smile by the performer sends mixed signals: it inspires doubt and mistrust in the audience and those who see and hear you through the audience.

There is a reason why the audiences at the US presidential debates are asked to remain silent until the end of the program. These two illustrations are some of the reasons. The reaction of the physical audience has a far greater influence than most people realize. Take these examples: In the 1980 and 1984 presidential debates, Ronald Reagan used humor to counteract his opponents. The audience inside the building of both events laughed joyfully, prompting the audience at home to react in the same manner to the Republican candidate. Not only were these two occasions the most frequently shown on television during the debate analyses, but they were also credited to having been critical to Reagan's victories.

During the 1988 vice-presidential debate, the Republican candidate, Indiana senator Dan Quayle, responding to criticism of his lack of experience, tried to compare himself to one of the most popular figures in the history of American politics, John F Kennedy. His opponent, Democratic vice-presidential nominee, Texas senator Lloyd Benson, humorously downplayed his comparison by telling his colleague: "Senator, I knew Jack Kennedy. Jack Kennedy was a friend of mine. Senator, you are no Jack Kennedy." Here again, the audience approvingly laughed, and the rest is history. Quayle personally never recovered from the ridicule of the debate although he and George H. W. Bush went on to win the presidential elections.

That moment marked a very dark spot on Quayle's record. Through the four proceeding years as vice president, he was the object of ridicule and jokes. When he ran for the presidential nomination of the Republican Party, he attracted very little attention and more jokes. In the end, he never came close to being a serious candidate, despite his resume and the traditional advantage that former vice presidents hold. He lost and went into political retreat.

More recently, an obscure forty-seven-year-old lady from Scotland blew everyone away with her performance when she participated on a British television contest called *Britain's Got Talent*. The judges and the audience couldn't wait to speak to Susan Boyle as soon as she finished her song; such was their surprise that a plain woman could be such a wonderful singer. The audience was exuberantly happy; everyone was on their feet. Even the judges were caught unexpected. "This was the biggest surprise I have had in three years of this program," said one judge. "It was an absolute privilege to hear you sing," said another. "Susan, you can go back to your home village, head high, proud of receiving the approval of all of us," they continued. Boyle's YouTube videos attracted tens of millions of hits, she received an overwhelming amount of requests for television interviews, and she was on her way to stardom, hopefully, as these lines were being written. That is the power of a smile.

Laughter is an amazing instrument in the development of a magnetic personality. As the German poet and philosopher Goethe writes, "Nothing shows a man's character more than what he laughs at." By laughing and consequently inducing laughter, you are opening your heart to others to see your insides at the same time as you are forcing them to open theirs so you can read their needs and aspirations while you try to lead them harmoniously.

One of the most important functions of laughter that is rarely observed is its ability to repair relationships. A Yiddish proverb goes like this: "What soap is to the body, laughter is to the soul." Do I need to explain further? Is there anything a man needs more than a clean soul? Who would not like to deal with people whose souls are clean? Who would not like to be a part of a company of soul-cleaned people? This is not a joke when you notice that some of the most complicated social conflicts are more often than not resolved without negotiation or bullets, but by a mere laugh between two antagonists.

Laughter is the finest nonviolent way of solving problems, as Frank A. Clark, onetime president of the Des Moines Area Religious Council, once said, "I think the next best thing to solving a problem is finding some humor in it." That is the power of laughter; that is why it is sometimes called "a tranquilizer with no side-effects." Humor and laughter are two of some of best kept secrets of personal magnetism, and in the words of Atkinson, they make you look "bright and interesting and cheerful . . . [a] distributor of hope, trust, sympathy, and brightness."

Noble Characters

Personal magnetism is an inner gift of the ability to attract for the public good. As such, a magnetic person is an individual who has the ability to attract people not for selfish reasons but for the service of others. Community service is a very complicated task; it is never a straightforward task, because those who are served naturally have diverse and often conflicting interests, regardless of the apparent demographic homogeneity. Age, gender, and social class are enough to produce different and conflicting interests, even in a small, closed, homogeneous society. For this reason, it is crucial that a leader be surrounded by people of noble character: "men and women who" in the words of Atkinson "will stand for what is right, first, last, and all the time. Men and women whom money cannot buy."

A leader who surrounds himself with people of unconquerable spirit and virtues; people who consider character and knowledge to be more important than money and pleasure; people who speak truthfully to the best of their knowledge; people who would say nothing to please anyone or anything that would be against their own consciences; fearless people who would rather give everything than compromise high ideals; people who have conquered their passions, ambitions, fears, and doubts; in short, people who have conquered themselves. All of those people are potential leaders of personal magnetism who have chosen to serve a leader who serves others.

Close partners reflect a lot about the character of the person they represent. Not only do representatives mirror the character of the leader, they are also key players in the success of any given leader and his agenda. Just as no generous leader can succeed surrounded by less intelligent people, no brave and skillful general can win a war if his regiment is made up of cowards and frightened soldiers.

For a successful leader, noble character above everything else should be the basis of his associations, especially when it comes to the selection of very close friends. The choice of close friends or confidants based on noble character will not only determine success or failure, the individuals themselves will determine greatness and competence or weakness and incompetence of any leader.

Strong Will

When a vehicle is out of energy, the only location where it is likely to replenish that energy is a gas station; when man is hungry or thirsty, the most likely place where he can get food or water is in a kitchen or a restaurant. A leader who feels weak needs to strengthen his will by finding joy in whatever he is doing. True joy comes from inside. But it is also said that joy, like optimism, is contagious. Thus, a leader whose inner circle contains joyous and optimistic people will also find himself surrounded by strong-willed people; as a result, he will have an inexhaustible source of energy to strengthen his confidence.

A major reason why society has leaders and followers is because the majority of the people are fearful of facing life or the potential chaos that comes with uncertainty of the future. Roger Simon, chief political columnist of a popular political website, politico.com, had this in mind and put it in much better words. At the surprise victory of the Republican Party in the congressional election in 2002, politico.com website reported the following:

> Strength has been an especially potent force in our politics even since the attack of Sept. 11, 2001. When Republicans picked up seats in the congressional elections of 2002, Bill Clinton had a simple analysis: "When people are insecure, they'd rather have someone who is strong and wrong than someone who's weak and right." (www.politico.com/news/stories/1007/6490.html)

Not to defend ignorance, but the first mission of any leader is to drive fear out of the people. A fearless people will always find their way out of trouble, regardless of apparent difficulties. A leader who instills fear in one way or the other, sooner or later, pays greatly. The masses are driven by emotion and feeling; leaders are driven by beliefs and purpose. Belief and purpose are strengthened by self-confidence and association with people of strong belief.

Humans being human, there is always time for weakness in all of us, including our leaders. This time of temptation can break or make strong-willed people as well. In times of weakness or self-doubt, a leader draws his strength from the strong-willed people around him. This is why it has been said again and again that behind a successful man there is a strong woman. This archetypal woman derives her strength from mental, emotional, and spiritual power of her own, and puts it into the service of inspiring, encouraging, believing in, and visualizing her mate's success to the fullest of the dream. To the extent that he lets her into his confidence, the dream will come true.

Decision-making is the expression of a strong will. People do not like nor do they trust someone who hesitates in making decisions, but they prefer someone who has the guts to take a position and stick with it as long as it has been done in the best interests of the group or organization and then lets the chips fall where they may. Strong-willed confidants play a major role in assisting the leader in making tough decisions, while trying to minimize the possibility of making mistakes. Any decision made by anybody has the potential to achieve two results: success or failure. Success, of course, produces happiness and joy, but failure hits man at the very center of life, the heart, with one of the most perilous of all its weapons, discouragement.

All of us face discouragement in the face of a seemingly insurmountable obstacle, and a leader is no exception. Unlike for the majority of people, the discouragement of a leader can have broad consequences. A leader will enhance his personal magnetism by surrounding himself with realistic but strong-willed people as an alternative source of strength and power to overcome trials and distress.

A magnetic person is always a student of himself and the world around him, discovering his shortcomings and filling them with the strengths of others, like an ocean forever satisfying an ever-demanding shore with waters from rivers, lakes, and rain. Acknowledging one's own lapses and learning from others is strength not weakness, and it is the secret of the strongest.

High Ideals

Ask any farmer what happens when you mix a decaying fruit with good ones? It destroys the rest of the crop in a very short time. Ask a doctor what happens when you infect some people with a virus: the virus will spread. It is amazing the power of evil over good, wrong over right. One rotten orange can destroy hundreds, even thousands of perfectly good oranges; one infected person can spread a virus in whole locality and beyond, however millions of perfectly good apples cannot help a decomposing apple to recover. That is the apparent power of evil over good, but isn't truth or good more powerful than evil?

Indeed, goodness—or truth—is what sustains life; evil does not. Light is always stronger than darkness. Evil always bows to good; good may withdraw when necessary, but it never bows to evil. It is dark not because the sun bowed to darkness but because it has withdrawn. It is light because darkness has bowed to the higher power of light. Evil has a destructive power and good a constructive one. Evil requires no power to be sustained, but good does. All it takes to destroy a mighty building is to abandon it, and it will eventually crumble down, but it takes care to maintain good.

The power of evil is acquired almost effortlessly and mindlessly. The power of good is acquired through effort and diligence. The power of evil is common; the power of good uncommon; the power of evil is weak, while the power of good is strong; the power of evil requires low ideals, while the power of good requires high ideals.

What happens when you face a mirror to the sun? It definitely will not create another sun, but it will reflect the light of the sun with the same blinding light. A truly magnetic person is a mirror of good—he takes high ideals and makes them his own. Like a mirror, he does not reflect darkness, but light. He goes not after the common, but the uncommon, not the easy, but what is worthwhile, regardless of the price to be paid. He never ceases to discover and rise above himself. He discovers himself by measuring social or high ideals, by conquering himself, and by adopting the good that he finds in others. Thus, in his search for high ideals, a leader who is seeking to enhance his personal magnetism will always surround himself with people whom he admires, those who are capable of challenging and exceeding his intellectual and moral prowess. Always seeking the company of good apples and avoiding the bad ones at all costs. Efficient leadership is the art of placing yourself in the center of those who are not necessarily like-minded people, but who are capable and good people. A magnetic leader learns more about himself before learning anything about others. To know and understand that knowledge is found everywhere, but most of all within you, is the first step toward acquisition of an immense personal magnetism.

Chapter Twelve

Golden Keys and The Crown

Golden Keys

The power of attracting man's attention is the most mysterious power there is. Winning people's attention and devotion is the most elusive endeavor imaginable. Gods and goddesses have been trying since the dawn of time to attract human hearts by using both the carrot and the stick. While we do not know the level of their success or failure, we know that many of them can only barely be remembered, let alone mentioned.

Prophets and philosophers have come and gone, using sophisticated and simple language to no avail, and many of them did so at the expense of their own lives. Kings, despotic rulers, and warlords conquered lands and tried to bend human will by the sword to force people to pay attention to them, just to end up in mass killings and eventually retreat after losing all the conquered lands and, in many cases, their power at home as well.

Communism tried the "equality formula" just to end up with prison camps, poverty, widespread dissatisfaction, and eventually colossal failure. The ongoing "democracy experiment" rather than being what it is supposed to "self government" is quickly becoming government by and for the "big brother" with its almost excessive taxation and excessive restriction of personal liberties. It (democracy) is too ambiguous, to say the least, and extremely hard to implement, making balanced allocation of commonwealth practically impossible, thus leaving it almost entirely in the hands of the few.

It is a dangerously becoming literally a big "business scheme," relentlessly building court houses, mushrooming private prisons, and massive law enforcement entanglements used by the few to scare or force the majority into obedience. It is in fact a paradox, on one hand, a real life expression of natural selection or survival of the fittest theory, on another, the rich have become the object of envy and the subject of insecurity, and the famous have become victims of their own success, leaving everyone to defend for himself and private civilian security firms at all levels, from individual to governmental as well as international levels booming as harmony and happiness farther stay out of reach of social contract.

Very few people have succeeded in mastering the art of personal magnetism. And those who did succeed; did so not because they were the chosen ones, but because they cultivated some crucial understanding that, when well-utilized, helped soften human resistance and paved the way to the magic of personal magnetism.

In this work, we have strived to discuss what we know and feel to be the golden keys (what has been presented so far) of personal magnetism. And of course, they are golden only when in the hands of an astute mind and poised intellect. Just because they are golden does not mean they are easy to use. Just like the physical substance of gold is hard to find but, once found, makes commercial exchange easier, the golden key, once understood and diligently exploited, becomes a sun of every heart and a fountain of pure water.

These golden keys will fail to open any door when held by a stiff hand and arrogant heart, but they will open any door when held by a soft hand and humble heart. They are the germs of personal magnetism when seen through the eyes of the master self within you. They have been carefully researched and are given here with minimum explanations, with the sole hope and intention that leaving to your heart the liberty of going beyond the surface and deep inside yourself to find the true meaning and the practical ways of getting the most benefits out of these eye openers.

The first and most important element a student of personal magnetism must understand is that before you can attract anyone, you must first attract yourself. You must love yourself before anyone can love you. You must pay tribute to yourself before anyone will pay tribute to you. You must get along with the man or woman within you, that person who speaks the language that only you can understand, before you can even try to get along with people of the outside world who speak a language you may or may not understand. These people want you to always read between the lines but not so with your inner self (your best and most loyal friend above and below) whose language is plain and simple.

Sound selfish? Not at all. Attracting yourself means attracting the master of all masters, and this master can be found nowhere else in the universe but inside you. He is your master self, the silent voice heard only by your heart, the one and only true center of your universe, the humble and gentle man inside who loves, guides, and protects you when you listen and trust him.

Unless you acquire the habit of voluntarily going in the silence to listen to your inner master self, personal magnetism will come to you the hard way, if it ever comes at all. This has been practiced by all of the most charismatic people who ever lived. Charismatic people are also solitary people for this reason. Moses, Plato, Alexander the Great, Jesus, George Washington, Napoleon, Abraham Lincoln, and Gandhi were all obedient listeners of their inner masters.

You will know it is your master self speaking when he is not judgmental or critical of you and others, does not instill in you fear, hate, doubt, impatience, vengeance, discouragement, anger, or any other destructive feeling. If you let the inner master have the total freedom to express himself through you, stars will be brought down to earth and bow before you. This is what the first commandment in the Bible is all about, that is what the sages of ancient times meant when they said, "Knowledge is to be found everywhere but most of all within yourself." I will let you go deep down to scoop more for yourself.

Personal magnetism is not always a by-product of common sense but uncommon sense and uncommon wisdom. There is a good reason why the most charismatic individuals are also the most despised by a great deal of people. This is so because one of the first things a magnetic person learns is to challenge them to break or bend the common wisdom. Leading people in a new direction often requires understanding this truth taught by ancient teachers as one author wrote: "Things are not always as seen, and wisdom often appears to us in a guise that we find, at first, unrecognizable. Truth is not necessarily your experience and limited knowledge; it is everything beyond the veil of your illusion."

Personal magnetism is built by seeing things beyond images reflected in your eyes, understanding the meaning behind the audible sounds, feeling beyond the reach of your senses. By so doing, you will discover something that captivates people's imagination. Charismatic people do not always go with the flow; they do not always follow the herd; they stand aside, pursue a different course, and let the herd follow them.

They do not see the south, north, east, or west the same way most people do. They understand Japan is northeast of China but west of Alaska; the United States is north of Mexico but south of Canada. For them, the glass can be half full and half empty at the same time. They understand fortune can come in the form of pain and misfortune can come in the form of joy. They understand that true knowledge is not acquired through physical senses but poured directly into our hearts in great silence when all physical senses are completely shut down and those of the heart, mind, and intellect are alone activated. They understand that the love of silence is wisdom; knowledge and illumination that prompted Newton and Einstein to discover laws that had never been taught in school, and an uneducated Shakespeare became the greatest writer the world had ever seen. I will let you go deep down to scoop more for yourself.

Charismatic people understand that personal magnetism is a prize, not a present; it is earned, not given; and it is won, not inherited. They understand the wisdom taught by ancient teachers. Seekers of personal magnetism are well-off knowing that men who desire being important are numerous, but those who succeed or excel are always few. They are guided by the true and deep feeling that men who see what most people see with the physical eye only see the world, and that they are the vast majority; but those who see with the inner or divine eye, and ultimately see what the vast majority do not see, make up a very small number, for they see the treasure that makes men a magnet of both men and gods, and then everything in between.

Thus, they look at things, people, and the world; they listen to speechless thought or inner speeches and speeches from their fellowmen differently from the rest of the world. They seek to understand the causes rather than just the effects, until they discover the cause of all causes, the first and final cause, the causeless cause.

They strive to understand the scariest thing the vast majority of people fear most, and that is death, the only thing that makes man pay attention and devotion to anyone who can shield him from the tyranny of that monster. So they think, speak, act, and stand fearlessly before any threat of death, thus giving their fellowmen the appearance of a conqueror of the fear of death and their best hope of protection.

They build their greatness and immortality by dedicating themselves to the defense of the good of their neighbor, community, country, and humanity. They find this holy secret hidden not beyond the stars or beneath the oceans, but in their own hearts, where the first and last true battles of life are fought and permanently won or lost. They realize that personal magnetism is the sweetest fruit there is, and as such, to harvest it one must climb a thorny ladder of patience, because to be worthy of it one must be persistent.

They discern that, in order to receive help from the universe or to keep gods from being turned off, reward or punishment should not be the motive of their good thought, feeling, words, or deeds, but the deeper joy of serving others. You can go deep in your heart and scoop more of these gems.

Truly magnetic people are disciples of truth because they know that the untruth can only keep magnetism for so long, and it is not long at all. Therefore, they arm themselves with the best weapon there is, a teachable spirit. They are truly avid learners of the truth and superb manipulators of the light that enlightens the hearts of men.

They control and purify their thoughts by thinking only what is good, right, and constructive. They avoid and shut down all negative thoughts, feelings, sounds, and images by suffocating them with hope, faith, and love.

They recognize what the old-school thought teaches, in the words of one thinker: "Life can be perilous; 'soldiership' must be proven to rise in rank, and fear of no trial is the spirit of the conqueror." They work both hard and smart; they perfect their faith through actions, because in the end, only the action counts; and without it, hope and faith are fruitless.

They live and lead by example; they do what they say and say what they do. They hold themselves to a higher standard than they hold others. They give praise and thanks to the worthy and admirable, living and dead, and deny the same privileges to the unworthy, dead or alive. They honor good men, shun bad ones, but serve everyone indiscriminately. You can go deep and scoop more for yourself.

A magnetic person comprehends that man lives in two worlds: visible and invisible. He understands man's fascination with the invisible world and his love-fear of the invisible. Thus, a magnetic person tends to be a private person and a discreet one, to keep the aura of mysteries and myths around him, and therefore keeping people coming back for more. He understands that his personal magnetism will last only as long as his mysterious or mythical aura is shining. This is the real reason many democratic constitutions prohibit elected leaders from serving after a certain number of years, because fake magnetic leadership can only last for so long. He reveals a little truth to a very small number of people who truly and sincerely appreciate its inestimable value. I know it sounds heartless or maybe arrogant, but the mass of people is nothing but a herd of swine, unworthy of the truth. This is simply to say that the truth is a privilege, not a right, it must be earned not given, and the majority of us do not work diligently enough to be worthy of it.

Even the most generous man who ever lived, the man who gave the gift of life to the dead, healed the sick, and fed the hungry—Jesus Christ—called the mass of people (allegorically of course) swine and dogs, undeserving of the truth, and hence His need to teach them in parables. Matthew reads, "Never give what is holy to dogs or throw your pearls before swine. Otherwise, they will trample them with their feet and then turn around and attack you," (Matthew 7:6: ISV 2008).

The truth has always been guarded with the most lethal weapons available. Secret societies impose the harshest punishment to members who are careless or dare to reveal the secrets with which they have been entrusted. Secret services charged with searching and keeping government secrets kill or jail for life anyone who unlawfully reveals government secrets—even in this country treason is subject to the death penalty.

Silence is the great teacher of a magnetic person. He spends his sacred time and leisure in his heart and in the universe. He frees his heart to receive inspiration from the universe to think, feel, imagine, and act upon it. He obeys his heart when it gives him constructive instruction and thanks the universe for generous gifts. This way he receives the truth, keeps improving himself to the better while helping the few around him to improve themselves as well. Follow the lead or find your way deep and scoop more.

A charismatic person must be more forgiving, more generous, less selfish, less envious, less ungrateful, and more serving. He must consider his work the mission of his life. He should not be a lazy person but someone who truly earns his living through the work of his head and hands. He must make sure his duties are always performed to the fullest and not half way. Doing his best must mean to him going to the limit of his ability. He must be both a teacher and a student, both sun and planet. Just as the sun gives light freely and joyously to planets and planets receive and enjoy sunlight, a magnetic person must help those around him and humbly receive their help whenever necessary.

He must be susceptible to the truth and hard like a rock to superstition and falsehood, for these two lead to ignorance and distraction. The importance of vulnerability to the truth by a magnetic person can never be overstated. Trusting one's sincere and honest fellow man is the only one way to open oneself to the truth, because Heaven will never come down here to reveal the truth; besides your heart, no one except truth's messengers, your fellowmen, will reveal it to you. You can find more on this if you dig deep down in your heart and scoop.

The list is already too long without mentioning every single one of them here, but we cannot close this section without mentioning two more golden keys of charisma, and they are happiness and attention. Happiness within a magnetic person is truly a great key that turns and keeps the door of personal magnetism wide open. Happiness, you may have heard, is contagious and definitely not infectious. No one gets sick or bored for excessiveness of well-founded and sincere happiness.

"Life, liberty, and the pursuit of happiness" as it is written in the United States Declaration of Independence—the first two are either somehow guaranteed or protected (for all law-abiding citizens) by the creator or government, but only happiness is or should be created, guaranteed, and protected by the individual himself. That is why we keep running up and down in pursuit of happiness and even though we find some of it in material acquisition, we find authentic and lasting happiness in association with joyful people.

Sure, money can help but not always. For instance marry a wealthy person, and if that wealthy person is happy, so will you be, but if the wealthy person is not happy, his or her money is probably not going to make you happy, it is very likely going to make your life even more miserable than you expected.

Sad and angry individuals are the least magnetic people there are; on the other hand, the happiest individuals are the most magnetic people. Even the forces of nature are turned off by sad hearts and turned on by and attracted to joyous ones. The world rides on the backs of joyous souls who receive inspirations, aspirations, and willpower from Mother Nature more easily and more often than sad souls, who seem to see only troubles in every direction.

Happy souls are also great transformers of the inspiration and aspirations of Mother Nature into great deeds on which civilizations have been built. The secrets of nature are magnificent treasures, highly discerning, and as smart and wise as any intelligence and wisdom can be. They may be invisible to us, but they are not blind or deaf by any stretch of imagination. They choose their way carefully into worthy, deserving hands, and when deceived, they can fight back devastatingly with unparalleled firepower, if need be.

Of happiness and power of personal magnetism, French writer Albert Camus is quoted to have said:

When you have once seen the glow of happiness on the face of a beloved person, you know that a man can have no vacation but to awaken that light on the faces surrounding him; and you are torn by thoughts of unhappiness and night you cast, by the mere fact of living, in the hearts you encounter.

And Dr. Albert Schweitzer said,

Success is not the key to happiness. Happiness is the key to success.

The more enthusiastic you are about finding reasons or even excuses for being honestly happy inside out, the more magnetic or charismatic will you be. Naturally, people like being around happy people.

Both life and freedom are expressed and felt through happiness. Nurturing a feeling of happiness and, most importantly, being conscious of it is truly holding in one's own hands the golden key of personal magnetism, because as Mark Twain once said, "Whoever is happy will make others happy, too."

Is it not that what personal magnetism or charisma is all about? If you know how to spread happiness, you will be the king of the hearts of your fellowmen. People love and idolize happy human beings; they make or long to discover myths and legends around them. Eyes fall in love with the exterior of a person in hopes of finding happiness hidden inward, but once they find out that the inside person is disgusting rather than happy, they do not bother looking at *Ms.* or *Mr. Universe* for another second.

We are all vulnerable to happiness as Marcel Proust acknowledges in this heartfelt admission: "Let us be grateful to people who make us happy; they are the charming gardens who make our souls blossom."

The last golden key of personal magnetism to be mentioned here is attention. The importance of attention in life can never be overstated. I feel the obligation of apologizing up front before going any further, because I know no matter how hard I try, I will fall short of truly expressing the importance of this priceless power called attention. If attention is not the most important power that man has, it is certainly up there among the most important, and it is surely second to none, because it is synonymous to the being—"I am here and I am there."

Attention is the power that enables man to be simultaneously at the center and at the circumference, to be present where the physical organs are encased and anywhere else in time and space. It is the power that enables man to transcend time and space, the power that enables man to live in the now and here or there. It is this power that makes it possible for man to concentrate intensely on a specific time and location and either reconstitute history, predict events of the future, or explain laws of nature that affect life now.

Wherever man's attention is, there he is. This is the power used effectively by pioneers, people who discovered laws that had never been taught in schools or anywhere before. There is the power used by Archimedes, Pascal, Newton, Shakespeare, Einstein, and others to come up with knowledge that affected the trajectory of human life forever.

Whatever your attention is on, you become. People do not become what they merely desire but what their attention is persistently upon, and those whose attention wanders from point to point achieve very little in life. If it was a matter of desire only, everyone would be successful, since everyone has a desire for success, but it is even more a matter of attention to thoughts and feelings.

Attention is the essence of a mysterious natural law commonly known as the law of attraction. It is by paying close and consistent attention to something, an idea perhaps, that it will reveal itself to you and either inspire how you attract it or simply attract you to itself.

"Good things happen when you pay attention," said one thinker and in the words of philosopher and mystic Simone Weil, "The highest ecstasy is the attention at the fullest." Every marvel in any field that has affected human life for the better was paid for at the price of close attention—mostly to small things. The so-called geniuses are not necessarily the brainiest, but they are surely the most attentive among us. This is how a poor patent clerk like Albert Einstein came to symbolize brain power—not because he had more of it, but because he paid the closest attention to whatever he was doing.

The only time excessive use of attention may be problematic is when it comes to health. Because, as Plato notes, "Attention to health is life's greatest hindrance." This is true, because when man starts paying too much attention to health, he opens himself up to fear, doubt, and self-preservation to the point where he loses the self-confidence, courage, and faith required to surmount obstacles that stand in the way of success. He avoids taking risks that are not only imperative to grow and to succeed but also great teachers and door openers of the kingdom of happiness.

A magnetic person or a person who is in search of personal magnetism does not just understand and use effectively the power of attention; he pays close attention first and foremost to his feelings, then thoughts and actions, as well as the feelings and actions of others. The reason for paying attention to feelings and thought first is very simple: feelings and thought are self-created, and out of them comes everything. It is through feelings that the man inside lights our way of the outside world and through feelings we gain confidence to move on to action or patience to wait for more clarity.

By paying careful attention to his thoughts, feelings, and actions, he stays close to the man inside, the inner master who teaches and protects him better than anyone else. By paying attention to the inner self, you weigh every feeling, thought, action, and their impact on the happiness of others. In the secret chamber of his heart, he walks in the shoes of others, and they walk in his shoes; he basically practices the Golden Rule, the mother of personal magnetism.

Yes, the man inside is not only the best teacher, but also the defender of a man's life. Contrary to what many believe, man is not protected by his free will but rather his inner master; therefore, the imperative to pay very close attention to all promptings that come in the form of thoughts or feelings from the *kingdom of heaven* that we've been told is within, is the rule that comes from the man inside every man, the true image of God. Paying attention to the man inside multiplies one's charisma at a speed few of us can imagine.

The Crown

We have come a long way to this point. However, by no means is this the end of the road to personal magnetism; we are not even halfway to the grand prize, but we are certainly one or two steps in the right direction. Ending the journey or even relaxing from here would be like a basketball team of very talented athletes that declares victory after overwhelming the opposing team with a dozen unanswered three-pointers in the first quarter, and then letting the other team justify its relevance in the last three quarters. If history has taught us anything, it is that prematurely declaring victory, even against a weak but determined opponent, spells disaster. One lesson I hope my readers to get from this book is that reading alone will not make you charismatic, unless you understand, and most notably, you apply, apply, and apply the wisdom learned here and elsewhere in your private and public life.

The *imperativeness* of application can never be emphasized *strongly* enough. Of all the magnificent qualities, including love, intelligence, wisdom, and power, none makes one perfect except by the repetition of actions derived thereof. Application alone gives religion, science, and philosophy their relevance. All the lessons of philosophy, religion, and science are worthless unless they are applied. This book and others may serve the reader very little, if any at all, unless this advice is heeded. You can read all the books ever written on this subject, spend countless hours unearthing knowledge written by the wisest of men, but it will not do you much good unless you apply, apply, apply the wisdom learned. Just like the application of business knowledge makes a little-educated merchant accumulate wealth over time, the application of personal magnetism principles enables a potentially charismatic person a reservoir of personal magnetism that vibrates charisma like a dam-generated powerhouse.

The application of knowledge of personal development is like thought: people can give you material to think about, but you must think it through for yourself. No one can ever do it for you, regardless of how much love and admiration people have for you. The principles in this book and elsewhere must be personally applied inwardly and outwardly by anyone who is in search of personal magnetism until your star shines not just to your satisfaction but more importantly to the satisfaction of those you want to attract. Indeed, help can come from all corners, but application must be individualized.

To be successful, the application principles are facilitated by two conditions. The first is that you must acknowledge your ability to acquire and grow charisma; you must have desire for and faith in becoming charismatic. Without this acknowledgement, it will be hard to succeed. Anyone who underestimates himself is set to fail in almost everything he or she does, and nowhere is the value of self-worth more important than in the business of attracting people.

We are all naïve sometimes; we all want to be around people who feel good about themselves. Acknowledging your own ability to acquire and grow personal magnetism sends the first rays of light to others like a morning sun, announcing the ability of your heart to shine on theirs and supply them with sufficient energy to sustain life.

Morning sunlight has been the subject of worship throughout history and in almost every society. Before our mental abilities were invaded and abused by modern technology, thanks to morning sunlight, we planned and predicted the rest of the day's activities. There were few surprises and life was happier. The acknowledgement of our ability to acquire and grow charisma can serve as a weather forecast tool to others, help gather people around, and give us a chance to show what we are up to — and therefore, increasing our chances of success.

The second principle is that application must be *voluntary*. The secret of voluntary action is that it generates inner power that could not have existed otherwise. It stimulates balanced thoughts, increases the odds of success, and does a lot of good if the action is constructive. No wonder the judicial system allocates harsher punishments for crimes found to have been voluntary.

Voluntary application has a great potential for success, because two important forces lie underneath it. The first power is the power of search. "Seek and ye shall find," it is said in Matthew 7:7. Nothing builds momentum better and more certainly than the power of searching. The more you search, the stronger grows the momentum; the stronger the momentum, the more excitement one gets; the more excitement, the more self-confidence, faithfulness, and courage one gains; and the more confidence, faith, and courage, the more likely that success is just one step away. The second power of voluntary application is attention. As we said earlier, attention is true magic.

Now, let's move on to other light switches that will help to increase the illumination to the application. Aiming to attract all people is total foolishness for a man if you imagine that God has given Himself eternity to attract one human heart at a time. Attracting human hearts is not only an elusive business; it is a perilous one too. It is not really a road less traveled; it a dangerous road; even the few who dared to travel it have not all arrived safely to their destinations. It is a road filled with expected and unexpected hazards, a journey that sometimes ends tragically.

This, of course, is not to discourage or scare anyone, but rather to strengthen your resolve if you are really interested in the business of acquiring and growing personal magnetism. There are many brave hearts that stood and are standing firm today; those who refuse to give in to the storm no matter how threatening the clouds seem to be still go on and win the crown of the human heart. Despite the odds against them, they prevail and triumphantly secure the admiration of their contemporaries and future generations. They go on to become immortalized in the hearts of men and become synonymous with tradition.

Admiration won, immortality gained, and tradition created have carried the great names of charismatic people throughout civilizations past and present. We do not all have to be the heroes of civilizations, and this book is not written with that intention in mind. But we are all called to be the heroes of our own hearts while trying to influence positively those we can. No matter how small the number of people, and no matter how precarious it might be, the human heart is worth every effort to attract.

Effective leadership is worth all the effort of the heart, soul, and mind of man because it enriches life, and restores love, peace, freedom, safety, and security, without which true happiness can never be attained.

Constructive, magnetic leaders are the blessings and the saviors of the world. They are not just fathers of countries, founders of religions, or originators of schools of thoughts; they are fathers of civilizations, they are the second-best things here on Earth—second only to God; they change the lives of generations for the better, and regardless of the logic of Aristotle: "All men are mortal; Socrates is a man; therefore ..." Socrates is *immortal*. What? Yes, he lives forever in the hearts and lives of men whose minds he enlightens even as we speak.

The world has never ceased to improve or slow down toward progress; truth and justice keep getting stronger over evil and injustice ever since the great ones of old (who may have lost their lives to injustice in process) stepped out in public to live and teach these ageless principles of personal magnetism. Should they come back today and commit the same offenses for which they may have been sentenced to death then, all things being equal, they would very likely have better courts, better judges, better investigations, better juries, and they would undoubtedly be acquitted.

That is the victory of the ages. That is the wisdom that never fails. That is the power of personal magnetism. That is how a better world is built. That is how a new generation corrects the mistakes of the past generations. That is how you go beyond the golden rule. That is how you leave a better world than the one you inherited. That is the joy of a constructive application of these secrets of personal magnetism. That is what we hope this book will implant in your mind for these are **The Best Kept Secrets of Personal Magnetism.** They have been hidden well in the faithful breasts of the few, the self-chosen, the enlightened, and now made available to all sincere seekers.

Postscript

Dear Reader.

The ink of our physical pen may have run out here, unexpectedly or otherwise, but this work is by no means over. It can't be, and it shouldn't be. But before our ink completely runs out, we thought we should remind you of the immortal words of Heraclitus, an ancient Greek sage who more than 2,500 years ago said, "The unapparent connection is more powerful than the apparent one."

Well, this may be the *apparent connection* or end of our work, but the reality is that the *unapparent* connection is yours to craft. Do it diligently with an unlimited pen in the endless book of your consciousness and actions, until the Truth in you, your heart and mind shines brilliantly like the light of a thousand suns as it leads you confidently to happiness, great joy, and victory in all your noble and imperishable goals.

Thus, we say this work is . . . *to be continued in the Deepest Chamber of your Truest Being* . . .

However, while you are writing your unapparent connection for this book, the first of the *Hints of Wisdom* series, we wholeheartedly invite you to also read our three upcoming works: *Exalted Secrets of*

Brilliant Minds; The Central Mountain and *Emancipated Intelligence* respectively, the second, third and fourth of these series for more growth and enjoyment.

BIBLIOGRAPHY

ABC News. *Nightline.* August 8, 2008.

Allen, James. *As a Man Thinketh.* Kent, United Kingdom: Grand Books PLC, 2003.

Atkinson, William Walker. *The Secret of Success: Unleashing the Power Within,* New York: Cosimo Classic, 2007.

—. *Mind Power, The Secret of Mental Magic.* New York: Cosimo Classics, 2007.

Behrend, Genevieve. *Your Invisible Power: The Mental Science of Thomas Troward.* Holyoke, MA: The Elizabeth Towne Co. Inc., 1921 (original publication). Widely available in public domain reprints and online, including http://www.psitek.net/pages/PsiTekYIPContents.html.

Collier, Robert. *The Secrets of Ages,* New York: Jeremy P. Tarcher, 2007.

Covey, Stephen R., A. Roger Merrill, and Rebecca R. Merrill. *First Things First.* New York: Simon & Schuster. 1994.

De La Fontaine, Jean. *Selected Fables/Fables Choisies: A Dual-Language Book.* Edited and Translated by Stanley Appelbaum. Mineola, New York: Dover Publications, 1997.

Dumont, Theron Q. *Advanced Course of Personal Magnetism.* Domino Publishing Company, 1917.

—. *The Art and Science of Personal Magnetism.* Advanced Thought Publishing Co.; 1913.

—. *The Power of Concentration.* New Vision Publications, LLC; 2007.

Fox, Emmet. *The Sermon on the Mount.* HarperSanFrancisco 1989.

Haanel, Charles F. *The Master Key Arcana.* Wilkes-Barre, PA: Kallisti Publishing, 2004.

—. *The Master Key System.* New York: Jeremy B. Tarcher/Penguin, 2007.

Haddock, Frank Channing. *The Power of Will.* RGC Books, Inc., 1921.

Hicks, Esther, and Jerry Hicks. *Ask and It Is Given.* Carlsbad, CA: Hay House, Inc., 2004.

Holmes, Ernest. *The Art of Life.* New York: Jeremy P. Tarcher/Penguin, 2004.

_____. *Creative Mind and Success.* New York: Jeremy P. Tarcher/Penguin, 1919.

Johnson, Dennis D. "Leadership from Bottom Up." *Oregon Masonic News,* May 2008.

King, Godfre Ray. *The Magic Presence.* Schaumburg, IL: Saint Germain Press, 2008.

—. *Unveiled Mysteries.* Schaumburg, IL: Saint Germain Press, *2008.*

Kleinknecht, C.F. *The Kleinknecht Gems of Thought Encyclopedia* Vol. V. Washington, DC: Roberts Publishing, 1955.

_____.The Kleinknecht *Gems of Thought Encyclopedia* Vols. V-XV Washington, DC: Roberts Publishing, 1964.

Kouzes, James M. and Posner, Barry Z. *The Leadership Challenge.* Jossey-Bass, 1997.

Levi, Eliphas. *The Key of the Mysteries;* translated by Aleister Crowley

Machiavelli, Niccolo. *The Prince.* Translated by Daniel Donno.

Oxford American Desk Dictionary and Thesaurus, The. Second Edition.

Phylos the Thibetan (Frederick S. Oliver). *A Dweller on Two Planets.* Santa Cruz, CA: Evinity Publishing Inc., 2009 (1894).

Price, John R. *The Superbeings.* New York: Fawcett Crest, 1981.

Shinn, Florence Scovel. *The Power of the Spoken Word.* Camarillo, CA: DeVos Publishing, 1988.

Saint Germain Foundation. *The "I AM" Discourses.* Vol. III. Chicago: Saint Germain Press.

Trine, Ralph W. *In Tune with the Infinite.* Filiquarian Publishing LLC. 2007.

US News and World Report: Collector's Edition. "The Secrets of the Super Rich." July 2008.

Voice of "I AM." Chicago: Saint Germain Press, Inc., January 1945.

Wattles, Wallace D., III. T*he Wisdom of W. D. Wattles III.* New York: Barnes and Noble, 2007.

Websites

BBC News.
http://news.bbc.co.uk/2/hi/south_asia/7424302.stm

Bible Gateway. "Matthew" http://www.biblegateway.com/
passage/?search=Matthew%204:1-11 (Accessed 03/22/2009).

CNN.com. "Jonestown Factsheet." http://www.cnn.com/2008/US/11/12/jonestown.factsheet/index.html.

Crime Suite 101. "Anniversary of Jonestown Massacre in Guyana." http://www.crime.suite101.com/article.cfm/30th_anniversary_of_jonestown_massacre_in_guyana.

Idea Finder.
http://www.ideafinder.com/history/inventions/postit.htm

Merriam-Webster dictionary.
http://ww.merriam-webster.com/dictionary/poverty.

Pubwire.com.
http://www.pubwire.com/DownloadDocs/AFABLES.PDF. (Accessed 12/25/2011).

Politico.
http://www.politico.com/news/stories/1007/6490.html.

Spiritwire.com. *http://www.spiritwire.com/* (May 2008).

Wikipedia. "Cambodia under Pol Pot." http://www.en.wikipedia.org/wiki/Cambodia_under_Pol_Pot.

—. "Federal Government Shutdown of 1995." http://www.en.wikipedia.org/wiki/federal_government_shutdown_of_1995.

—. "J. K. Rowling." *http://www.en.wikipedia.org/wiki/J._K._Rowling.* (April 2008).

—. "Talleyrand." http://www.en.wikipedia.org/wiki/Talleyrand.

Wisegeek.com. "What Is a Temporary Insanity Plea?" *http://www.wisegeek.com/what-is-a-temporary-insanity-plea.htm (Accessed 03/29/2009).*

About the Author

Wisdom J.O.Y. Makano, is a philosopher, a poet, and a lifelong student of ancient religious, creative and esoteric mythologies, learning, along the way, what impels those immovable seeds of human race to go for the perilous "quest for the road that leads to the place all wish to find*. He lives in the serene Pacific Northwest of the United States of America with his lovely wife and five children. ***The Best Kept Secrets of Personal Magnetism*** is Makano's first book. He is also author of three forthcoming books: Exalted Secrets of Brilliant Minds; ***The Central Mountain*** (both manuscripts currently under review) and ***Emancipated Intelligence*** (manuscript in progress.) Makano holds an associate's, a bachelor's, a Master of Public Administration, and a Master of Art in Teaching degrees from Clackamas Community College in Oregon, Washington State University, Portland State University, and Lewis and Clark College respectively. You can reach Makano by email at makanologos@yahoo.com or visit his website, www.makanologos.com

Pacific Book Review

Author, Wisdom J.O.Y. Makano is a poet and a philosopher. He has worked a lifetime studying ancient sources of knowledge, the wisdom of the sages, religious text, philosophy, and other esoteric volumes. His extensive research and wealth of knowledge has now culminated into his first book, The Best Kept Secrets of Personal Magnetism. The principles herein are based on the Golden Rule, "treat others as you would like to be treated." The author says this is the "finest rule of conduct and the key to influencing people." He explains this ancient doctrine was made famous by Jesus Christ and is still "the highest principle in the remotest of societies," and how this rule was also taught by prophets and ancient wise men from many sects including the Hebrews, Greek, Chinese and the Indians.

There are explanations for how to use the laws of human nature and the golden rule for dynamic social or business change. You see that integrity, gratitude, and a genuinely, "caring attitude" can open doors to the success of the practitioner. The ultimate message is--a person does not have to be chosen or special, but can come from any walk of life, however humble, and still achieve their hearts desire by using these principles. However, the principles must be used for good, and not to manipulate others. Great men and women throughout time have used these proven techniques to change their personal lives and to change the world for the better.

This is also a book about leadership and how to develop a winning style for any situation. Since we do not achieve success alone we must learn how to influence others who can help us achieve our goals and dreams. This is a guide and reference book for how to do that and the truths found here can be tested, instantly, with the people in one's life. They work equally as well with family and friends as with business associates. The author invites the reader to test all that he has written to their own satisfaction before accepting his statements. Now, there's a winning formula in itself!

The Best Kept Secrets of Personal Magnetism has quickly become one of my favorite personal achievement books since Think and Grow Rich, was popular (again) in the 1970's. While Think and Grow Rich, by Napoleon Hill, and Og Mandino's, The Greatest Salesman in the World had a business feel about them, The Best Kept Secrets of Personal Magnetism, written by Wisdom J.O.Y. Makano, has a more holistic feel from the moment you open the book. The book is warm, inviting, uplifting, and naturally motivating in the sense it offers new hope for whatever one wants to accomplish, whether that is great leadership, more charm and charisma, or just wanting to be a happier person. The author says his book is for anyone who wants to set themselves apart by developing their own personal magnetism, not for the purpose of manipulation, but for the purpose of sharing their gifts with the world. I believe it is also for the truth seeker, the philosopher, the teacher, the salesman and almost anyone who wants to improve any area of their life. It is for the inspired and for those who want to be inspired, again. Author, Wisdom J.O.Y. Makano, has three more books soon to be published, Exalted Secrets of Brilliant Minds, The Central Mountain, and Emancipated Intelligence. I believe each of these will be a treasure for any who seek the best in themselves and others.

S. Marie Vernon, Jacksonville, Alabama, for Pacific Book Review

CPSIA information can be obtained
at www.ICGtesting.com
Printed in the USA
FSOW02n1650160715
8939FS